LITERATURE AND IDEAS SERIES
Irving Howe, *General Editor*

# The
# Elizabethan
# Age

EDITED WITH INTRODUCTION BY
## DAVID L. STEVENSON

*A Fawcett Premier Book*

FAWCETT PUBLICATIONS, INC., GREENWICH, CONN.
MEMBER OF AMERICAN BOOK PUBLISHERS COUNCIL, INC.

## ACKNOWLEDGMENTS

"The Aristocratic Class Structure of the Renaissance," Chap. 2 from *Shakespeare and the Renaissance Concept of Honor* by Curtis Brown Watson. Copyright © 1960 by Princeton University Press. Reprinted by permission of the Princeton University Press.

"English Treason Trials and Confessions in the Sixteenth Century," from the *Journal of the History of Ideas*, October, 1954 (XV, 471-498). Also from the *Journal of the History of Ideas* are: "Physiology and Psychology in Shakespeare's Age," January, 1951 (XII, 75-89); "On Elizabethan 'Credulity'," April, 1940 (I, 151-176); "God and Expansion in Elizabethan England: John Dee, 1527-1583," January-March, 1964 (XXV, 17-34). Reprinted by permission of the *Journal of the History of Ideas* and the authors.

"Body and Soul," Chap. 14 from *Science and Religion in Elizabethan England* by Paul H. Kocher, copyright 1953. Reprinted by permission of the Henry E. Huntington Library and Art Gallery, San Marino.

"Man in Nature: The Renaissance Conflict." Reprinted with permission of The Macmillan Company from *Shakespeare and the Nature of Man* by Theodore Spencer. Copyright 1942, 1949 by The Macmillan Company.

"The Order and Continuance of Nature." Reprinted by permission of the publishers from Geoffrey Bush, *Shakespeare and the Natural Condition*, Cambridge, Mass.: Harvard University Press, Copyright, 1956, by the President and Fellows of Harvard College.

"The Tragic Picture," from Chap. II, *Shakespeare's Tragedies, and Other Studies in Seventeen Century Drama* by Clifford Leech, 1950. Reprinted by permission of the Oxford University Press and Chatto & Windus Ltd., London.

"Jacobean Tragedy," the Introduction from *Jacobean Tragedy, The Quest for Moral Order* by Irving Ribner, 1962. Reprinted by permission of Methuen & Co. Ltd., London.

"The Society of the Shakespearean Moment," Chap. IV from *The Shakespearean Moment* by Patrick Cruttwell, 1955. Reprinted by permission of Columbia University Press and the author.

Library of Congress Catalog Card Number 67-16879

First Fawcett Premier printing, January 1967

Published by Fawcett World Library,
67 West 44th Street, New York, New York 10036

PRINTED IN THE UNITED STATES OF AMERICA

# PREFACE

The essays in this collection, with the exception of Geoffrey Bush's "The Order and Continuance of Nature," Clifford Leech's "The Tragic Picture," and Irving Ribner's "Jacobean Tragedy," simply supply historical information about the Elizabethan Age. They are a series of long historical annotations meant to remove those elements of strangeness in Elizabethan literature resulting from the fact that it flourished in a different time with somewhat different ways from our own of looking at the world.

The reader should note that there was no "correct" dictionary spelling in the sixteenth century to which every writer and every printer adhered. As a result, when passages from Elizabethan books are quoted by the writers in this collection, they sometimes use the original spelling, sometimes modernize it. Shakespeare's spelling is almost always in modern form, that of John Donne almost never. Spenser invented his own half-archaic spelling and is always quoted in this spelling. For the rest of the Elizabethans, there is little consistency as to the spelling used; both that of the sixteenth century and that of the twentieth are employed.

I have not included a bibliography of suggested readings because the footnotes to the essays themselves supply a rich reference to important books and articles concerned with the Elizabethan Age and its literature.

DAVID L. STEVENSON

*Hunter College, July, 1966*

# CONTENTS

# INTRODUCTION

## 1

### THE HISTORICAL FRAME OF REFERENCE

The purpose of this collection of essays is to serve as an introduction to the historical dimension in the literature of the Elizabethan Age. By definition that age is obviously co-extensive with the reign of Elizabeth I (1558-1603), but it stretches forward in time to affect at least the early work of John Milton. The essays included here are scholars' explorations of significant ways in which this age differs from our own in its assumptions and views of the social and political order, of the nature and purposes of knowledge, of man's role in the scheme of nature. Such differences are often interesting in themselves and placate our historical curiosity. They are also part of the information which a reader needs to acquire in order to understand more fully both the historical moment which produced the literary giants of the Elizabethan Age, and their relationship to it.

The climate of idea and opinion of time past, which is always embedded in literature, becomes important, I think, when aspects of this "climate" have actually entered into a work of art as a controlling part of its meaning. Thus one may concede that four centuries hence no one could intelligently analyze and evaluate present-day American fiction and drama unless he were supplied substantial information about the effect of Darwin and Freud on twentieth-century attitudes toward the nature of being. Likewise, we cannot feel that we wholly comprehend Hamlet and his problems unless we are made aware of Elizabethan-Renaissance theological and philosophical speculations which inform and set boundaries to Hamlet's questioning of the order and value of existence.

It is only fair to note, however, some of the obvious limitations and difficulties which this historical dimension creates. It may help us to recapture local conditions which made a given piece of writing important to its own age. But the retrieval of such information cannot be said to reestablish the viability of all the writing of the age. We can never make great art out of Lyly's comedies and his novel *Euphues* by understanding the reasons for their popularity in the 1580's. Moreover, the relationship between an acknowledged work of art (e.g., *King Lear*) and the views of its age is not one that is defined with easy precision. A writer's era is an aspect of his private life and also of his literary achievement. It is, further, only a piece of the environment within which he worked, not the total environment. It is one of the factors which may have partly shackled his genius, partly set it free. Yet we pursue the historical factor in literature because it is a tangible one, and an aspect of a writer's environment which is amenable to investigation and discussion. It is also that part of his age which he shares with the other writers of his time.

Any honest discussion of the value of the historical dimension in literature involves one, in addition, in the contemporary quarrel between the rival claims of the "pure" literary historian and the "pure" textualist critic. It is assumed as a matter of course by the absolute historian that the more we know about an age in which a particular writer lived, the closer we come to a full comprehension of his work. It is assumed as equally self-evident by the absolute textualist that the literary work of art, as art, cannot be discussed at all until it has been deliberately isolated from the local views of its age, until it has been stripped bare of any local frame of reference.

As I see it, these two views, when one is set up to exclude the other, are not so much false approaches to interpretation and evaluation as they are self-limiting oversimplifications of the very piece of literature to which they are being applied. In order to read Sidney's or Donne's love poetry with any insight at all, we surely need to know that it exists in a complex interrelationship with the romantic conventions of the Renaissance. We dare not

10

attempt a single canto of Spenser's *Faerie Queene* without the aid of elaborate historical annotation. Even Shakespeare's most self-contained plays (e.g. *Othello* or *Twelfth Night*) need at least a hint or two from the literary historian in order to better place the romantic ideas relating them to their moment. But if we read with any discrimination at all, we also must know that the writings of Sidney, Spenser, Shakespeare, and Donne are less united by their articulation of shared attitudes or concepts of the time than they are separated by the special qualities of the personality and talent of each writer.

Because of the genuine problems and difficulties it raises, I should like to make as clear as possible what seems to me to be the undeniable importance of the historical dimension in literature. In order to do so, I should like to present two passages, one from Milton and one from Shakespeare, as each might be explicated first by a textualist critic, then by a literary historian. In each instance, I think, the lines in question would be intolerably diminished in meaning and effect if we were to omit the insights of either explanation. But my point, of course, is to demonstrate the extra and enriching value given to each passage by framing it in historical perspective.

My first example is from Milton's "Lycidas" (1637):

> Fame is the spur that the clear spirit doth raise
> (That last infirmity of noble mind)
> To scorn delights and live laborious days;
> But the fair guerdon [reward] when we hope to find,
> And think to burst out into sudden blaze,
> Comes the blind Fury with the abhorred shears,
> And slits the thin-spun life.          (ll. 70-76)

If one denudes these lines of any framing by sixteenth- and early seventeenth-century thought concerning the purposes of human life, one could argue that they are a clear assertion of the timeless paradox that men do use fame as a spur in their struggles for secular, human glory. One might observe that such struggling can be called part of the infirmity or sickness of being, in that life is chancy and one may not live to achieve the fame one seeks. One could further note that even if one achieves the glory one

11

seeks, it turns out to be a commodity as utterly transient and insubstantial as an individual's life itself.

But these lines, if they do illustrate what a textualist critic might call a "concrete universal," have also a strong Elizabethan undertow of eschatological implication, derived from the theological concerns of the age: glory and fame belong to the afterlife. One cannot strip Milton's lines of this implication and leave them whole. Lucretius or Camus could conceivably have given voice to similar paradoxical views concerning the illusions of existence. But such other theoretical paradoxes would surely have their own special and indispensable time-framing.

It should also be observed as a matter of literary history that Milton's lines assume, I think, our awareness of other Elizabethan literary speculations as to the value of secular, intellectual, or poetic achievement. Spenser, a favorite with Milton, had opened the Elizabethan literary philosophizing on fame in the October Eclogue of his *Shepheardes Calender* (1579). Shakespeare had played a kind of game with the notion of fame in the first scene of *Love's Labor's Lost* (1594?). Samuel Daniel had brilliantly defended the legitimacy of man's quest for poetic fame in his own time, in his poem *Musophilus* (1599). Sir John Davies had taken the opposite stand in the same year, in his poem *Nosce Teipsum* ("Know Thyself"). Fulke Greville's poetical treatise, *An Inquisition Upon Fame and Honour,* printed posthumously in 1633, is closest in time to Milton's "Lycidas," and closest in view to his concern with the purposes of human striving in a Christian, post-lapsarian world.

My second example is the final sentence from Hamlet's letter to Ophelia:

> Thine evermore, most dear lady, whilst this
> machine is to him,
> 
> Hamlet.     (II.ii)

The line falls harshly on modern ears because the word "machine" (Latin "machina") no longer carries the general meaning of "any sort of device or contrivance." But with this one word properly annotated for us, we can take

Hamlet's terse whimsical reference to his body as a mere device or thing out of its time context and regard it for what, in a way, it is: a curious, tense playing with the concept of the human mind and will timelessly caught in the fragile, perishable contraption of the flesh. Crudely paraphrased, the line thus means "I will be faithful to you as long as my body holds together"; or "as long as I can make it."

But Hamlet's way of putting the transiency of life is not just personal caprice. It is also very much of its age, a version of many other such comments to be found elsewhere in Shakespeare and in other Elizabethan writings. It is essentially Elizabethan-Christian in its overly-self-conscious insistence that the body is an entity separate from the soul, and is a *thing,* a mere mechanism inhabited by the soul. Lorenzo, in *The Merchant of Venice,* teases Jessica, while he makes love to her, by referring to the body as "this muddy vesture of decay" (V.i). Shakespeare asserts the separateness of the body from the soul more personally, using it as the basic image of sonnet 146. Bosola, in Webster's *The Duchess of Malfi,* employs this Elizabethan-Christian dichotomy savagely, in the lines:

> And though continually we bear about us
> A rotten and dead body, we delight
> To hide it in rich tissue: all our fear
> Nay, all our terror, is lest our physician
> Should put us in the ground to be made sweet.     (II.i)

John Donne carries this Elizabethan way of looking, as one might expect, to the extreme of depicting the human body, over and over, as some sort of fantastic container for the soul (see "The Extasie," and "Aire and Angels"). In lines from his "Of the Progresse of the Soule, the Second Anniversarie," he uses what is wry comment in *Hamlet* to induce the "metaphysical shudder":

> . . . in a beheaded man,
> Though at those two Red seas, which freely ranne,
> One from the Trunke, another from the Head,
> His soule be sailed, to her eternall bed,
> His eyes will twinckle, and his tongue will roll,

13

As though he beckned, and called backe his soule,
He graspes his hands, and pulls up his feet,
And seemes to reach, and to step forth to meet
His soule.                                         (11. 9-17)

There may be very little in the Elizabethan literature
that we continue to read as an exciting, sturdy part of
Western letters that cannot be understood, in a way, outside its time frame. Yet one should never flee the historical
erudition of the professional literary scholar as if one were
running from hidden mysteries, unrelated to literary art.
His findings are always merely information intended to be
useful. What the "historical" readings of the two passages
cited above do illustrate, then, is that a retrieval of their
historical dimension puts them into a context in which
their meaning takes on an added richness of implication.
Moreover, if he is doing his job properly, and not claiming
too much for it, the literary historian gives us the sense
that we are "getting things right." We accept the evidence
that Milton's lines are not just a concrete universal, but
that they are clearly involved with the assertion of an early
seventeenth-century concept of the nature of being. Likewise, we accept the evidence that Hamlet's lines to Ophelia
are more than a demonstration of personal whim. In their
turn-of-the-century way and mood, they embody a conception of the soul and the body peculiar to their moment.
It is a conception that would have been expressed more
harshly, and less speculatively and tauntingly, in the "learn
to die" poetry of the fifteenth century; and a conception
not at all likely to occur to any serious writer today (except
to the T. S. Eliot of *The Four Quartets*).


2


## THE ELIZABETHAN AGE


The eleven essays which I have selected for this anthology
are all by contemporary scholars. The first ten essays come
in pairs, two to each of the first five sections. They are

concerned with what seemed to me the aspects of the Elizabethan Age that most need stressing in a general introduction to it. The final essay, in a sixth section, Patrick Cruttwell's "The Society of the Shakespearean Moment," stands alone. It serves as a general summary of ideas and views already encountered in the first ten essays, and gives a unique and incisive account of the general effect of the age on its literature. In an Appendix, "The Elizabethan Voices," I have included Francis Bacon's profile or brief sketch of Queen Elizabeth's life, and William Camden's account of her death and his personal eulogy of her as a monarch. It seemed fitting to allow two of the most perceptive and scholarly minds of the Elizabethan Age to express their personal views.

What follows are my own comments, section by section, on each of the essays in this collection. The essays, themselves, are more or less self-contained. But I thought it helpful to demonstrate ways in which the information in them might be shown to be particularly relevant to a student of Elizabethan literature. I have not engaged myself in any arguments as to the validity of the views expressed. I have, hopefully, made these views of greater use to a person coming to them for the first time.


Section I: The Social and Political Order

I have placed Curtis B. Watson's essay, "The Aristocratic Class Structure of the Renaissance," first in the book, because it gives the essentials of differences between the social and political order of the Elizabethan Age and that of our own. The differences are not absolute, to be sure, and in the social snobberies of the twentieth century we may see a kind of watered-down version of those based upon birth and social class of the sixteenth century. But the differences in terms of hierarchical power are absolute. Queen Elizabeth herself, and the two Stuart Kings who succeeded her, were officially and in reality above statutory law. They had an unquestioned right of life and death over those below them. Moreover, in the descending hierarchy of their highly structured order, those on the lower rungs

15

had little recourse, legal or otherwise, against those above them. It was a society, indeed, in which a man of our century might find it difficult to breathe.

This is not to say that so rigid an order did not show stresses and strains. William Camden (1551-1623), the Elizabethan scholar referred to above, and author of the first history of his own Elizabethan Age, quotes the Queen's Lord Treasurer, Burghley, as observing in 1598 that under pressure of taxation, "the nature of the common people of England [was] inclinable to sedition." He observed, further, "that there was an inbred disaffection in the vulgar towards the nobility" (third ed., 1675, p. 555). But the old order held firm until the civil war of the seventeenth century, and the beheading of King Charles I in 1649.

One sees reflections of this aristrocratic society wherever one touches upon the relations of one person to another. It is implicit in Shakespeare's painfully self-conscious dedication of his *Venus and Adonis* (1593) to the Earl of Southampton, and just as evident in the dedication of the Shakespeare First Folio (1623) to the two sons of the Countess of Pembroke. It is obvious in Spenser's careful choice of aristocrats for the seventeen dedicatory poems with which he prefaces the 1590 edition of *The Faerie Queene*. It is equally explicit in the famous clash between the Earl of Oxford and the mere knight Sir Philip Sydney, as to whether the Earl had the right of rank to order one of lesser nobility off the royal tennis court. As the biographer of Sidney, Fulke Greville (1554-1628) describes it, Queen Elizabeth herself intervened between the two men to prevent a duel. She cautioned Sidney as to "the difference in degree between earls, and gentlemen; the respect inferiors ought to their superiors; . . . how the gentlemans neglect of the nobility taught the peasant to insult upon them both" (*The Life of the Renowned Sir Philip Sidney*, 1652, Ch. VI).

The literature of the Elizabethan Age, as a matter of course, reflected this class structure as frequently and as innocently as our literature reflects that of the twentieth century. It is worth observing, indeed, that the characters in Elizabethan tragedy retain part of their interest for us

16

because they are so frequently men and women of high place. The fact of their genuinely greater autonomy in their society creates part of our interest in them. They possess a freedom of will denied us. No sheriff can arrest Hamlet and bring him to trial for the killing of Polonius. Hamlet himself passes his own judgment on the deed: "Thou wretched, rash, intruding fool, farewell!/I took thee for thy better." Lady Macbeth faces no jury for her role in the killing of Duncan; she destroys herself. Such characters become involved with the consequences of their decisions and deeds in a way fascinating to lesser mortals, denied their freedom from restraint.

One observes that the Elizabethan class structure is in evidence in literature usually by implication only. The aristocratic condescension with which Shakespeare's Theseus and Hippolyta, in *A Midsummer Night's Dream,* attend the play put on by the rustics, Bottom and Company, is there only by the tone of their remarks. In *Twelfth Night,* Olivia is graciously bewildered, without pausing to examine why, when she discovers that her steward Malvolio had imagined marrying her. In Webster's *Duchess of Malfi,* it is the fact that the Duchess chooses to marry her steward that arouses her brother's fury and brings on the tragedy. These evidences are everywhere. Two of the subtlest, most ironic playings with the established order, I think, are to be found in the debates in *The Winter's Tale* [1610-1611] between Perdita and Polixenes as to the propriety of marrying outside one's class (IV.iv), and in the portrait of a classless society sketched by Gonzalo in *The Tempest* [1610-1611] (II.ii). These two scenes take on an extra edge of force because they were in plays later produced [1612-1613] before the very divine right King James and his court as part of the wedding festivities preceding the marriage of his daughter to the Elector Palatine. Part of their charm for a wholly aristocratic audience was surely the self-indulgent laughter their teasing of an absolute order provoked.

The second of the essays in this section, Lacey B. Smith's "English Treason Trials and Confessions in the Sixteenth Century," follows as a kind of demonstration of the second half of Watson's essay, that loyalty to the

17

political and social order was the essence of an Elizabethan's sense of honor. Smith's portraits are of sixteenth-century aristocrats, caught out in the system, who faced execution and yet remained loyal to the system of which they were the victims. Their "confessions" at the headsman's block he cites as evidence of their ultimate allegiance, their ultimate tribute to their belief in a hierarchical order (or to their inability to imagine any other). Theirs was a loyalty that cannot be translated by the modern phrase "playing the game." It sprang from a strong sense of the divine necessity of an aristocratic ordering of society.

The only strong current of idea working against their views, in the Elizabethan Age, was that voiced occasionally by the Presbyterian Scots. When Queen Mary was deposed, for example, a delegation to Elizabeth defended the action, as Camden reports it, with the statement that "the Scottish people are above their Kings; yea and by the authority of Calvin, that popular magistrates are constituted everywhere to bridle the lusts of kings, and that it is lawfull for them to restrain bad kings by imprisonment, and to depose them" (p. 155). It was this stubborn Scottish view which has, of course, prevailed in the modern world. It was given classic seventeenth-century expression by John Milton, in his "The Tenure of Kings and Magistrates" (1649), his defense of the deposition of Charles I. He argued that "all men naturally were born free, being the image and resemblance of God himself"; and that "the power of kings and magistrates is nothing else but derivative, transferred, and committed to them from the people to the common good of them all, in whom power yet remains fundamentally, and cannot be taken from them." But by the time Milton wrote this, the Elizabethan Age was over.

If the Elizabethan aristocrat was willing to die for the hierarchical order which sustained him, men of lower rank often demonstrated equal loyalty to it, equally convinced of its divine necessity. John Stubbs, as an example, had personally outraged Queen Elizabeth by publishing a book, in 1581, which argued against her marriage to the Duke of Anjou. Stubbs was apprehended for merely having had opinions about those above him. A lawyer, Dalton, who defended his right, was committed to the Tower; his lenient

18

judge, in the Court of Common Pleas, was forced to resign from the bench. And Stubbs (and Page, who had distributed the book) were punished, as Camden reports it, by having "their right hands cut off with a cleaver, driven through the wrist by the force of a mallet, upon a scaffold in the marketplace at Westminster."

But Stubbs publicly accepted his punishment by a show of allegiance to the system as "honorable" as that of an Essex at the block. As Camden describes it, "I remember (being there present) that when Stubbs, after his right hand was cut off, put off his hat with his left; and said with a loud voice 'God save the Queen'; the multitude standing about was deeply silent" (p. 270). Stubbs was to die in loyal service to the Queen, eight years later, as part of the English expeditionary force which she had sent to aid the King of Navarre.

In the literature of the Elizabethan Age, the breaking of allegiance to the social order, especially where unquestioned loyalty to the monarch was concerned, was everywhere taken for granted as a breaking of the divine authority of the state. Perhaps the clearest literary reflection of such views is to be found throughout Shakespeare's play *Richard II,* as Lily B. Campbell has shown in her book, *Shakespeare's Histories, Mirrors of Elizabethan Policy* (1947). At the very beginning of the play, indeed, Richard's uncle, John of Gaunt and Duke of Lancaster, puts the concept of allegiance to the crown and to the whole social and political hierarchy as succinctly as it could be done. Gaunt refuses to respond to the taunts of his sister-in-law, Duchess of Gloucester, that he should revenge her husband's murder which had been arranged by King Richard. Gaunt voices an old man's comfort that his inaction is the only honorable course:

> God's is the quarrel; for God's substitute,
> His deputy anointed in His sight,
> Hath caused his death; the which if wrongfully,
> Let Heaven revenge; for I may never lift
> An angry arm against His minister.      (I.ii)

Shakespeare's contemporary, the poet Michael Drayton, in his epic *The Barons' Wars,* has Edward II proclaim his

19

divinity as King as he faces his barons who would murder him:

> You must think Heaven sufficiency hath wonted,
> And so deny it power, by your oppression,
> That into question dare thus bring
> The awful right of an anointed King.
> (Canto V, st. 15, ed. 1637)

Samuel Daniel's long work on the War of the Roses is a thesis poem on Elizabethan political views. As he stated it, in his dedication to the Countess of Pembroke, the penalty exacted by God against England for "the breach of the due course of succession by the usurpation of Henry IV" was a century of civil war.

In *Much Ado About Nothing,* Shakespeare plays the lightest game with the Elizabethan concept of the hierarchy of obligation. Count Claudio's private confession of love to Benedick is jokingly demanded by Don Pedro on Benedick's "allegiance." In Sir Walter Raleigh's poem "The Passionate Man's Pilgrimage," we get the most bitterly ironic lines of the period in which this hierarchy of obligation is expressed. Raleigh's aristocrat (himself) says his farewell to the system, at the block, thus:

> . . . this is my eternall plea,
> To him that made Heaven and Earth and Sea,
> Seeing my flesh must die so soone,
> And want a head to dine next noone,
> Just at the stroke when my vaines start and spred
> Set on my soule an everlasting head. (11. 51-56)

## Section II: Elizabethan Science

Patrick Cruttwell's "Physiology and Psychology in Shakespeare's Age," in this second section, is largely an essay in annotation, in pointing out ways in which Elizabethan literature makes use of a medieval scientific terminology to explain causal relationships between bodily function and mental or emotional states. It should not be difficult to understand the Elizabethans' unthinking acceptance of their own views that emotional stability comes from a proper balance of four fluids or humours in the body. One need only remind oneself that we also take as much for granted our own notions of evolution, of the determinism of the genes, and of multi-levels of human awareness sliding down into the subconscious. Cruttwell's essay forces us to face the question, indeed, as to whether Shakespeare's age was in any way less perceptive of secular man in all his vagaries than our own, merely because of its "inaccurate" physiology and psychology.

Shakespeare uses the Elizabethan concept of the four elements (earth, water, air, fire), along with the accompanying notions of the balance of the humours, with convincing elegance as metaphor in his pair of sonnets, 44 and 45. And Cruttwell's essay is very helpful in supplying the information that lets us know what Shakespeare is about. His sonnets work, lose all sense of oddity of metaphor, as soon as the annotation is supplied. Cruttwell comments on the half-punning way Shakespeare uses the Elizabethan word "spirit" in sonnet 129 to suggest ejaculation. Donne also visited this half-physiological territory in his poem "Farewell to Love." He joins in Shakespeare's game with the physiology of his age to explain male sadness after the act of sex as an awareness of the loss of "spirit," by a reminder that "each such Act, they say/ Diminisheth the length of life a day." But in large matters of understanding, one guesses, Elizabethan literature was as lightly tethered to its conception of a science of the body and soul as ours is to its conceptions of a science of the soma and the psyche.

Lily B. Campbell, in *Shakespeare's Tragic Heroes* (1930), worked out descriptions, according to Elizabethan science, of Shakespeare's tragic protagonists as they could be seen from the point of view of the humours, or bodily-fluid terminology of his time. Indeed, she found passages from Timothy Bright's *A Treatise of Melancholie* (1586) which pretty well "explained" Hamlet's state of mind. But the reality, the essence and power of the character Hamlet surely eluded Timothy Bright's theories as easily as it has eluded those of Dr. Ernest Jones in our time, in his *Hamlet and Oedipus* (1949). If in addition one thinks of the

21

fascination which the characters in Webster's *The White Devil* or *The Duchess of Malfi,* or in Middleton's *The Changeling* still have for us, one sees how easily Shakespeare's contemporaries disregarded their own physiological theories of behavior in order to portray the infinitely subtle realities of the human condition.

Paul H. Kocher's essay in this section, "Body and Soul," demonstrates how much the relationship of the body to the soul preoccupied men during the Elizabethan Age, how obviously it entered into everyday thinking, and into literary metaphor. But of greater importance to a continuing problem in Western thought is his discussion of the fact that an Elizabethan "science" of the human body was implicitly antithetical to the Elizabethan-Christian concept of the freedom of the human will. Carried to its logical conclusion, the medical-psychological doctrine of the humours set up as rigid a determinism for its time as does the doctrine of behavioral psychology for ours.

Shakespeare makes constant dramatic use of the possibility of human choice and human exercise of will throughout his plays. But if he thought much about how far a balance of humours determined significant actions, his plays fail to reveal it. Hamlet does speak to Horatio of "some complexion (i.e. the over-balance of some humour)/Oft breaking down the pales and forts of reason" (I.iv). But the problem facing Hamlet is set on a vaster stage than can be encompassed by derangement of bodily fluids. Shakespeare's heroes all seem to be involved in choices that are not predetermined by chemistry. Curiously, however, it is Iago, of all Shakespeare's creations, who most consciously shuns the determinism of Elizabethan physiology. His favoring the theological position of free will is almost pre-Miltonic. As he says to Roderigo, " 'tis in ourselves that we are thus or thus. Our bodies are our gardens, to the which our wills are gardeners" (I.iii).

Perhaps the Elizabethan Age, partly under the prodding of its theologians, always compromised with its own physiologically based determinism. It is a compromise that we still feel essential not only to the creation of great literary art, but essential to the enjoyment of existence. Somehow, we also have managed to shrug off the determinism of our

22

own time, for it would deprive us, too, of the exhilaration and the joy of our illusions of autonomy.

## Section III: Elizabethan Credulity and Belief in the Occult

One is tempted, in the presence of Madeleine Doran's most carefully objective essay in this section, "On Elizabethan Credulity," to accuse the Elizabethans of mere ignorance, and not of any special bias toward the marvelous. They may write as if they believed in spontaneous generation, in unicorns, in the phoenix. But if the skeptical Sir Walter Raleigh could give a clear account, in his *The Discoverie of . . . Guiana* (1596), of men with "eyes in their shoulders, and their mouths in the middle of their breasts," why should Shakespeare boggle at allowing Othello to fascinate Desdemona with a description of "men whose heads/Do grow beneath their shoulders" (I.iii). We are still ready, in our scientific twentieth century, to believe in flying saucers and little men from space at the flashing of a light on a dark night.

The three categories by which Miss Doran separates levels of Elizabethan response to the marvelous in life and in literature (pp. 155-156) seem to me essential ones for the honest reader who does not wish to invent some simple-minded "average" Elizabethan always agape at new wonders. She helps us enormously in placing such things as the ghost in Elizabethan drama, such mysterious narcotics as that given Juliet by the Friar, and such non-worldly creatures as Robin Goodfellow and Ariel. Indeed, she tempts us to speculate that certain Elizabethans—William Camden, Ben Jonson, Francis Bacon—would rather generally have preferred the skepticism of her second category or the outright rejection of her third when faced with most contemporary accounts of the marvelous.

When we turn to literature, we find that Edmund Spenser, of all his contemporaries, plays the most sophisticated tricks with levels of credulity. In his introduction to Book Two of *The Faerie Queene,* he argues that his fable will be regarded by some readers as only "th' abundance of an

23

ydle braine," and a "painted forgery." But he appeals to recent discoveries in the new world, "Indian Peru," the Amazon river, "fruitfullest Virginia," as evidence that anything may be true, even the legends of his *Faerie Queene*.

Spenser is inviting his sixteenth-century readers to consider the legendary fabric of his epic as something not wholly separate or apart from its "meaning." He seems to be saying that even though, in a way, the story be fanciful, yet it is "true" as part of the whole intention. That is to say, Spenser makes odd and extraordinary use of his age's concern with the marvelous. He wishes the reader to entertain the possibility of the events of his epic, without literal or actual belief in them. He wishes the deep seriousness, the deep concern with that which ought-to-be-possible to take strong hold of the reader's imagination in the presence of his work.

The second of the two essays in this section is Walter I. Trattner's sketch of the early career of Dr. John Dee (1527-1608), an Elizabethan mathematician, geographer, and investigator of the occult. I have included it because it reports the chaotic and fragmentary "scientific" results which occurred when a man with a brilliant scientific mind was turned loose in the sixteenth century. There were no clear boundaries, no known landmarks in the physical sciences. An investigator like Dr. Dee, working pretty much alone, was perhaps somewhat in the position of a man with the musical genius of a Mozart, but born into the world before there were sophisticated musical instruments, players, or a systematic method of musical notation.

Dr. Dee casting the horoscope for the young Queen Elizabeth to determine a proper inauguration day, recording his conversations with spirits, putting together the largest personal library of his time, reminds us both of Marlowe's Dr. Faustus and of Shakespeare's Prospero. Both dramatic characters lack a certain relevance in our twentieth-century world, even though we are willing to accept them on Miss Doran's third level: we are willing to entertain them and the fictions in which they live, imaginatively. But the mere existence of a genuine Dr. Dee gives us an historical referent for Marlowe's and for Shakespeare's magician, and lends them new dignity and substance.

I do not wish to understate the credulity of the Elizabethans and to make them more knowing than they really were in matters we think today susceptible to scientific proof. Sir John Davies, for example, the author of *Nosce Teipsum,* had the misfortune to marry a wife in league with the dark powers. She predicted the date of his death, and he seems to have died right on time. Queen Elizabeth, as we have seen, consulted Dr. John Dee. King James I, her successor, published a defense of the occult in his *Daemonology, in Forme of a Dialogue* (London, 1603).

William Camden, on the other hand, in all 661 pages of his history, seems to shun the marvelous and the occult as carefully as would David Hume, as a leading skeptic of the eighteenth century. Camden records a new star seen in the constellation Cassiopeia in November, 1572, a dramatic earthquake in Herefordshire which raised a hill in 1571, and a whole series of earthquakes in England in 1580 and again in 1583, without looking on them as signs and portents. Yet he, too, is half-willing to concede to the occult powers that the storms at sea which prevented the arrival of Anne of Denmark for her marriage to King James, in 1588, were their work, the result of "sorceries and evill practices of magicians and witches" (p. 438). He was writing his history under King James who himself believed in such things, however, and Camden may merely have been trying to be careful.

Madeleine Doran's discussion of the credulity of the Elizabethans, and Trattner's short life of Dr. Dee do give us, at any rate, sufficient information to help us place the meaning of the marvelous and the occult in sixteenth-century literature. Such essays in literary history make us more comfortable in our confrontations with what, at first, may seem very strange views indeed expressed in the writings of the Elizabethan Age.

Section IV: Intellectual Ferment in the Elizabethan Age

The first of the essays in this section is Theodore

Spencer's carefully articulate "Man in Nature: The Renaissance Conflict." In it he describes two rather different bases for the intellectual ferment which permeates the Elizabethan Age and its literature. The first of the conflicts was wholly within the theologically rationalized Christian view of the nature of reality, and arose between an optimistic reaction to fallen mankind and a pessimistic one. The optimistic view saw a hierarchical ordering of the bodies of the heavens (all turning around the earth as the center of the universe), a hierarchical ordering in society with a semi-divine monarch at the head of it, a hierarchical ordering in the animal kingdom, with man poised between the angels and the beasts. According to this view, man, though ejected from Paradise and living on in his less attractive state, was still at the center of the universe and of God's concern. By his own efforts of will, and by God's grace, he could get through life and return to Paradise.

The pessimistic view, while accepting the universe as divinely organized into a series of analogous orders, stressed the impotence of the individual in his post-lapsarian predicament. It saw man as born into a corrupt, sinful world where the quest for fame and honor was a paradoxical part of the corruption. As corollary, this pessimistic view also stressed the weakening of man's reason, his greater corruption, because of the age of the world of God's special creation, and its steady declination into darkness.

In the literature of the age, Edmund Spenser, in *The Faerie Queene,* seems to be wholly on the optimistic side. One sees this in the general moral intention of his epic, as he announced it, and by the fact that book by book each of his virtues is a demonstration of how it can survive in a naughty world. (One sees only a glimpse in him of the other, pessimistic reaction, at the beginning of Book Five where the discourse concerns the aging of the world and its greater wickedness.) If one reaches beyond the Elizabethan Age to Milton's great epic of his maturity, *Paradise Lost,* we find him supporting the theologically hopeful position to the point of suggesting that good actually came out of the evil of "man's first disobedience." This Miltonic view travels in twentieth-century criticism as "the paradox of the fortunate fall."

Perhaps the Elizabethan aspect of this theological conflict which now seems most remote is the negative, pessimistic view, since its opposite has rather generally prevailed, at least in the modern Protestant church. One finds it expressed in many places, but it dominates the work of Fulke Greville, for example. It reaches its most profound Elizabethan expression in his often quoted lines spoken by the Chorus Sacerdotum, at the end of his closet drama *Mustapha*:

> Oh wearisome condition of humanity!
> Born under one law, to another bound:
> Vainly begot, and yet forbidden vanity,
> Created sick, commanded to be sound:
> What meaneth Nature by these diverse laws?

In John Donne's poetry we seem to get now one side, now the other, according to the needs of the particular poem. He shows nothing like the fairly consistent optimism of Spenser or the complete Christian pessimism of Fulke Greville. In Donne's "Satyre II," for example, he outdoes anything that Calvin or Hooker might have said about human depravity, after the fall, in his salute to contemporaries:

> . . . which use
> To out-swive Dildoes, and out-usure Jewes;
> To out-drinke the sea, to out-sweare the Letanie;
> Who with sinnes all kindes as familiar bee
> As Confessors; and for whose sinfull sake,
> Schoolemen new tenements in hell must make.

Donne's memorial poetry to Elizabeth Drury is scathing in its references to human evil and the increased corruption in a fast withering world. From even before the moment of man's fall, corruption

> . . . seis'd the Angels, and then first of all
> The world did in her cradle take a fall,
> And turn'd her braines, and tooke a generall maime,
> Wronging each joynt of th' universall frame.
>
> ("An Anatomy of the World," 11. 195-198)

27

Yet in perhaps his best-known religious sonnet, "Death be not proud," Donne, unconcerned with human depravity and earthly decay, is wholly engrossed with the certainty of salvation:

> One short sleepe past, wee wake eternally,
> And death shall be no more; death, thou shalt die.

In Shakespeare, we get many casual references to the fall and to mankind in a post-lapsarian state, simply, one supposes, because the concept was one his age lived with as unconsciously as ours does with the superego and the id. In his very early *Comedy of Errors,* for example, Aegean refers to his pregnant wife as "almost at fainting under/The pleasing punishment that women bear" (Genesis 3, 16). In a comedy of his middle years, *As You Like It,* the Duke, in one of those typical Shakespearean simultaneously mocking and accepting lines, tells his rural court "Here feel we not the penalty of Adam,/The seasons' difference" (II.i); and then goes on to tell how they do. In the late play, *The Winter's Tale,* Polixenes argues in jest that could he and Leontes have retained their youthful innocence, "we should have answered Heaven/Boldly, 'Not guilty,' the imposition cleared/Hereditary ours" (I.ii). Shakespeare does not, however, often weight his dialogue with serious reference to the Christian pessimistic view, after the fashion of Donne or of Greville.

The second of the conflicts that Theodore Spencer discusses is quite different, and a product of that strange secular energizing of the human mind which we associate with the Renaissance. In one of its manifestations, it is a product of the new Copernican astronomy which, verified by Galileo, disrupted the old, comfortable analogical way of relating order in the heavens with order in the social and political spheres. The second of its manifestations is what we might today call a new, non-theological epistemological concern. It enters the thinking of the Elizabethan Age pretty much with Montaigne's *Essays* (translated into English, 1603), and is the beginning of our modern reliance upon the human mind, limited as it is, rather than upon tradition or revelation, as the basis for all knowing.

28

The third manifestation is a new secular concern for the basis of the authority of men in political power. It comes vividly alive in Machiavelli's amoral, atheological *The Prince,* a sharply perceptive, wholly this-worldly examination of the nature of political power in the state. His views, of course, are diametrically opposed to notions of a hierarchical society based upon a divine plan, a divine chain of being.

Theodore Spencer's essay amply suggests the impact of this three-pronged new secularism on the old Christian frames of reference, and the way in which it gave pattern to the intellectual ferments of the late sixteenth and early seventeenth century. He also gives many examples to show its effects on the literature of the time. I would like to add to his examples three more from Shakespeare to suggest the wide diffusion of this ferment.

In *Love's Labor's Lost,* Shakespeare's comedy which teases the new learning, the character Biron comments adversely, if very lightly, on the new fascination with astronomy:

These earthly godfathers of heaven's lights,
 That give a name to every fixed star,
Have no more profit of their shining, nights,
 Than those that walk and wot not what they are. (I.i)

Shakespeare's Richard III is a deliberate Machiavellian villain, almost a taunt to the Elizabethan cries of horror at Machiavelli's challenge to the old social order. But Shakespeare's taunt, if it was one, fascinated his age and made the play one of Shakespeare's most popular. It went through five separate printings during his lifetime. Finally, when Hamlet remarks to Rosencrantz that "there is nothing either good or bad, but thinking makes it so," and tells Guildenstern that the world, so beautiful to others, is to him "a foul and pestilent congregation of vapours," Shakespeare touches the new way of looking, as initiated by Montaigne.

The second of the essays in Section IV, Geoffrey Bush's "The Order and Continuance of Nature," sets Shakespeare's work somewhat to one side of the intellectual conflicts of his age. Bush regards Shakespeare as committed largely to the nature of things-in-themselves, in his plays, and not especially to the ways in which they may illustrate a philosophy or theology of Nature, or Being. A quality of detachment in Shakespeare from the local intellectual issues of his day Bush regards as a constituent element of his view and of his genius.

One needs to annotate words and phrases in Shakespeare to show how he worked within the vocabulary and the ideas of his time. But if, as Ben Jonson tells us, he was really "not of an age, but for all time," then we need to look as closely at those aspects of his art discussed by Geoffrey Bush as we do at his involvement with the local issues of his day. As Bush points out, the Elizabethan "doctrine of order has not survived: we no longer believe in degree and hierarchy." But *Hamlet* and *King Lear* have survived: they belong to a different enterprise of the mind, concerned with matters more personal, more obscure, and more exacting of our fears and affections."

## Section V: Elizabethan Intellectual Ferment and the Tragic Drama

Both essays in this section illustrate the significance for our understanding of certain aspects of early seventeenth-century tragedy of the kind of historical information presented by Theodore Spencer in his essay in *Section IV*, "Man in Nature: The Renaissance Conflict." Clifford Leech's "The Tragic Picture" points out relationships between the tone and mood of the waning Elizabethan years and the tragedies of Shakespeare and his contemporaries. He touches upon most of the bases of the intellectual ferment of the whole age. But his focus is really upon the private tragic mood which this ferment induced in certain playwrights of the period, their rather sudden and heavy "preoccupation with an irredeemable darkness" in all human existence. Irving Ribner's essay, his "Introduction" to a study of six Elizabethan-Jacobean writers of tragedy other than Shakespeare, is a much more specific analysis of the relevance in their works of conflicts underlying this intellectual ferment of the time. Each critic makes his own use of the interrelationship between an historical frame of reference and the very great Elizabethan achievement in dramatic tragedy. Each essay is self-contained and needs no editorial comment.


## Section VI: The Elizabethan Age, A Synthesis

Patrick Cruttwell's essay, "The Society of the Shakespearean Moment," summarizes many of the aspects of the Elizabethan Age discussed in the ten preceding essays. But it does more than that: it gives us a sense of the special tone of the aristocratic Elizabethan Age, of what it must have been like to those alive in it. Cruttwell's purpose, as his title suggests, is precisely to make clear interrelations between the literature of the age, the men that inhabited it, and the ideas or concepts of the time. Since he succeeds so well, he leaves me no room for further comment.


## Appendix: The Elizabethan Voices

Francis Bacon's most important writings, *The Advancement of Learning* (1605), and *Novum Organum* (1620), advocated a new method of investigating the nature of the physical universe. He grew up under Queen Elizabeth, but achieved his greatest worldly power under her successor, King James. He was appointed Lord Chancellor in 1618, and Viscount St. Albans in 1621. He probably saw Queen Elizabeth, and conversed with her, as often as any contemporary not a part of her personal staff. What he has to say about her, therefore, is based upon a lifetime's personal knowledge and observation, and is the admiration of one kind of genius for another. Ben Jonson considered Bacon to have had one of the brightest and most observant minds in Western civilization, and no one has ever cared to challenge Jonson's view.

The final selection in this anthology is the brief account of Queen Elizabeth's death by William Camden. I have often referred to his *History* of his age. He was Headmaster of Westminster School, Ben Jonson's teacher and lifelong

31

friend, and Clarenceux King at Arms, in which post he was responsible for the coat-of-arms drawn up for Shakespeare. He was the scholar to whom King James was willing to entrust the task of writing the account of Queen Elizabeth's reign. It seemed fitting, therefore, to give the reader of this anthology his portrait of the woman who gave her name to the greatest period of English literature. We see her at age seventy, and the year was 1603.

# I

## THE SOCIAL AND POLITICAL ORDER

*Curtis Brown Watson's two-part essay, "The Aristocratic Class Structure of the Renaissance," and "The Renaissance Concept of Honor," is taken from his book* Shakespeare and the Renaissance Concept of Honor. *In Watson's book, this essay appears as Chapter* 2.

*Lacey Baldwin Smith's "English Treason Trials and Confessions in the Sixteenth Century," was first published in October,* 1954, *in the* Journal of the History of Ideas (*XV*, 471-498).

## THE ARISTOCRATIC CLASS STRUCTURE OF THE RENAISSANCE

### By Curtis Brown Watson

1

#### THE DEFINITION OF NOBILITY

"I grant that not only in respect of our beginning, but of our ending too, we are all equals without difference or superioritie of degrees, all tending alike to the same earth from whence we sprong . . . but in the middle course . . . we are over-runne by our betters and . . . must needes confesse that some excell and are more noble than others."[1] The basic aristocratic assumptions of Renaissance society are admirably summed up by this passage from James Cleland's *The Institution of a Nobleman,* which so clearly indicates the vast gulf separating the democratic ideals of Western European civilization in the 20th century from the aristocratic ideals of that same civilization in the 16th century. The inequality of men, the fundamental superiority of some and inferiority of others, and the acquiescence of the vast majority of Elizabethans in being "over-runne by their betters" are as basically the political and social assumptions of Renaissance society as the notions of a social and political equality of all men, of a classless society—with consequent resentment of any attempt to assert class superiority—are the fundamental ideals of our own democratic society.

Despite the fact that Renaissance Europe represents one of the strongest influences in our own cultural heritage, we must recognize our profound antagonism toward many of its basic moral, social, and political assumptions fully to comprehend its concepts and its sensibility. Particularly when we examine political and social ideas of aristocratic superiority, of degrees of moral "nobility" and of social worth, must we recognize deeply rooted beliefs totally alien to us, for it is in just these aristocratic assumptions that the Renaissance concept of honor is rooted. Hence, an adequate analysis of this concept depends on a thorough comprehension of the aristocratic, hierarchical structure of Elizabethan society, and, in particular, a clear idea of the meanings it assigned the concept of nobility.

A central problem of every Renaissance work on moral philosophy was to define the nature of true nobility. An abundance of material on nobility exists which has been studied with painstaking thoroughness by Ruth Kelso in her able and informative book, *The Doctrine of the Elizabethan Gentleman.* Although there is bewildering complexity and sometimes even outright contradiction in the definitions of the concept, they can be reduced to three essential notions. The first of these is based on the idea of virtue and moral worth, but it places its emphasis par-

[1] p. 2.

ticularly on outstanding and preeminent virtue, superior moral excellence, manifested by undertaking lofty enterprises, civil or military, in the service of the state. The second results from the inheritance of noble blood from a long line of aristocratic ancestors. Finally, there is "nobility dative"—the particular titles of nobility which could be acquired by the accomplishment of deeds of outstanding public service.

Each of these was an aspect of the Renaissance concept of nobility. The apparent complexity of discussions of them results from a given writer's stressing one at the expense of another, usually for the didactic effect an exaggerated emphasis would produce. Thus Sidney writes in his *Aphorisms*:

> I am no herald to inquire of men's pedigrees; it sufficeth me, if I know their virtues.[2]

Montaigne makes a sharper distinction between personal worth and inherited nobility, placing a higher value on the first. Nobility and virtue, he says,

> have affinitie; but therewithall great difference: their names and titles should not thus be commixt: both are wronged so to be confounded. Nobilitie is a worthy, goodly quality, and introduced with good reason, but in as much as it dependeth on others, and may fall to the share of any vicious and worthlesse fellowe, it is in estimation farre shorte of vertue.[3]

The two men are not as indifferent to aristocratic ancestry as they appear to be. The tendency of the Renaissance moralists, culling eclectically from the pagan moralists, to involve themselves in paradox, contradiction, and outright inconsistency, should be recognized from the start.

Yet, although Renaissance moral ideas were seldom original and lacked the systematic integration and logical consistency which a single man, Aquinas, could give to 13th century thought, we find remarkable agreement on many essential points. The problems discussed so exhaustively in the books of moral philosophy were also receiving attention in the literature and drama of the Renaissance, were shaping the ideas and opinions of the men of the age,

[2] Sir Philip Sidney, *Aphorisms*, London, 1807, I, 3.

[3] *The Essayes of Michael Lord of Montaigne*, trans. John Florio, London, 1910, III, 5. (These references are to book and chapter.)

and hence were reflected in the social customs of the time. The extent to which central ethical concerns were unified in moral theory, literature, and life, is revealed in Renaissance discussions of true nobility. Henry Medwall's *A Goodly Interlude of Fulgens . . . and Lucrece* (1497) is nothing more than the presentation of such nobility in dramatic form. To trace its sources is rewarding as an indication of the truly international nature of humanist ideas and of the many links in the chain which connect the English manifestation of them with their classical sources in Italy. The original document was a dull treatise on the nature of true nobility, *De Vera Nobilitate,* written by Bonaccorso in 1428. Jean Mielot composed a French version of the book which was in turn translated into English by John Tiptoft, Earl of Worcester, and printed by William Caxton. Medwall makes use of the English translation.

The central moral and social issue of the play is simple enough. Lucrece, daughter of a noble senator of Rome, has to choose between two suitors. The one, Gaius Flaminius, is of common stock but great moral worth; the other, Publius Cornelius, although of aristocratic origin, is morally corrupt and ill-mannered. In Tiptoft's version, the daughter refers the suitors to her father, who in turn appeals to the Roman senate to decide which of the two men is the worthier suitor. The story ends inconclusively without any resolution of the dilemma. In Medwall's version, on the other hand, although Lucrece hesitates for some time before arriving at a decision, her final choice is unequivocally in favor of the plebeian but virtuous Flaminius. She decides,

> As the more noble man sith he this wise
> By means of his virtue to honor doth arise.

> I said this before
> That a man of excellent vertuouse conditions
> All though he be of a pore stoke bore
> Yet I will honour and comende him more
> Than one that is descendide of right noble kin
> Whole liffe is all dissolute and rotide in sin.[4]

[4] Henry Medwell, *Fulgens and Lucres,* New York, 1920, fol. g. i.

36

The conflict between simple virtue and inherited nobility is revealed with even greater dramatic force in the account of the trial of Lord Essex. During the trial Essex saw fit to mention that Cecil's grandfather had been an innkeeper, while Essex himself could boast of a pure and illustrious aristocratic heritage. Whereupon Cecil arose with great indignation and replied:

> My Lord of Essex . . . the difference between you and me is great. For wit I give you the preeminence, you have it abundantly; for nobility also I give you the place —I am not noble, yet a gentleman; I am no swordsman—there also you have the odds; but I have innocence, conscience, truth, and honesty, to defend me against the scandal and sting of slanderous tongues, and in this Court I stand as an upright man, and your Lordship as a delinquent.[5]

Although Cecil suggests that he is a more virtuous man than Essex, he nonetheless defers to no inconsiderable extent to Essex, since Elizabeth's erstwhile favorite could boast of aristocratic lineage. Indeed, as Johan Huizinga points out in his informative book *The Waning of the Middle Ages,* even when the nobleman was sentenced to death, he was still accorded all the respect to which his rank entitled him. The cloth placed over his eyes and the cushion on which he knelt were of crimson velvet as symbols of his high station.[6]

The basic assumption of aristocratic theory was, further, that the nobleman would be less likely to be vicious than the common man. As *The Courtier's Academie* suggests, "the noble seemeth borne with a better inclination, and disposition unto vertue, then a plebeian, or one extracted from the common sorte."[7] Several arguments were advanced to support this idea. One of them bears a striking resemblance to racial doctrines of our own 20th century, although the purity of blood desired was that of a class elite rather than one of race. In the words of Cornwallis, "since Time hath distild our bloods and separated us from

[5] *The Life and Death of Robert Devereux Earl of Essex,* ed. G. B. Harrison, New York, 1937, p. 307.

[6] London, 1937, p. 34.   [7] p. 185.

the crowde, I holde nobility bound not to commit any action tasting of a degenerate humor."[8]

Another argument stressed that a noble line of ancestors provided an incentive to emulate their renowned and preeminent virtues. The aristocrat had not only his own reputation to consider, but also the good name of his family. Castiglione, for example, insists that his ideal courtier must be born of noble stock:

> For it is a great deale less dispraise for him that is not borne a gentleman to faile in the actes of vertue, then for a gentleman. If he swerve from the steps of his ancestors, hee staineth the name of his familie.[9]

Conversely, as *The Courtier's Academie* points out, the plebeian inherits a predisposition to lesser virtue and can only convince the world of his unusual worth and merit by the greatest effort: "As it is knowne that the one is nobly borne, and the other not, with every one he ignoble shal be lesse esteemed, than the other noble; and it is necessary, that one ignoble, by many endeavours, and in long time, imprint in the minde of men, a good opinion of himselfe."[10]

The third major argument used by the aristocratic theorist to support his notion that the sons of the aristocracy were, almost inevitably, superior to the sons of the middle or working class, was that of breeding and education. Thus La Primaudaye observes:

> The Nobilitie is the ornament of everie Commonwealth. For commonly the Nobles are of greater abilitie, of better behaviour and more civill than the common people, than artificers, and men of base estate, because they have beene brought up from their infancie in all civilitie and amongst men of honor.[11]

As this passage indicates, honor and nobility were restricted to the aristocratic class largely because that class had sufficient leisure for a humanistic education in the liberal arts and the moral disciplines. "To acquire vertue, quiet, and leasure is requisit."[12] This leads Count Romei,

[8] William Cornwallis, *Essayes,* ed. D. C. Allen, Baltimore, 1946, p. 39.

[9] Baldassare Castiglione, *The Book of the Courtier,* trans. Thomas Hoby, London, 1928, pp. 31-32.

[10] p. 224.    [11] *The French Academie,* p. 687.

[12] Count Romei, p. 199.

in *The Courtier's Academie,* to make a sharp distinction between the education of the gentleman in the liberal arts and the training of the lower classes in the mechanical arts.

Nobility, then, could mean exalted moral worth or it could mean exalted class position. As the above quotation from *The French Academie* suggests, the two were usually closely linked—a man of noble blood would, presumably, receive the proper training in morals and manners, and hence would, in all likelihood, be noble and worthy of honor because of both his rank and his character. Even though the moral philosophers made due allowance for nobility without virtue, and for virtue without nobility, the ideal gentleman would be able to boast both of his noble lineage and of his virtue. Mulcaster agrees, noting that if he adds

> desert in his own person . . . [he] doth well deserve double honour among men, as bearing the true coate of right and best nobilitie, where desert for vertue is quartered with discent in blood, seeing aunciencie of linage, and derivation of nobilitie is in such credit among us and alwaye hath bene.[13]

Every Renaissance work on moral philosophy reaches this conclusion when it discusses the nature of true nobility. Each kind of nobility is desirable, but as an ideal neither is sufficient by itself. The more exalted one's rank or one's virtuous qualities, the more one is deserving of receiving honor. In the words of Elyot,

> Severite . . . Magnanimitie . . . Constance . . . Honour . . . Sapience . . . Continence. . . . These qualities . . . do expresse or sette out the figures of very nobilitie; whiche in the higher astate it is contained, the more excellent is the vertue in estimation.[14]

## THE POLITICAL HIERARCHY

The Renaissance moralists, in accordance with their pyramidal and hierarchical view of degrees of superiority in the social body, found an especial correlation between

[13] Richard Mulcaster, *Positions,* London, 1581, p. 200.
[14] Thomas Elyot, I. 21.

the exalted elite of heroic and magnanimous men of outstanding virtue and those who belonged to the highest
political ranks. The monarch, in theory at least, was both
politically and morally supreme, and the great lords of the
realm were presumably the high-minded, great-hearted
souls whose preeminent virtue made them the heroes of
the age. Count Romei sums up this ideal correlation when
he suggests that political degrees "have amongst themselves like proportion of nobilitie, as in them of vertue
there is supposed."[15]

For the aristocratic society of the Renaissance, the positions of the greatest social importance were the "seven
degrees of superioritie" described by Segar in *Honor
Military and Civill,*

> Of Gentlemen, the first and principal is the King, Prince,
> Dukes, Marquesses, Earls, Viscounts, and Barons.
> These are the Nobilitie, and be called Lords, or Noble-
> man. Next to these be Knights, Esquiers, and simple
> gentlemen, which last number may be called *Nobilitas
> minor.*[16]

This classification includes all the groups which could
rightly consider themselves members of the aristocracy.
The sharp line the Elizabethans drew to distinguish the
upper from the lower classes appears in Markham's remarks on gentility.

> *Honor or Nobilitie* which the Grecians doe call *Eugenia,*
> and signifieth liberal and good Birth, is nothing else but
> *Gentrie,* or the true title of Gentleman; which, howso-
> ever it alter by multiplication of Titles, yet that is the
> first and most auncient; as being the only Ground-worke
> or Base, from whence is raised and built up the goodly
> Pyramed or Collosses of all other great denominations,
> for it can Support and beare up it selfe of it selfe, when
> without it all other Titles fall, vanish, and are nothing.
> And whether we derive it from *Generosus,* or *Gentilis,*
> that is, from *Honor* or good familie, yet it is the first
> witnesse of Vertue, and makes the person in whom it
> dwels capable (by merit) of all other Honors whatso-
> ever.[17]

[15] p. 227.
[16] William Segar, *Honor Military and Civill,* London, 1602, II, 51.
[17] Francis Markham, *The Booke of Honour or Five Decads of
Epistles of Honour,* London, 1625, p. 44.

40

The famous incident of Sidney's challenge to Oxford on the tennis court in front of the French ambassador indicates how important it was to Queen Elizabeth to maintain degrees of rank. She rebuked Sidney as an inferior challenging a superior; obviously she was more concerned with a proper and due respect for superior rank than she was with the propriety of a challenge to a duel, though, as we shall see, the Renaissance monarch was opposed to that particular Renaissance ritual.

*The Monarch.* The monarch stood at the apex of Renaissance society. His position became more and more exalted as the national states took shape and, directly or indirectly, challenged the supreme power of the medieval church. At this point, Christian and pagan-humanist theory coalesce, both bestowing on the regal position an almost divine character. In Christian theory, the king was the direct representative of God on earth, hence his position was sacrosanct. A challenge to the king's authority was a challenge of the divine order of things; sedition and atheism were often linked by the political philosophers of the 16th century. Indeed, it was sometimes assumed that even a wicked monarch was to be given unquestioned obedience since many Renaissance Protestants took it for granted that God could have selected an evil tyrant only if he wished to scourge a nation for its sins. Guazzo gives apt expression to the religious injunction which lay behind the political absolutism of the age.

> I have alwayes blamed in my minde, those which will appoint lawes and orders of life to Princes, who are Lordes over Lawes, and injoyne them to others. And therefore by my will we will not apply the humilitie of our Philosophie to the Majestie of Princes: for that beeing Gods on earth, it is to bee thought, that all which they doe is done well; and that to reason of and call into question their dooinges, is nothing else but with the Giants, to lay siege to heaven.[18]

Guazzo therefore admonishes his Courtier to give the Prince "the love, fidelitie, diligence, and reverence whiche is due to Princes"; the Prince being "a God on earth, it

[18] M. S. Guazzo, *The Civile Conversation,* trans. George Pettie, London, 1581, II, 47.

behoveth him to doe him honoure as to a sacred thing."[19]

Pagan-humanist theory likewise held that the monarch deserved the highest esteem since monarchy and aristocracy were the two forms of government which received the fullest approval of the pagan philosophers. According to the ideal theory of pagan-humanist philosophy, the prince excelled in virtue and valor to the same extent as he was preeminent in social rank. He was, as Hurault said, "the chiefe and most excellent of all."[20] Hence he should be the first to be admitted to that select circle of heroes and demigods who surmount all other men in virtue. In the words of Count Romei,

> Seeing honours and prerogatives, are imparted to nobilitie correspondent to the vertue, which in their kind is presumed to bee . . . the last, wherin vertue heroicall is supposed, being that of Kings . . . is most superior.[21]

Hurault in like manner quotes from Aristotle's *Politics* to support his admonition that a king "ought to be esteemed as a God among men."[22]

To justify this exaltation of the monarch, the pagan philosophers argued that the first men to become kings were selected for their goodness and virtue. Hurault, quoting from the *Offices* of Cicero, states that "the first chusings of Kings, was for the estimation which men had of them, that they were good and just men."[23] This, of course, gave added sanction to the monarch's position, since it suggested that the royal families passed on their superior virtue from generation to generation. In their political theory, the pagan humanists made a sharp distinction between the king, who by his very title was a good man, and the tyrant, whose government was among the worst. Tyrannicide had its place in the ethics of the Greek and Roman philosophers. In the Renaissance, certain Calvinist writers (Philip Mornay, Bishop Pynet, and George Buchanan, for example), and the Jesuits supported it; the majority of political theorists, however, accepted the Christian view for which La Primaudaye speaks in the following passage:

[19] *ibid.*, III, 55.
[20] Jacques Hurault, *Politicke, Moral and Martial Discourses*, p. 5.
[21] p. 227.
[22] p. 5.    [23] *ibid.*, p. 187.

42

whatsoever they are, they have their authoritie from God onely: the good as mirrors of his goodnes, the bad, as scourges of his wrath to punish the iniquitie of the people. . . . Therefore in respect of obedience and reverence, we owe as much to the unjust, as the just prince.[24]

The exalted position of the Renaissance sovereign, in short, entitled him to the utmost respect, even to a semi-divine reverence. It is easy for us to read our own cultural values into this matter and to view the zealous concern with which the Renaissance monarch guarded his high prestige as but the expression of haughty pride. But both the Christian and the pagan-humanist ethics assumed that the monarch would display an imperial dignity. When Queen Elizabeth writes, for example, that "as a Queen Sovereign" she expects to have "our royal superiority preserved," she is only giving expression to the cultural values of her age.[25] Because the great lords of the realm felt themselves similarly entitled to the highest respect and esteem, it is in the clashes of will between Queen Elizabeth and her great lords that we can observe the high aristocratic dignity of the Renaissance leaders presented in its most colorful and dramatic form.

Some of her most powerful favorites, particularly Essex, dared at times to resent her claim that even the greatest lord was a "creature of her own."[26] It is not merely the fiery temperament of Elizabeth which leads her into a high rage at Essex's conduct. When she rebukes Essex, either by a slap or by written rebuke, she speaks for the political supremacy which her age allowed her. Thus she writes Essex, "Can you imagine that the softness of my sex deprives me of the courage to resent a public affront? The royal blood I boast could not brook, from the mightiest Prince in Christendom, such treatment as you have within the last three months offered to me."[27] Elizabeth felt that she was being presented to the world as the "spectacle of a despised princess" and she would not tolerate such treatment.[28]

[24] p. 576.
[25] *Letters of Queen Elizabeth,* ed. G. B. Harrison, London, 1935, p. 243.
[26] *ibid.,* p. 170.      [27] *ibid.,* p. 218.      [28] *ibid.,* p. 219.

43

*The Great Nobles.* The extent to which the great nobles were aware of their own lofty stature has been indicated; Essex and Peregrine Bertie, in particular, refused to accept an affront from anyone, not excepting the Queen. The French Ambassador, De Maisse, was urged by Essex to call on Burleigh, Essex's great enemy. De Maisse was tremendously impressed by this display of magnanimity and wrote of the great English nobles, "They have great respect for each other."[29] These nobles, unless attending court, lived on large country estates in a magnificent style appropriate to their high position. The Earl of Pembroke, for example, had more than a thousand servants all clad in his livery. Indeed, even at the end of the 16th century, a few of the feudal families remained who were treated with a deferential respect almost equal to that shown the English monarch. The crown, of course, did not meekly accept this haughty independence of the old nobility, for it threatened the unity of the nation and contradicted the patriotic spirit of the first great age of European nationalism. Nonetheless, the lord's retainers often felt a greater loyalty to their own master than to their Queen.

*The Professions and the Merchants Class.* In the Renaissance the profession of learning in general, and the practice of law in particular, were held in the highest repute, even though the scholar was not necessarily of noble blood. Indeed, the final chapter of *The Courtier's Academie* presents a debate on whether the military profession or the profession of letters is entitled to the higher prestige. The resolution of the debate is as convenient and happy as the ending of a Shakespearean comedy. The soldier, it is decided, is more deserving of honor; the scholar should be revered, rather than honored, but held in equal esteem.[30]

Whether the mercantile class could also consider itself worthy of respect was a question of great importance. Fynes Moryson points out how greatly the French and the Italians differed on this matter. Speaking of the French, he says,

[29] André Hurault Sieur de Maisse, *Journal,* ed. G. B. Harrison and R. A. Jones, London, 1931, p. 114.
[30] Count Romei, p. 295.

44

The Nobility high and lowe, I meane lordes and gentlemen, are altogether free from Impositions or Tributes
because they serve the king in his Warrs (as well in
person as with a certaine number of horsemen according
to their quality) without taking any pay. And this Im-
munity little diminisheth the kings profitt, because the
Nobility scornes to be Marchants, thincking such
traffique ignoble, according to the Heraults rules,
howsoever the Italians even the very Princes disdaine
not traffique by the great, leaving only the gaine of
Retailing to the people.[31]

It will be seen that here ideals are being brought into
conformity with the realities of the social structure of a
particular country. Italy was not primarily a nation of
warriors, but rather of learning and trade, as is indicated
by the influential role of the Medici family. Therefore the
scholar and merchant acquire greater prestige than in other
European countries. True, Castiglione does adhere to the
humanist dictum that anyone who worked for gain was
ignoble:

You know in great matters and adventures in wars the
true provocation is glory: and who so for lucres sake or
for any other consideration taketh it in hande (beside
that hee never doth any thing worthie praise) deserveth
not the name of a gentleman, but is a most vile mar-
chant.[32]

Count Romei also admits that "the Philosopher affirmeth,
that the life of marchants is base, and contrary to vertue."[33] Yet he is confronted by the fact that the Venetian
Republic was held in the highest esteem throughout Renaissance Europe. He ponders the gulf between theory and
reality:

I would willingly understand, if to practice marchandise
wer any obstacle of Nobility: For if that should be true,
the Venetian nobility so highly esteemed of, wold be
nothing worth, in that there be seldome any of their
nobles, which are not also marchants.[34]

The resolution of this dilemma involves an interesting
compromise. The motives of the particular merchant are
scrutinized; insofar as public service, benefit to the state,

[31] *Shakespeare's Europe: Unpublished Chapters of Fynes Moryson's
Itinerary,* ed. Charles Hughes, London, 1903, pp. 171-172.
[32] p. 70.    [33] p. 204.    [34] *ibid.*

45

can be ascribed to him, he is exonerated from the charge of baseness since the humanist philosophers had always exalted patriotism.

> For marchandise may be practised two manner of waies, the one, by causing to be brought out of farre countries, those commodities which are not in their own, to their own gaine, and for benefit also of the common-wealth, the other, by not respecting publike benefit, but onely to enrich himselfe.[85]

The conclusion is obvious. The merchant motivated by a desire to serve the state is to be considered noble and worthy of praise, but he who is motivated simply by self-interest is utterly ignoble, "this being grounded upon avarice, and a sordide gaine, as it is from vertue farre remote."[86]

*The Working Class.* A close correlation exists in pagan-humanist writings between baseness, as a description of one's low social standing, and baseness in its moral sense. Here again, the Renaissance moralists use Aristotle as their authority.[87] In the *Politics* he had observed, "it is therefore clear from these considerations that in the most nobly constituted state, and the one that possesses men that are absolutely just, not merely just relatively to the principle that is the basis of the constitution, the citizens must not lead a mechanic or a mercantile life (for such a life is ignoble and inimical to virtue)."[88] In accordance with this social theory, Count Romei makes a sharp distinction between the upper and lower classes and argues that virtue belongs almost solely to the aristocracy. "The practice of mechanicall and vile trade, is proper to him ignoble," he observes, and hastens to add "that the life of mechanicall

[85] *ibid.*, p. 205.   [86] *ibid.*
[87] Aristotle is "the Philosopher" in both the 13th and 16th centuries. That he is the authority (the "moral pilot" of Europe, in Eliot's phrase) in both centuries does not mean that there is any necessary parallel in interpretation of Aristotle by Dante's and by Shakespeare's contemporaries. As Henri Busson points out "the greatest enemy of the Christian faith in the 16th century is precisely the person who had been its main support in the 13th—Aristotle." Henri Busson, *Les Sources et le Développement du Rationalisme,* p. 9.
[88] H. Rackham, trans., Cambridge, Mass., 1944, vii, 8.

46

artificers is base, degenerating from vertue, and unworthy a civill man."[39] Elsewhere he is even more sweeping in his indictment of the lower classes. "He which is employed in base practises cannot exercise vertue: and there is no doubt, but all common wealths, as well ancient, as moderne, distinguish by this character, the noble from the vulgar sort."[40] Again and again, the Renaissance moralists emphasize this major social theme: that the greatest gulf exists between the aristocratic and the lower classes, and that this is as it should be. Our use today of such insulting epithets as "boor," "rustic," and "farmer" indicates the extent to which our terms of opprobrium in a democratic society had their origin in the aristocratic and hierarchical class distinctions of the Renaissance.

It would overstate Renaissance attitudes, however, to suggest that no allowances were made for the possibility that the lower classes might be virtuous. One of the three definitions of nobility was purely in terms of virtue, per se, as has been indicated. The aristocrat might have a greater inclination to lead a virtuous life, and he might possess the virtues more abundantly, but no Renaissance moralist would completely deny that a peasant or artisan could at least possess the simple virtues. As Cornwallis says, "I am not so precise to call no Actions noble that carry not with them a rumour or a glittering. To my meaning, nobility and honesty meane al one; and thus may a paineful Artisan be noble, if he follows his vocation painefully and constantly, he is honest, and so noble, being a Limme of a state though no maine Organ."[41] Similarly, in *The Steel Glas* Gascoigne exalts the virtues of the simple plowman. Indeed, he warns that Peerce Plowman may climb to heaven before the priest since he may possess greater humility. Hence he admonishes: "Behold him, priests, & though he stink of sweat/Disdaine him not."[42]

Whatever the allowances of this sort, no book or treatise on ethical and political philosophy concealed the tone of disdain and contempt with which the aristocrat referred

[39] p. 195.  [40] *ibid.,* p. 202.
[41] p. 198.
[42] George Gascoigne, *Complete Works,* Vol. 2, p. 170.

to his social inferiors. For Plato, Aristotle, and Cicero, democracy rivaled tyranny as an example of the worst of governments precisely because the lower classes, viewed as a whole, were considered ignorant, irresponsible, and hence utterly incapable of self-government. The masses were to be feared, distrusted, held in scorn, and kept in their place. They were usually described in such derogatory terms as "base," "vulgar," "fickle," and "foolish." Insofar as they knew their proper station, respected their betters, and were true and loyal subjects of their sovereign, they were entitled to his love. But in an age in which such a great Lord as Leicester was referred to by his Queen as a "creature of her own," the common people could hardly expect the monarch to display anything more than the condescending and paternalistic love of a father for an infant child.[43] On this issue the Graeco-Roman philosophers had been in complete agreement. Whether Academic, Peripatetic, or Stoic, the writer of antiquity had held that the multitude would be deficient in the rational faculties on which all the the classical virtues were based. Bryskett's reference to the "vulgar sort, whose judgement is so corrupt and crooked, that they cannot discerne what true honor and dignity is," is but reiteration of the view of antiquity.[44]

2

DEFINITION OF THE CONCEPT OF HONOR

The best definition of the Renaissance concept of honor, as it affected the individual, comes from Rabelais. In speaking of the order of free will in his Thelemite monastery, he describes the simplicity of its rules of virtuous behavior:

[43] *Letters of Queen Elizabeth,* ed. G. B. Harrison, p. 170.
[44] p. 191.

In all their rule, and strictest tie of their order, there was but this one clause to be observed:

## DO WHAT THOU WILT

Because men that are free, well-borne, well-bred, and conversant in honest companies, have naturally an instinct and spur that prompteth them unto virtuous actions, and withdraws them from vice, which is called honour.[45]

As is so often the case, we are here confronted with a contradiction in the ethos of the pagan humanists. It is suggested on the one hand that the desire for virtue is innate, but on the other hand it is pointed out that the Renaissance aristocrat is carefully instructed in the moral disciplines and refrains from intercourse with any who is not of a like virtue. Virtue is hereditary and in the blood, but it will not, apparently, bear wholesome fruit if the soil is not as carefully selected as the seed.

The sense of honor, the desire for virtue, is then deeply implanted in the soul of the Renaissance gentleman. He is not concerned primarily with the opinion of others, but with his own conscience, his own inner sense of integrity. Insofar as Renaissance moral treatises followed the humanist philosophers of antiquity, first emphasis was placed on the individual's acquisition of a sense of his own value and moral worth. Both Aristotle and Cicero placed major stress on the fact that virtue was not implanted by the gods but resulted largely from a man's own inclination and training. Stoic philosophy developed this theory of individualism and self-reliance to its extreme, but Epictetus is uttering a mere truism of pagan philosophy when he says, "Fidelity is your own, virtuous shame is your own."[46]

According to pagan-humanist theory, however, the sentiment of honor was to be found only in the aristocratic classes. Aristotle had said that arguments:

[45] François Rabelais, *Gargantua and Pantagruel,* trans. Sir Thomas Urquhart and Peter Motteux in *Great Books of the Western World,* Vol. 24, Chicago, 1952, I, 57. (These references are to book and chapter.)

[46] *The Discourses of Epictetus,* trans. George Long in *Great Books of the Western World,* Chicago, 1952, Vol. 12, p. 25.

are powerless to stimulate the mass of mankind to moral nobility. For it is the nature of the many to be amenable to fear but not to a sense of honour, and to abstain from evil not because of its baseness but because of the penalties it entails.[47]

This remark becomes a Renaissance commonplace. Repeatedly a distinction is made between those who are motivated "for vertues sake, for feare of reproch, for love and reverence to honestie" to lead upright and virtuous lives, and those who are compelled to goodness and virtue "for feare of punishment to be inflicted on them by the magistrates."[48]

To the modern mind, confronted by three centuries of egalitarianism and scientific scepticism, Renaissance concepts of virtue, conscience, and honor not only tend to have a fuzzy vagueness because they are so abstract, but also fail to evoke any passionate emotional response because our values are, in theory at least, largely democratic. For the man of the Renaissance, on the other hand, they involved his whole being. Honor was related to the intellectual faculties, but was equally an "ardent heate which enflameth the minde of man, to glorious enterprise, making him audacious against enemies, and to vices timerous."[49]

The Renaissance has often been described as an age of exuberant Falstaffian licentiousness and of Marlovian immorality—an age in which the lust for power and the love of sensual delights overflowed all ethical restraints and justified itself simply in terms of animal vitality and emotional intensity. To deny these aspects of the Renaissance spirit would be folly, but they should be subjected to a rarely made qualification. The intensity of Renaissance feeling, while it overflowed with torrential energy the banks of its two main ethical streams, was to a large extent held within the channels of these two rivers. Indeed, the very fact that Renaissance emotion was so channeled, and so directed, gave it much of its intensity. The death of More as a Christian martyr and of Sidney as a soldier fighting for country and honor were as typical as the death of Marlowe in a tavern brawl. Even Montaigne, who at times

[47] *Nicomachean Ethics* x. 9.
[48] Bryskett, p. 138.
[49] Count Romei, p. 78.

seems the very embodiment of the sceptical attitude toward life, highly esteems this sort of moral integration: "The reputation and worth of a man consisteth in his heart and will: therein consists true honour: Constancie is valour, not of armes and legs, but of minde and courage."[50] Only an age which, generally speaking, had an unquestioned faith in the reality of good and evil—be it Christian, or pagan-humanist, or most frequently a mixture of the two— could mold its elite to such a single-minded, intense devotion to virtue and honor.

Honor, as an inner quality, was then first of all a sentiment and passion; it is only when we exhume its corpse from the dreary pages of Elizabethan ethical treatises and breathe into it the living fire with which it possessed the heart, soul, and mind of the English gentleman that we can appreciate its real significance. But the definition of the ethical concept is also important. Honor results from the pursuit of virtue and is inextricably connected with it. A favorite metaphor endlessly quoted by the eclectic Renaissance moralists compared the inseparability of virtue and honor with that of the body and its shadow.[51] It was often suggested that one should seek virtue, and honor will follow like a shadow, whereas it would be folly to pursue honor for its own sake. An equally popular description of the inseparable connection between honor and virtue is that of La Primaudaye:

> For this cause the auncient Romans built two Temples joined together, the one being dedicated to Vertue, and the other to Honor: but yet in such sort, that no man could enter into that of Honor, except that he passed through the other of Vertue.[52]

Robert Ashley's *Of Honour,* which was produced sometime between 1596 and 1603, the period in which Shakespeare was writing many of his greatest plays, is the most compact work on the subject to appear during the English Renaissance. In this work is to be found one of the fullest definitions of honor (one almost identical with the definition in Du Vair's *Moral Philosophy of the Stoicks,* to which I have already referred in the Introduction). Ashley observes that

[50] III, 6.
[51] See "Introduction," n. 3 Watson.     [52] La Primaudaye, p. 233.

51

neither to be praised, nor to be reverenced, nor to be esteemed is for it self to be desired; but that we may behold the Testimonie which good men and wise have geven of our vertue and be delighted therwith, as having not so much confidence in our selves herein as in the judgement of others.[53]

The excellence of this definition lies in its close and precise distinction between honor as an inner quality and honor as a sign of public respect. The opinion of others is not to be ignored as in the ancient Stoic or medieval Christian scheme, but is to give satisfaction by confirming one's inner sense of honor.

### THE INDIVIDUAL VIRTUES

Since most of the Renaissance moralists were agreed that honor results from the pursuit of virtue, they felt it essential to define virtue itself. For Renaissance moral philosophy, as for the philosophers of antiquity from whom they drew their inspiration, four cardinal virtues were of primary importance—prudence or wisdom, justice, fortitude, and temperance. Cicero's statement in the widely quoted *Offices* demonstrates why these were considered "cardinal" virtues:

For, since all moral rectitude springs from four sources (one of which is prudence; the second, social instinct; the third, courage; the fourth temperance), it is often necessary in deciding a question of duty that these virtues be weighed against one another.[54]

These four virtues were the keystones of every Renaissance book on moral philosophy. The Aristotelian virtues expanded beyond them, but largely by building on them. Thus, the virtue of magnanimity arises out of that of fortitude. For the Renaissance moralist, extensions beyond the cardinal four were rarely systematic; he was seldom concerned to copy exactly the twelve Aristotelian virtues. Often, as in *The Faerie Queene,* Christian virtues are mixed with classical. But, as T. S. Eliot has observed, there is an overtone of Christian piety and pity in medieval

[53] *Of Honour,* p. 59.
[54] I. 43.

literature not usually to be found in Elizabethan verse.[55] Hurault and La Primaudaye, however, closely identify magnanimity with the Christian virtue of patience. Almost invariably a Renaissance work on moral philosophy included magnanimity or greatness of soul, liberality, magnificence, modesty, and courtesy, in addition to the four cardinal virtues. Whether or not Christian values were also discussed depended on the extent to which the author was concerned with religious as well as secular morality. La Primaudaye's *French Academie* is largely religious in tone; Count Romei's *Courtier's Academie* is, like so many Italian treatises, primarily secular.

## PATRIOTISM AS AN ASPECT OF FORTITUDE

Patriotism was usually considered one of the essential aspects of the cardinal virtue of valor or fortitude which was also often linked with the all-embracing virtue of magnanimity. The warlike and patriotic spirit of the Elizabethan age is fully delineated in Raleigh's account of *The Last Fight of the Revenge*. Not only does the courageous behavior of the English sailor illuminate his pages, but equally Raleigh's intense patriotic zeal and concern for the reputation of England.

The rise of nationalism in the sixteenth century is a historical truism; the change in sensibility which resulted from an exaltation of national sentiment in wars between Christian nations has often been overlooked. The spirit of Renaissance nationalism is a far cry from medieval attitudes, where, whatever the military realities, war was often justified as a crusade against the infidel or heretic. Loyalty to country and to one's monarch replaces, to no inconsiderable extent, loyalty to the one universal (Catholic) church. The Elizabethan attitude toward the Papists was as much the result of fear of their political might as it was of a distaste for their dogma. Elizabeth might sympathize

[55] "Seneca in Elizabethan Translation," *Selected Essays,* New York, 1932, pp. 87-88.

53

from the religious point of view with the French Huguenots, but her sympathies did not interfere with her more central concern that the principle of royal supremacy and of the iniquity of rebellion be fully recognized throughout Europe. Her remonstrance to the French King about the massacre of her fellow Protestants was but a mild rebuke.

The patriotic sentiment of the Renaissance drew great moral support from the humanist philosophy of antiquity. The intense patriotic fervor of the Roman writers in particular was rapidly picked up by the 16th century moralists. Cicero's definition of glory in *The Philippics* as "praise won by honourable deeds, and great services toward the state" reveals the close correlation between individual achievement and social obligation, the twin poles of Renaissance morality.[56]

## HONOR AS HONESTY, INTEGRITY

The ideal Renaissance gentleman was a man of absolute honesty and integrity. Hence, one of the traditional privileges of the aristocrat had been his right to testify in court without bond and without witnesses. The mere word of a gentleman was, presumably, as trustworthy as the sworn testimony of a man of the lower classes. From this belief arose the conventional form of insult—to give a man the lie—which was a part of the etiquette of the dueling code. The sense of honor and of honesty were equally involved in these cardinal aspects of the dueling code.

Indeed, honor and honesty were practically interchangeable in the Renaissance, although the shading of meaning which distinguishes the two words today had begun to differentiate them. The Latin word *honestas* meant worth, virtue, honorable character, probity. As Guirino, one of Count Romei's courtiers, observes, "by the definition of honour . . . it seemeth that honour and honestie are inseparable."[57] Hurault also maintains that the man who has lost his credit (i.e., honesty, integrity) "hath no more to

[56] Walter C. A. Ker trans., Cambridge, Mass., 1957, I, 12.
[57] p. 117.

54

lose, because the whole welfare and honour of a man dependeth thereupon."[58]

The emphasis on honesty was so great that the pagan philosophers seemed to prefer an honest simpleton to a man who proved to be even slightly deceitful, however brilliant he might be. The humanist philosophers held nothing in greater abhorrence than the feigning of emotions not felt; open enmity is infinitely preferable to pretended love. Cleland is expressing one of the fundamental Renaissance precepts when he says that a friend is "such in his hart as hee appeareth in action, without al dissumulation or deceit, loving nothing but honest, faithful, plain, and simple dealing."[59] Montaigne suggests that nothing shows greater ignobility than deceit:

Of all vices, I finde none that so much witnesseth demissenesse and basenesse of heart. It is a coward and servile humour, for a man to disguise and hide himselfe under a maske, and not dare to shew himselfe as he is. . . . A generous minde ought not to belie his thoughts, but make shew of his inmost parts: There al is good, or at least all is humane. Aristotle thinkes it an office of magnanimitie to hate and love openly, to judge and speake with all libertie.[60]

In this passage, the close integration of various Renaissance virtues is indicated; openness and lack of all pretense are considered indispensable attributes of the magnanimous man. In Renaissance England simplicity may have possessed the pejorative meaning which the word now has but it meant equally a quality of the highest nobility. "In vertue may be nothing fucate [L. "fucatus," = "painted"] or counterfayte. But therein is onely the image of veritie, called simplicitie."[61]

In no aspect of its creed is humanism more dogmatic than in its concern for absolute truthfulness. Anything short of perfect honesty is viewed with dismay; "an honest man . . . never crackt his credit, but is wel known for such an one, and this man is truely worthy of honor, and deservedly honored."[62] Bryskett designates "the bright-shining

[58] p. 93.
[59] p. 195.
[60] *Essayes,* III, 13.    [61] *Elyot,* IV, 4.
[62] Count Romei, p. 108.

vertue of truth" a moral virtue, and adds that "this is that excellent vertue that is of al others the best fitting a Gentleman, and maketh him respected and welcom in all companies."[63] Ben Jonson lays particular emphasis on this quality in his description of Shakespeare, finding him "(indeed) honest, and of an open, and free nature."[64]

If one feels unquestioned confidence in the honesty of others, then a sense of loyalty and fidelity is but a logical concomitant and accessory virtue. For if one accepts the assumption of the humanist moral philosophers that the aristocrats will be guided by a creed of honorable righteousness, then one can rely on the complete confidence of their followers who will have absolute trust in them. Elyot, indeed, insists that trust and loyalty are one and the same virtue:

> That which in latine is called *Fides,* is a parte of justice and may diversely be interpreted, and yet finally it tendeth to one purpose in effecte. Some time it may be called faithe, some time credence, other whiles truste. Also in a frenche terme it is named loyaltie. And to the imitation of latine it is often called fidelitie. All which wordes, if they be intierly and (as I mought saye) exactly understanden, shall appere to a studious reder to signifie one vertue or qualitie, all thoughe they seme to have some diversitie.[65]

In a world which of necessity involved much unpredictable mishap, brought on by fickle Fortune or callous Fate, which contained a relatively small proportion of virtuous men and a multitude who were ignorant, deceitful, treacherous, malicious, and vicious, the pagan humanist depended on the mutual integrity which he felt could exist between men of honor and good will. This was the cord which held human society firmly knit. Thus Hurault asks,

> How could mans frailtie be upheld among so many waves and storms, if there were no firmnesse in the doings and saiengs of princes? Among fellowes, faithfulnesse maintaineth friendship. It maketh servants to obey their maisters with all integritie."[66]

Loyalty, integrity, and trustworthiness were indeed the

[63] p. 243.
[64] *Works*, ed. C. H. Herford and Percy and Evelyn Simpson, Oxford, 1943, Vol. 8, p. 584.
[65] III, 6.  [66] p. 90.

primary virtues of the servant class. Since they were people of low birth, one could not expect them to be heroic—not even honorable in the full sense of the word. Guazzo observes that, though one's servants be "not all of the civillest, yet they are faithfull and trustie, which is a thing more to bee set by, then civilitie, finenesse, or bravery."[67]

If simple honesty and faithfulness are such cardinal virtues in the pagan-humanist ethics, it is not surprising that the greatest attention is paid to the vice of fraud and deceit. Elyot defines fraud as "an evill disceite, craftely imagined and devised, whiche, under a colour of trouthe and simplicitie, indomageth him that nothing mistrusteth."[68] The fear of this vice led classical moralists to write endless pages of advice as to how the true friend could be distinguished from the flatterer and false one. Cleland, in his *Institution of a Nobleman*, lines up the qualities of the two side by side, so that they can be compared with the greatest ease:

> A freind is such in his hart as hee appeareth in action, without al dissimulation or deceit, loving nothing but honest, faithful, plain, and simple dealing.
>
> Where your flatterer under the appearance of a modest grave, and holy countenance, and under the skin of a gentle lambe, shal be ful of fraude and falshood like the foxe.[69]

The Renaissance moralist labored no theme with greater emphasis than that of the disaster which lay in store for the man who could not distinguish between these two types. Since integrity and faithfulness between men of honor were the bonds which cemented human society, the man who masked his self-interest and viciousness under the pretense of good will was considered particularly dangerous. The English admired and distrusted Italy, a land which to them symbolized both the link with a classical past which was becoming more and more meaningful to Northern Europe, and the source of all the sophisticated vices of a pleasure-loving, epicurean civilization. Fynes Moryson, for example, praises the Italians for their good breeding and courtesy on the one hand, but damns them on the other for their lack of integrity. His

[67] III, 53.    [68] III, 4.    [69] p. 195.

57

is a typically English view which finds its most eloquent expression in his *Itinerary*.

> Touching the manners of the Italians. They are for the out side by natures guift excellently composed. By sweetnes of language, and singular Art in seasoning their talke and behaviour with great ostentation of Courtesy, they make their Conversation sweete and pleasing to all men, easily gaining the good will of those with whome they live. But no trust is to be reposed in their wordes, the flattering tounge having small acquaintance with a sincere heart, espetially among the Italians."[70]

Ironically, this is the country which first rediscovered the classical heritage of European civilization and whose books on the humanist ethics, etiquette, and moral philosophy were constantly being translated, and whose civilizing influence on England in the late 16th century was much greater than that of France.

# ENGLISH TREASON TRIALS
# AND CONFESSIONS
# IN THE SIXTEENTH CENTURY

## By Lacey Baldwin Smith

The western world has been alarmed and baffled by the state trials and the abject confessions to a variety of crimes which have been emerging from behind the Iron Curtain during the last few years. The reports of these trials even after they have been judicially edited by discriminating officials border upon comic opera while the confessions of the victims, to western ears at least, seem to deny the ideals which we hold most high—the rights and dignities of the individual. Communists who once held important positions, who have appeared in the annals of their party as the most loyal of servants, are suddenly transformed by their own confessions into vicious counter-revolutionists, bourgeois spies and secret collaborators with Anglo-American imperialism. Moreover, if we are to believe what we read, those who have succumbed to the insidious if deca-

[70] p. 415.

dent lure of western materialism freely confess their heinous crimes and carefully present themselves as examples of the awful consequence of straying from the straight and narrow path of the party line.

The West has endeavoured to discover some explanation for behavior so alien to its own way of thinking, to find some reason why men will admit offenses they have never committed, will sacrifice themselves to the will of the party organization, and will without murmur or complaint subject themselves to the discipline required of the communistic world. The hope of reprieve, the fear of jeopardizing the future of one's family, the use of drugs, the application of physical coercion, not to mention the more sophisticated torture of endless questioning and calculated loss of sleep have all been offered in explanation. Whether these are the correct causes for actions totally foreign to western experience is far from certain, but the fact that such things do occur in communist areas of the world should not be dismissed as something viciously and uniquely Russian and communistic; much the same type of phenomenon has happened within our own historic tradition. It may come as something of a shock to the English-speaking world that the land we tend to regard as the home of liberalism and democracy experienced a similar affliction: that England of the sixteenth century had her state trials and her incomprehensible confessions.

England during the age of the Tudor despots and especially under Henry VIII had in a less developed form most of the instruments of oppression which exist today behind the Iron Curtain. Trial for treason was the device by which the government struck down both great and low, and one foreign traveler in 1558 remarked that one could not be certain from one day to the next who might be closest to the King's confidence and who degraded, stripped of his possessions and imprisoned awaiting the death of a traitor,[1] "as horrible to tell as frightful to see."[2] As in modern

[1] Étienne Perlin, *Description des royaulmes d'Angleterre et d'Escossa . . . par 1558* (London, 1775), 27.    [2] *Letters and Papers, Foreign and Domestic, of the Reign of Henry VIII*, ed. J. S. Brewer, J. Gairdner, and R. H. Brodie, 21 vols. in 33 parts (London, 1862-1910), XV, No. 737. Henceforth referred to as *L.P.*

Russia, the victims were subjected to immediate incarceration, long periods of imprisonment and endless hours of interrogation, and although Englishmen prided themselves that torture was a thing unknown to the common law, those accused of treason were exposed to any form of persuasion the government cared to use. The fear of being charged with high treason was a constant threat from which no man was free, for the statutes regulating the nature of treason were so vague that they could be construed to include almost any word, expression, wish or deed. The Act of 1534 extended the punishment for the most frightful crime that an Englishman could commit to verbal offenders; to all who "do maliciously wish, will or desire, by words or writing, or by craft imagine," the King's death.[3] The closer the proximity to the crown, the greater the danger, for the law could be used not only to punish those who indulged in overt acts of rebellion, but was considered an instrument to remove those who had become too powerful or too dangerous in an era which could tolerate no rivalry with the King. Anthony Waite probably gave voice to the fears of his entire generation when he wrote Lady Lisle in 1535 saying

it is rumored that a person should be committed to the Tower for saying that this month will be rainy and full of wet, next month, death, and the third month, war. He will be kept there till experience shows the truth of his prophecy.[4]

The appalling spectre of being indicted for subverting the commonwealth hung over every head, for anyone could accuse his neighbor of treason. "Here in England," wrote the French ambassador to his sovereign,

if two witnesses will swear and affirm before the council that they have heard a man speak against his duty to his King, or contrary to the articles of religion, that man may be condemned to suffer death with the pains appointed by the law, although he be absent or ignorant of the charge, and without any other form of proof. Innocence is no safeguard when such an opening is offered to malice or revenge . . . . There is no security

[3] *Statutes of the Realm* (London, 1817), III 26 Henry VIII, cap. 13, 508-509.

[4] *L.P.*, VIII, pt. i, 771, p. 290.

60

for any man, unless the person accused is brought face to face with the witnesses who depose against him.[5]

As Charles de Marillac remarked, innocence was "no safeguard" against being charged with treason, for with an instrument of destruction so loosely phrased as the Act of 1534, any man could be accused of "maliciously" wishing, willing or desiring, by word or writing, the King's death; it all depended on the construction given to the words. Richard Hilles gave an accurate if horrible description of Tudor standards when he wrote Henry Bullinger:

> But, to say the truth, people did not inquire much, as it is no new thing to see men hanged, quartered or beheaded for one thing or another, sometimes for trifling expressions construed as [being] against the King.[6]

In the sixteenth century the intent to do treason was regarded as being just as heinous as the act itself. The determining factor in most cases was not whether the individual had committed treason, but whether he was too dangerous to the state to be allowed to live. When this had been decided, it was a simple matter to "infer" from words or writings that the victim had treasonous intentions, and to "construct" from the evidence a damning case against him. Tudor monarchs were usually scrupulously careful to conform to the letter of the law and to go through the form of a trial, but justice and fairness rarely entered into their considerations.

Kenneth Pickthorn has pointed out that the trial of Anne Boleyn and her accomplices was notable because treason was " 'constructed' with great freedom,"[7] but it is important to remember that the case was far from unique. With an array of details which would do justice to the yellow tabloids of today, the government indicted the Queen for "despising her marriage, and entertaining malice against the King, and following daily her frail and carnal lust." She was said to have "falsely and traitorously" procured "by base conversations and kisses, touchings, gifts and other infamous incitations, divers of the King's daily and famil-

[5] William Thomas, The Pilgrim, edited by J. A. Froude (London, 1861), Note F, 152.
[6] L.P., XVI, No. 578, p. 272.
[7] Kenneth Pickthorn, Early Tudor Government: Henry VIII (Cambridge, 1934), 289.

iar servants to be her adulterers and concubines. . . ." Moreover she was charged with having "incited her own natural brother, George Boleyn, Lord Rocheford" to incest, and with having "conspired the death and destruction of the King."[8] The actual evidence against them for such a massive and detailed accusation was, as the Imperial ambassador observed, very meagre. All but the groom, Mark Smeton, (who had confessed presumably under torture) "were condemned upon presumption and certain indications without valid proof or confession." The evidence against the Queen, the ambassador went on to say, was based primarily upon the supposition that there had been "a promise between her and [Henry] Norris to marry after the King's death, which it thus appeared they hoped for; and that she had received and given to Norris certain medals, which might be interpreted to mean that she had poisoned the late Queen [Catherine of Aragon] and intrigued to do the same to the Princess [Mary]. . . ." As for the Queen's brother, he "was charged with having cohabited with her by presumption, because he had been once found a long time with her, and with certain other little follies."[9] The case for the crown can be reduced to the syllogism that since the Queen had talked to Norris of marriage, she therefore meant to marry him; since she had marriage in mind, she must have desired the death of the King and conspired to attain it. Thus her traitorous intent had been proved beyond a shadow of doubt.

The key to Tudor trials and the reaction of the juries was the question of intent. If the government could prove the "maliciousness" of the desire or action of the victim, in other words the intention of the culprit, the case for the crown was almost invariably sustained. The full extent of this can be seen in another royal trial when the fifth of Henry's queens was executed in 1541. At that time the French ambassador, Marillac, reported that Thomas Culpeper had been condemned of high treason for having carnally known Queen Catherine Howard "although he had not passed beyond words; for he confessed his inten-

[8] *L.P.*, X, No. 876, sec. vii.    [9] *Ib.*, No. 908, pp. 377–378.

tions to do so, and his confessed conversation, being held by a subject to a Queen, deserved death."[10]

There was little that was secure during these "perilous times," and even silence could not protect a man from being charged with harboring secret malice—a fact which Sir Thomas More discovered to his grief. At More's trial in 1535 Christopher Hales, the Attorney General, argued that "though we should have no word or deed to charge upon you, yet we have your silence, and that is a sign of your evil intention and a sure proof of malice."[11] Very likely the Attorney General was correct in suspecting that More was endeavouring to conceal his dislike of the King's claims to the Supreme Headship of the Church of England behind silence, but once the government had decided that the safety of the state necessitated a man's death, not even silence could save him. Possibly John Vives in writing to Erasmus placed his finger on the true temper of early Tudor England when he said "the times are difficult, and one can neither speak nor be silent without danger."[12]

The subjects of the Tudor despots were well aware of their constant peril. The maxim that "the King's wrath is death" was a principle of government constantly proved by facts, and every courtier and government official must have known by experience the contemporary proverb *"Lubricus est primus locus apud reges."*[13] A change in government policy, the sudden cooling of the King's affections, the damning presence of royal blood in one's veins or merely disagreement with the royal purpose could end in high treason. Sir Richard Empson and Edmund Dudley were sacrificed at the commencement of Henry VIII's reign because they seemed to personify the financial extortion of the government of the first Tudor, and Empson complained bitterly that Henry had abandoned him to his enemies "without other cause than that he obeyed his father's commands, and upheld the regal authority."[14] This, in fact, was exactly their crime; they had been too zealous in a

[10] *L.P.*, XVI, No. 1426, p. 666.     [11] Thomas Stapleton, *The Life and Illustrious Martyrdom of Sir Thomas More*, trans. by P. E. Hallett (London, 1928), 192.
[12] *L.P.*, VII, No. 635.     [13] *Ib.*, XIV, pt. ii, No. 750, p. 278.
[14] Edward Lord Herbert, *The History of England under Henry VIII* (London, 1870), 113.

government from which the new king was attempting to disassociate himself, and though the legality of their past actions was recognized to the extent that they were not indicted for financial extortion, "new and strange crimes were found and objected against them" as that "their intent was to seize upon the person of the new king, and so to assume the sole government."[15]

Those who suffered for treason because they had lost the royal favor and were regarded as a potential menace to the state were almost as numerous as those who were executed as a consequence of outright rebellion. Thomas Cromwell, Richard Empson and Edmund Dudley died as scapegoats; Sir Thomas More and the Abbots of Glaston-bury and Reading because they were quiet if persistent dissenters from the royal religious policy; the Earl of Surrey and the Duke of Buckingham because their titles and dignity encroached too closely upon that of the crown; the Marquis of Exeter, the Earl of Suffolk and the Countess of Salisbury for their fatal touch of royal blood; and Anne Boleyn because she could no longer control her husband's fickle passions. In none of these cases is there any clear indication of overt treason. Their crime was their fall from royal grace; the evidence arrayed against them was the secret malice of their hearts and their traitorous intent.

From the standpoint of statecraft Tudor disregard for justice is understandable, but what will perhaps always remain a mystery is the reaction of the victims themselves. Both innocent and guilty at the moment of death almost invariably acknowledged their real or imaginary offenses in terms of glittering generalities. Although the culprits occasionally did request their audience not to judge too severely the causes which had brought them to the scaffold, they nevertheless proclaimed their worthiness to die. The form of these confessions followed a fairly set pattern. Those about to suffer announced that they had come hither to die, and they were careful to point out to the surround-ing multitude that they had been judged by the laws of the land and that they were content to accept the penalties which the law required. After granting the legality of their execution, they usually went on to hold themselves up as

[15] *Ib.*, 117.

64

examples of the frightful fate in store for those who dared to sin against God and their king. Finally, they ended by requesting their audience to pray on their behalf that God and king would mercifully forgive them their trespasses, and then, in a closing burst of loyalty, they expressed the hope that their gracious sovereign might long and happily reign over the kingdom in peace and tranquility. Rarely was a word of complaint or bitterness heard at these executions, and usually both the innocent and guilty humbly prostrated themselves before the royal will and confessed the iniquities of their lives.

Even those who were the victims of the most completely fabricated evidence admitted their guilt, and all those who had been involved in the fall of Queen Anne Boleyn conceded the justice of their executions. William Brereton, although he asked his audience not to judge the reasons for his fate too harshly, avowed that he had "deserved to die if it were a thousand deaths"; Sir Francis Weston announced that he "had thought to have lived in abomination yet this twenty or thirty years and then to have made amends." "I thought little," he confessed, "it would have come to this."[16] Mark Smeton merely stated that "he was justly punished for his misdeeds."[17] Strangely enough the man who had the greatest cause to complain made the most abject and demeaning confession. "I was born under the law, and I die under the law," George Boleyn said, "forasmuch as it is the law which hath condemned me . . . I deserve death even though I had a thousand lives—yea, even to die with far more and worse shame and dishonor than hath ever been heard of before . . . ." and, he concluded, his death should be a warning to his many friends to "take heed not to fall into the error of my ways."[18]

The Queen's final remarks were far shorter than her brother's and on the whole considerably less demeaning. Like Brereton, she implied that she was guiltless of the crimes for which she was being executed, but she was

[16] George Constantyne, "Memorial to Thomas Lord Cromwell," *Archaeologia: or, Miscellaneous Tracts relating to Antiquity* (London, 1831), XXIII, 65.     [17] *L.P.*, X, No. 1036, p. 431.
[18] *Lettre d'un gentilhomme portugais . . . sur l'exécution d'Anne Boleyn, Lord Rocheford, Brereton, Norris, Smeton, et Weston,* edited by F. Michel (Paris, 1832), 10.

careful to say that she had come to the scaffold ready "to yield herself humbly to the will of the King." She then concluded by beseeching all men "to pray for the life of the King, my sovereign lord and yours, who is one of the best princes on the face of the earth, and who hath always treated me so well that better could not be."[19] These are surprising sentiments from the lips of a discarded wife who was paying the price for her failure to keep the royal eye from wandering.

Anne Boleyn and those who died with her were not the only victims of laws manipulated to suit the royal purpose; nor were they the only ones who died wishing a long life and a happy reign to the man who had instigated their death. Both the Duke of Buckingham and Thomas Cromwell suffered; the former because of that fatal royal blood which made him a possible candidate for the throne should Henry die without a male heir; the latter because the king needed a scapegoat in 1540 for his discarded religious and foreign policies of the previous few years. Both men vigorously denied that they had committed treason. When the Duke's indictment was read against him in May of 1521, Buckingham categorically stated that it was "false and untrue and conspired and forged to bring me to my death,"[20] and when the Duke of Norfolk announced the fearful sentence after the trial, Buckingham answered that he was no traitor and scornfully remarked that he would "never sue to the King for life."[21] Yet on the scaffold the Duke was far less defiant, and he acknowledged that "he had offended the King's Grace through negligence and lack of grace, and desired all noblemen to beware by him, and all men to pray for him, and that he trusted to die the King's true man."[22]

As for the unlucky Thomas Cromwell, when he was arrested for combined heresy and high treason, the French ambassador reported that "in a rage [he] cast his bonnet on the ground, saying . . . that this was the reward of his services," and he appealed to the consciences of his arrestors "as to whether he was a traitor."[23] Unfortunately for the Vicar-general it was exactly his services to

[19] Ib., 13.
[20] Edward Hall, *Henry VIII*, edited by C. Whibley (London, 1904), I, 224.    [21] Ib., 225.    [22] Ib., 226.    [23] L.P., XV, No. 804.

the crown which resulted in his undoing, and he was shortly to learn one of the cardinal principles of Tudor government—that though the King could do no wrong, the royal accomplice could, and consequently had to accept the punishment. Despite Cromwell's violent denial of his traitorous behavior, however, he humbly submitted himself to his destiny after he had been condemned by an act of attainder, and he announced on the scaffold that he had "come hither to die, and not to purge" himself, for, he said, "if I should so do, I were a very wretch and a miser." He had, he confessed, been

> a great travailler in this world, and being but of a base degree, was called to high estate," but being an ungrateful wretch he had offended his prince for which he begged forgiveness. He concluded by desiring all those present at his execution to "pray for the King's Grace, that he may long live with you in health and prosperity.[24]

Whether or not the second of Henry's Queens to be executed for adultery was guilty remains something of a mystery. The only indiscretion proved against Catherine Howard was that she had, quite understandably, failed to inform her royal lover that her life before her marriage had not been as pure as might have been expected of a queen. However, Catherine, like her cousin Anne, "made the most godly . . . end that ever was heard tell of," and in the words of one contemporary, the Queen and her accomplice, Lady Rocheford, accepted their fate with "wonderful patience and constancy," desiring "all Christian people to take regard unto their worthy and just punishment with death for their offenses against God . . . and also against the King's royal majesty." They were, they confessed, "justly condemned . . . by the laws of the realm and Parliament to die . . . ."[25]

Possibly the most tragic death of the mid-sixteenth century was that of Edward Seymour, Duke of Somerset. The Duke's death was the result of a bitter intra-party rivalry within the council of regency established to govern the kingdom during the minority of Edward VI. The climax was finally reached when the Duke of Northumberland maneuvered Somerset into a position where he could be

[24] John Foxe, *Acts and Monuments,* ed. G. Townsend (London, 1843–49), V, 401.    [25] *L.P.,* XVII, No. 106.

caught on a technical charge of felony. The condemned minister's real crime, at least in the eyes of Northumberland, was his popularity with the populace of London, and consequently the ruling clique of the council took care that the Duke's execution should take place in the early hours of the morning before the city was fully aware of what was happening. Somerset, however, did not protest the actions of his enemies. Instead he bowed to the inevitable and said: "I am condemned by a law whereunto I am subject, as we all [are], and therefore to show obedience I am content to die." Then, after claiming that it was "the ordinance of God thus to die," he requested his audience to "pray together for the King's Majesty, to whose Grace I have always been a faithful, true, and most loving subject."[26] That gracious and loving sovereign had not raised a finger to save his maternal uncle and merely reported laconically in his Journal that on the 22nd of January "the Duke of Somerset had his head cut off upon Tower-hill between eight and nine o'clock in the morning."[27]

If it seems strange that those who were the victims of fabricated evidence; who were sacrificed upon the high altar of state necessity, should go to their death professing the worthiness of their fate, it is equally inexplicable that the men and women who had actually indulged in high treason should do the same thing. Treason, rebellion and sedition were common-place phenomena in the sixteenth century, and the executioner was kept busy with a steady procession of state enemies who had committed the most hateful crime known to Tudor times. Yet the men who entered into treasonous conspiracies with the full knowledge of the consequences of failure, who staked their lives on a venture which they must have felt was worth the risk of the disgusting death reserved for traitors, rarely protested at their execution. No attempt was made to explain the ideals on which their actions had been predicated; no endeavour was made to defy the tyranny and injustice against which they had presumedly given their lives.

[26] James Froude, *History of England* (New York, 1877), V, 360–362.     [27] Gilbert Burnet, *The History of the Reformation of the Church of England*, ed. E. Nares (London, 1839), IV, 226.

Except in the case of a few religious traitors, sixteenth century scaffold speeches are singularly free of such impassioned if vain words of defiance as those of Nathan Hale. It is true that Friar Forest when he was burnt in chains in 1538 for both heresy and treason is reported to have cried out "that if his body should be cut joint after joint, or member after member burnt, hanged, or what pain soever might be done to his body, he would never turn from his old profession."[28] These are brave words, but they are also exceptional words, for expressions of either defiance or innocence are indeed rare. Another instance of open challenge is that of the Countess of Salisbury who was executed in 1541, but unfortunately the source of this story is questionable since it is related by the seventeenth-century historian Lord Herbert, and is not substantiated by contemporary reports.

> The old lady, being brought to the scaffold . . . was commanded to lay her head on the block; but she . . . refused, saying, "So should traitors do, and I am none"; neither did it serve that the executioner told her it was the fashion; so turning her gray head every way, she bid him "if he would have her head, to get it as he could": so that he was constrained to fetch it off slovenly.[29]

Although examples of open refusal to humble oneself to the "fashion" must have existed,[30] the great majority of so-called traitors died resigned and compliant, while even those who suffered for their religious faith were careful to express their obedience and beg forgiveness. In 1539 the elderly Abbot Richard Whiting, who in the words of Thomas Cromwell had been sent down to Glastonbury to "be tried and executed,"[31] entreated the witnesses of his

---

[28] John Stow, *Annales or a General Chronicle, of England,* ed. E. Howes (London, 1631), 575.

[29] Herbert, 650; cf. *L.P.,* XVI, No. 897.

[30] The most obvious example of refusing to confess one's guilt is the case of Sir Ralph Vane who vigorously maintained his innocence at his execution on 26 February, 1552 and died still cursing the man who had instigated his death, the Duke of Northumberland, claiming that "his blood would make Northumberland's pillow uneasy to him." *Cobbett's Complete Collection of State Trials,* ed. T. B. Howell (London, 1809), I, 523. Henceforth referred to as *State Trials.*

[31] *L.P.,* XIV, pt. ii, No. 399.

execution to "desire the King's Highness of his merciful goodness and in the way of charity to forgive him his great offenses by him committed and done against his grace."[32] Years later, Edmund Campion, the Jesuit martyr, made a similar confession when he admitted that "if you esteem my religion treason, then am I guilty." He never wavered in his faith, but like so many before him, he prayed for Protestant Elizabeth, "your Queen and my Queen, unto whom I wish a long quiet reign with all prosperity."[33] In a sense the laconic words of Sir Thomas More sum up the attitude of religious traitors of the sixteenth century when he protested at his execution that he died "the King's good servant but God's first."[34] As More's biographer, R. W. Chambers, has pointed out, both the ex-Chancellor's brevity and choice of words are exceptional, and very likely they are, as the author suggests, "the most haughty ever spoken on the scaffold."[35] However, despite More's defiance, no word of complaint passed his lips—he still died "the King's good servant."

More typical are the confessions of John Dudley, Duke of Northumberland, Sir Thomas Wyatt, Sir John Gates, and Henry Grey, Duke of Suffolk. All of these men carefully followed the prescribed formula for scaffold addresses, admitting the worthiness of their death, denying the righteousness of their cause, and holding themselves up as fearful examples of the just fate reserved for traitors. The Duke of Northumberland and his associates in treason avowed their crimes against God and crown for having attempted in vain to disturb the legitimate succession of Queen Mary by setting Lady Jane Grey upon the throne. The Duke acknowledged that he had "been an evil liver" and had "done wickedly all the days" of his life and had sinned most of all against the Queen's highness, of whom, he said, "I here openly ask forgiveness." Then the man who had vigorously proclaimed his Protestantism and had imprisoned and deprived a large portion of the old

[32] Thomas Wright, *Letters relating to the Suppression of the Monasteries,* Camden Society publications, Vol. 26 (London, 1843), No. cxx, p. 261.
[33] Richard Simpson, *Edmund Campion* (London, 1867), 319, 321.
[34] R. W. Chambers, *Thomas More* (London, 1948), p. 349; *L.P.,* VIII, No. 996.     [35] Chambers, 350.

Henrician espiscopacy denied his faith and admitted that the "chiefest occasion" of his villainy had been "through false and seditious preachers" who had induced him to err "from the Catholic faith and the true doctrine of Christ."[36] Likewise, Sir John Gates, one of the Duke's supporters in the plot against the Queen, went to his execution abhorring his treasonous actions and confessing his religious sins. Sir John had good cause to resent his lot, for others of higher station than he had been involved in Northumberland's schemes and yet had escaped the unpleasant sequel of the Duke's failure, but Gates did not voice his grievances and instead confessed: "My coming here this day, good people, is to die; whereof I assure you all I am well worthy; for I have lived as viciously and wickedly all the days of my life as any man hath done in the world."[37]

Thomas Wyatt and the Duke of Suffolk died for their rôle in the famous rebellion against Queen Mary in 1554. Both men deserved their fate, the Duke as a persistent if ineffectual conspirator who had learned nothing from his close escape in the failure of the Northumberland plot the previous year; and Wyatt as a turbulent rabblerouser whose plea before the bar of history that his leadership of the revolt of 1554 was done in the name of Protestantism and nationalism does not ring true. However, both men made "a good and godly end," and if we are to believe their own statements, they both had sudden change of heart as to what constitutes the true behavior of a loyal and dutiful subject. Wyatt abjured his vicious life and conceded that he had been "lawfully and worthily condemned, for," he said, "I have sorely offended against God and the Queen's Majesty, and I am sorry therefore."[38] The Duke was even more abject.

"I have offended the Queen and her laws, and thereby am justly condemned to die, and am willing to die, desiring all men to be obedient. And I pray God that my death may be an ensample to all men. . . ."[39]

[36] Patrick Tytler, *England under the Reigns of Edward VI and Mary* (London, 1839), II, 230–231.
[37] John Bayley, *The History and Antiquities of the Tower of London* (London, 1825), II, xlix.
[38] *The Chronicle of Queen Jane,* ed. J. G. Nichols, Camden Society publications, vol. 48 (London, 1850), 73.      [39] Foxe, VI, 545.

One might imagine from this that high state officials and those of noble blood had a monopoly on scaffold disclosures; however, those of humbler origin were equally addicted. Thomas Blount reported to Cromwell in 1538 the case of eight men and two women who were so moved by the eloquence of Dr. Taylor, the chaplain of the Bishop of Worcester, who preached at their death, that they actually thanked "the King and his officers for their just execution."[40] Elizabeth Barton, better known as the Nun of Kent, was equally compliant at the moment of her demise. Her crime was that she had prophesied that Henry "would not live a month after his marriage" with Anne Boleyn.[41] Even under the most favorable circumstances the government could not have allowed such a prognostication to go unpunished, but worse than this for the unfortunate Maid, her prophetic powers were supported by a sizable number of influential people who were regarded by the government as being enemies of the King's marriage and his religious policies. Consequently it was of paramount importance that the Nun be proved a fraud and executed, if only as a means of attacking her more distinguished partisans. At her execution in 1534 Elizabeth Barton humbly resigned herself to the government's purpose and obliged the crown by confessing that the real responsibility for her fraudulent prophecies rested with more important and powerful company.

> "I am not so much to be blamed, considering it was well known unto these learned men that I was a poor wench without learning. . . . But because the things which I feigned were profitable unto them, therefore they much praised me, and bare me in hand that it was the Holy Ghost and not I that did them."

It was this false and treasonous advice, she said, which had brought her to the scaffold and a traitor's death.[42]

These then are the facts of the case—that men and women of the sixteenth century debased themselves before the inscrutable will of the crown, confessed to deeds of which they were innocent, denied the justice of the ideals for which they were dying, and read statements which have all the earmarks of having been either actually written or at

[40] *L.P.,* XIII, pt. i, No. 1509.     [41] *L.P.,* VII, No. 72.
[42] Hall, II, 259.

least carefully perused by the government which was decreeing their death. The question immediately arises as to why men should have accepted their fate in silence, compliantly acquiesced in this travesty of justice, and acted out this final farce to its bitter end?

The possible explanations for the scaffold disclosures of the sixteenth century are almost as numerous and just as varied as those offered to resolve the mystery of our more modern phenomenon. Needless to say, they are also just as uncertain and inconclusive. The explanations themselves can best be grouped into three general categories: physical pressure brought directly to bear upon the victims; Tudor ideas concerning a subject's duty towards his sovereign and his society; and finally the importance of certain religious and fatalistic ideals of the age.

The first and in some ways the most intelligible interpretation is that of physical coercion. It is undoubtedly true that Tudor governments had at their disposal innumerable ways of inducing "traitors" to confess, and certainly torture was used especially on persons of low degree and on the so-called religious traitors. However, there is no evidence that physical torment was inflicted on either of Henry VIII's Queens, on Thomas Cromwell, on Buckingham or even on Robert Aske, the leader of the northern rebellion in 1536. Moreover, in many instances, the government had subtler if no less effective methods of persuasion. Endless interrogation and months of imprisonment under the most squalid conditions were often enough to break the most stubborn spirit, and one of the constant pleas of the victims was, in the pathetic words of Thomas Cromwell, "not to make him languish long."[43] Moreover, both great and low were exposed to the enormities of a traitor's death—the excruciating agony of being "laid on a hurdle and so drawn to the place of execution, and there to be hanged, cut down alive, your members to be cut off and cast in the fire, your bowels burnt before you, your head smitten off, and your body quartered and divided at the King's will, and God have mercy on your soul."[44] These were the words read at the condemnation of the Duke of Buckingham whose noble blood and high estate could not save even a Duke

[43] *L.P.,* XV, No. 804.    [44] Hall, I, 225.

from such a death. Only the King's gracious mercy could commute the sentence to the more humane execution of beheading, and that mercy was often conditioned by the willingness of the victim to comply with the royal desire. Neither knighthood nor noble status was a safeguard against being "hanged, drawn and quartered," for the traitor automatically lost both rank and title. The Duke of Buckingham after his condemnation referred to himself simply as "Edward Bowhen, the most caitiff of the world," while the bill of indictment against the Earl of Surrey in 1546 merely described him as "Henry Howard, late of Kennynggale, K.C., otherwise called Henry, Earl of Surrey."[45]

That fear of the unpleasant death reserved for traitors influenced the victims of Tudor tyranny was suggested as a possibility even by contemporaries, and when the disgraced Thomas Cromwell was sentenced "to suffer as a heretic or traitor, at the King's pleasure,"[46] Richard Hilles remarked to a friend that there was a rumor that the deposed Vicar-general "was threatened with burning at the stake instead of death by the axe if he did not confess his crimes at execution."[47] Also the traitor, Robert Aske, shuddered at the prospect of the death in store for him, and begged the King to "let me be full dead ere I be dismembered."[48] That gracious sovereign actually deigned to accept this humble petition, but whether or not a condition was attached to the royal mercy is not known. However, it is quite possible that Aske's compliance on the scaffold and the King's benevolence were related.

There was yet another instrument of coercion at the royal disposal. All the property of a traitor was automatically forfeited to the crown, thus leaving his family impoverished but at the same time liable for the condemned man's debts. On occasion the crown could be merciful and in the case of Cromwell's young son, Gregory, the government permitted him to retain his title and estates. Again, the question of whether or not there is a connection with the Vicar-general's behavior on the scaffold must be left

---

[45] *L.P.*, XXI, pt. ii, No. 697; Hall, I, 225.     [46] *L.P.*, XV, No. 498, sec. 60
[47] *L.P.*, XVI, No. 578.     [48] *L.P.*, XII, pt. i, No. 1224.

unanswered. However, contemporaries suspected that it was an "artifice in the King to confer his title and many of his domains while he was yet in prison upon his son Gregory . . . in order that he might the more readily confess his offenses at execution."[49]

Certainly the dread of a traitor's death and the fear of leaving one's family destitute and unprotected entered into the willingness of the prisoner to forfeit their ideals and accommodate themselves to the purpose of their sovereign. Also the hope of reprieve may have helped to determine the actions of those who suffered. It was rumored that Henry Norris, one of those accused of being Queen Anne's paramour, would be granted a full pardon if he would confess his crime,[50] but in most cases the hope of reprieve must have been a very slight one. When the Duke of Somerset's scaffold address was suddenly interrupted by the appearance of Sir Anthony Brown, whom the audience mistook as a messenger of pardon, the Duke exclaimed: "There is no such thing, good people; there is no such thing. It is the ordinance of God thus to die, wherewith we must be content."[51]

The theory that confessions were wrung from reluctant prisoners by fear, torture and the hope of reprieve leads to another possibility: that the disclosures were never actually spoken by the victims themselves, but were either carefully edited versions of their final words or were complete fabrications published by a government anxious to destroy the reputation of its enemies. This is an argument especially endearing to those who wish to vindicate or excuse the behavior of men and women for whom they have a high regard or who find their final expressions of self-debasement contradictory to their past lives. It is perfectly true, of course, that the dying words of many of the prisoners do not fit the pattern of their previous lives. Certainly in the instance of Thomas Cromwell, his humble acknowledgement of his faults before God and man and his words of devotion avowing that he was dying true to his faith are highly suspicious in the light of his career which proves, if

[49] *L.P.*, XVI, No. 578.
[50] Constantyne, "Memorial to Thomas Lord Cromwell," 64; *L.P.*, X, No. 1036, p. 49.      [51] Froude, V, 361.

nothing else, that the Vicar-general was anything but a religious man. However, it seems clear that those who were accused of high treason actually gave their confessions themselves. There were too many witnesses to these public executions to permit the government to circulate fabricated versions of the dying words of the victims. At Robert Aske's execution all the important personages of the northern counties were present including the rebel's own brother,[52] while the unfortunate Maid of Kent was forced to tour the realm making her disclosure of fraud at all important towns.[53] The only evidence of any contemporary doubt about the authenticity of these final dicta is found in a letter from Cardinal Pole to a friend saying that he feared "he was wrong in writing of Cromwell's coming to his senses, for his last words as printed do not give the same impression as the narrative of those who told of his end and last words."[54]

A government so determined to paint its victims as villains of the deepest dye was certainly capable of modifying their dying phrases to suit its purpose, but it must also be remembered that the Crown had a final and highly effective method of controlling its most stubborn prisoners. This was simply to demand that they forgo their "right" and say nothing at their execution. On the eve of Sir Thomas More's death, Sir Thomas Pope came to the Tower to warn the ex-Chancellor to prepare himself for the following morning, and he also informed More that it was the King's further pleasure "that at your execution you shall not use many words." "Master Pope," Sir Thomas answered, "you do well to give me warning of his Grace's pleasure. For otherwise, I had purposed at that time somewhat to have spoken. . . . Nevertheless, whatsoever I intended, I am ready obediently to conform myself to his Grace's commandments."[55] Evidently Henry suspected that More would endeavor to vindicate himself, and knowing that the ex-Chancellor could not be intimidated had found other means to silence him; More, as we

[52] *L.P.,* XII, pt. ii, No. 261.    [53] *State Papers, Spanish,* IV, pt. ii, No. 1154, p. 867.    [54] L.P., XVI, No. 40.
[55] William Roper, *The Life of Sir Thomas More,* ed. J. M. Clines (New York, 1950), 83.

already know, was obedient to this final royal demand. The government likewise anticipated that Queen Anne would maintain her innocence, for Sir William Kingston wrote Cromwell shortly before her execution saying that he had received the Vicar-general's letter ordering him to clear the Tower of curious onlookers including the representatives sent by the Imperial ambassador, and he agreed with Cromwell that the smaller the number present at the Queen's death the better "for," he said, "I suppose she will declare herself to be a good woman for all men, but for the King, at the hour of her death. . . ."[56] It was only at the last moment that the Queen was allowed to address the few witnesses of her execution and then only after she had "begged leave to speak to the people, promising to say nothing but what was good."[57] However, surprisingly enough, examples of men or women going to their death in silence are rare, and for the most part the victims were willing enough to say a few final gracious words before departing this life even if they were edited by the Crown.

Physical coercion, the dread of a traitor's death, family pressure and the agonies of imprisonment may, in the last analysis, be not only the simplest but also the most accurate explanation of the success of Tudor governments in enforcing their will upon those who encountered the royal wrath. Unfortunately however, there are too many cases of last minute reversals, of men and women who, despite all the pressure which could be brought to bear, arrogantly defied the Crown and at their trials insisted upon their innocence or mocked the jury of their peers, yet who, when they mounted the scaffold, suddenly avowed their sins and acknowledged their worthiness to die. Such was the case of John Oynyon, one of the monks of Glastonbury who suffered along with his Abbott. He "denied his crimes, casting his arms abroad and saying 'Alas, is this justice to destroy a man, guiltless?' professing to be as innocent as a new-born babe." This protest, as one of the witnesses of his execution related,

"he continued to the gallows, when his heart began to relent, and he and his companions, with their ropes about their necks, confessed that they had committed

[56] *L.P.*, X, No. 910.     [57] *Ibid.*, No. 911.

high treason, especially Oynyon, who said he had offended the King in such sort of treason that it was not expedient to tell thereof, and begged the people to pray for him and to desire the King to forgive his soul, else he was sure, he said, to be damned."

And yet, observed the narrator, "not an hour before, a man that had heard him speak would have thought him guiltless."[58] A similar story is told by Hugh Latimer of a man who continued to profess his innocence and was hung still maintaining it. He was cut down, the preacher said, "somewhat too soon, afore he was clean dead; then they drew him to the fire, and he revived; and then he coming to his remembrance, confessed his fault, and said he was guilty."[59] The worthy divine drew from this gory tale "a wonderful example" of the mysterious workings of God, but the fact remains that despite all the government could do to this prisoner, he refused to divulge his guilt until the very moment of death.

There remains yet another possibility: that a greater pressure than torture or intimidation was imposed upon these so-called traitors of the sixteenth century. It is almost inconceivable that the prisoners confessed willingly, but there is considerable evidence to indicate that they did so deliberately, as a final act of sacrifice to a power greater than themselves. One might almost describe it as the ultimate expression of obedience to a discipline and a way of thinking which had been inculcated from birth. Possibly the most revealing words ever spoken by a sixteenth-century Englishman are those reported by the Imperial ambassador as having been said by George Boleyn after hearing the verdict of his trial. After his condemnation he announced "that since he must die, he would no longer maintain his innocence, but confess that he had deserved death."[60] The modern reader will recognize in these words a touch of oriental fatalism, but there remains something more. There is obedience to the law, to the desire of the King and to the mandate of the nation which had willed his death. The victims of Tudor tyranny may have felt themselves innocent of the crimes immediately ascribed to

[58] *L.P.*, XIV, pt. ii, No. 613.
[59] Hugh Latimer, *Sermons* (Everyman ed., London, N.D.), 128.
[60] *L.P.*, X, No. 908, p. 378.

them, but if the law, administered as the will of the King, deemed them worthy to die, then the prisoners considered themselves guilty, deserving death as men no longer useful to society. Fully to comprehend this alien attitude, it is necessary to appreciate sixteenth-century mores which demanded absolute obedience to King, to law and to society. These three are a veritable trinity, being both separate and indivisible, representing the highest and most esteemed faith of the realm and closely associated with the religious ideals of the day.

The Crown was sacrosanct; the King himself, as the Lord's anointed, could do no wrong, and although Tudor England had no theory of divine right of Kings, it needed none, for those who doubted the divinity that "doth hedge a king" were voices crying in the dark. The brilliant aura of divinity, the inscrutable light of infallibility which emanated from the royal person was such that one contemporary dared "not cast [his eyes] but sidewise upon the flaming beams of [the King's] bright sun."[61] The King, wrote Tyndal in 1528, was above judgment, for the man who dared judged a King "judgeth God; and he that resisted the King resisteth God and damneth God's law and ordinance. . . . The King is, in this world, without law, and may at his lust do right or wrong and shall give accounts but to God only."[62] In less theological terms, Sir Thomas More voiced the same opinion when he said "from the prince as from a perpetual wellspring, cometh among the people the flood of all that is good or evil."[63] It was not for a miserable subject to judge between royal good and royal evil; his sole duty was to obey, and this was a doctrine to which all were expected to adhere.

Nor was it doubted that the King could lawfully command a man to die, and on this subject Stephen Gardiner, Lord Chancellor of England under Queen Mary, was quite explicit, for, he said, he "who has not obeyed his prince,

[61] Quoted in F. Le Van Baumer, *Early Tudor Theory of Kingship* (New Haven, 1940), 86.

[62] William Tyndale, *The Obedience of a Christian Man.* (London, 1582), 32.

[63] Sir Thomas More, *Utopia* (Everyman ed., London, 1951), 20.

let him die the death."[64] There could be no life, no status, no liberty outside the pale of the King's favor, and Tudor subjects, "as the grass from the ground, had all their nourishment from the King, from whom their glory proceeded even as the small star's light proceedeth from the sun alone."[65] A man "owed all things save his soul" to his sovereign,[66] and even his immortal soul was placed in jeopardy and faced the fires of eternal damnation if he turned to rebellion to ease his conscience. The august position to which the King was elevated by most Englishmen was noted by an Italian traveller when he commented that

> towards their King, they [the English] are wonderfully well affected; nor would any one of them endure hearing any thing disrespectful of the King, through the honor they bear him; so that the most binding oath which is taken by them is that by which 'the King's life' has been pledged.[67]

There is more truth than animosity in what Luther remarked about Henry VIII when in 1539 he wrote that "what Juncker Heintz wills must be an article of faith [for all Englishmen] for life or death."[68]

It is only in the light of this overwhelming sense of obedience to the royal will and this feeling that the King could literally do no wrong, that the compliant words of Anne Boleyn became explicable when she cried that she had "come hither only to die and thus yield herself to the will of the King, my lord." It must always be remembered, strange as it may seem, that the Queen may have actually believed and willingly stated that Henry was "one of the best princes on the face of the earth . . . and hath always treated me so well that better could not be."[69] The constant entreaties of the prisoners for forgiveness may have been sincere; the pleas to the populace to obey their sovereign and to take example by their fate may have been truthful. When a nation, as the French ambassador sagely noted,

[64] Pierre Janelle, *Obedience in State and Church: Three Political Tracts by Stephen Gardiner* (Cambridge, 1930), 181.
[65] *L.P.,* XIII, pt. ii, No. 1140.    [66] *L.P.,* VIII, No. 870.
[67] *The Second Book of Travels of Nicander Nucius of Corcyra,* edited by J. A. Cramer, Camden Society publications, vol. 17 (London, 1841), 16.    [68] *L.P.,* XVI, No. 106.
[69] *Lettre sur l'exécution d'Anne Boleyn,* 13.

makes of a man "not only a King to be obeyed, but an idol to be worshipped,"[70] then it must also be willing to sacrifice both innocent and guilty upon the altar of that faith.

This then is the first element of the trinity; obedience to the King. But it was not enough to have submission alone, merely to bear "with patience and humility" the punishment administered by the Lord's anointed; one had also to admit the justice and legality of that chastisement, for it was the law which transmuted the royal will from tyranny into legality, from personal whim into justice.

Englishmen were proud of the law of the realm which protected the rights of individuals and was the safeguard of the state. The Crown as a "perpetual wellspring" from which came all good and evil may in effect have been above the law, but usually the King followed the advice of Stephen Gardiner and made "the law his will."[71] The apologists of Tudor tyranny were quick to point this out, and one contemporary raconteur of the Reformation took pains to justify the execution of the Marquis of Exeter, Lord Montagu and their adherents on the grounds that "no person at all hath been condemned, but by twelve of his peers, irreprovable and indifferent," and "no noble lord without the special sentence of twenty four lords at the least," while the prisoners were "never put to execution till they had been indicted in their counties and afterwards arraigned, . . . and by the judges condemned." "Who," concluded this admirer of Henry's despotism, "can find in his heart, knowing this, to think the same Prince that so hath judgments ministered by the law and by the ordinary jurisdiction, to be a tyrant?"[72] The laws of the land, as Anne Boleyn complained, may have been cruel, but the inhabitants of Tudor England were born under these laws and had to abide by the tyranny of their own making. The law like the King must be obeyed for it was the voice of the nation and the will of the Crown.

It is only in connection with this pre-eminent respect for law that the ever-recurrent expression in Tudor confessions, "I am born under the law, and judged under the law,

[70] L.P., XV, No. 954.
[71] Foxe, VI, 46.    [72] Jeremy Collier, An Ecclesiastical History of Great Britain (London, 1714), II, No. xlvii, 39.

and die under the law," becomes comprehensible. The will of the state legally expressed through the laws of the realm was infallible, and Robert Devereux, Earl of Essex at his trial in 1601 was merely acknowledging a self-evident fact when he announced "that since I have committed that which hath brought me within the compass of the law, I may be counted the law's traitor in offending the law, for which I am willing to die, and will as willingly go thereto as ever did any."[73] Even the sixteen-year-old Lady Jane Grey admitted the law as having no kind of fault or flaw, and she proclaimed it as being "a never erring judge."[74] It was almost as if the law stood above personal ideas about guilt or innocence, and no matter how innocent the individual may have considered himself, once the law had passed sentence and found him guilty, then the victim was regarded by all, even by himself, as being worthy to die. As George Boleyn said, since he had been condemned by the law to die, "he would no longer maintain his innocence but confess that he deserved death."

Although the law was regarded as a "never erring judge," there was in Tudor England something which stood above both law and justice; this was the principle of state necessity, that in a moment of crisis the state should be bound neither by law nor morality. Kings no longer needed a papal dispensation in order to break their royal pledge for they could now do so in the name of statecraft. As Professor Pollard has pointed out, sixteenth-century England was proud that the common law denied the use of torture, yet the average subject considered it no contradiction that the rack should be utilized in cases of high treason.[75] The rights, liberties and privileges of the individual as safeguarded by the law had to be set aside when claim was made to the highest rule known to Tudor citizens —that of the welfare of the state. The will and need of society stood above the individual liberties of the people, and it is here, in the obedience that a subject owed his society, that the final element of the trinity is perceived.

[73] *State Trials*, I, p. 1365.     [74] N. H. Nicolas, *The Literary Remains of Lady Jane Grey* (London, 1825), 52.
[75] Alfred F. Pollard, *Henry VIII* (London, 1934), 432–433.

The modern world tends to view England of the sixteenth century as one of the first manifestations of rugged individualism, where society was mobile and men, as Lewis Einstein has written, were urged on "to dare all"[76] and proclaim to the world that "King of a molehill had I rather be than the richest subject of a monarchy."[77] Tudor society was undoubtedly fluid, and wealth and royal favor were forces which rivalled both birth and breeding. Upstarts and adventurers rubbed shoulders with pedigreed nobles, and as one contemporary complained: a gentleman could no longer be discerned by dress alone, for "they are like hatters' blocks that wear what is worthier than themselves."[78] All this may be true, but Tudor England lived too close to the medieval concept of life to differentiate truth from fiction, and they still maintained the fable of the medieval corporate society. "No man," said Richard Crompton, "is born only for himself but for his country also."[79] "Surely," wrote one good Englishman in 1548,

every honest man ought to refuse no pain, no travail, no study; he ought to care for no reports, no slander, no displeasure, no envy, no malice, so that he might profit the commonwealth of his country, for whom next after God he is created.[80]

The modern tenet that the state is created for the good of man was unknown to the denizens of the Tudor world who still clung to the ancient idea that men were born into a divinely ordained society with certain established privileges and duties.

Combined with this concept of a corporate state was a newer and more potent force, that of latent nationalism. In the face of the foreign enemy, of the French, the Spanish and the Scots, Englishmen were expected to maintain a

[76] Lewis Einstein, *Tudor Ideals* (New York, 1921), 114.

[77] George Peele, *The Battle of Alcazar,* printed in Alexander Dyce, *The Dramatic and Poetical Works of Robert Greene and George Peele* (London, 1861), 427.

[78] Sir William Cornwallis, *Essays,* No. 20, "Of Imitation." (London, 1632), 221–222.

[79] Quoted in Einstein, p. 190 from Richard Crompton, *The Mansion of Magnanimity,* Sig. E.

[80] British Museum, Lansdowne MSS., No. 238. This is John Hale speaking.

united front, and Archbishop Cranmer warned his countrymen to "remember the fable of Aesop, that when the frog and the mouse did fight together, the puttock came, and snatched them up both." "It is an easy thing," he added, "to break a whole faggot when every stick is loosed from another."[81] The crime of treason was therefore not only looked upon as a denial of the corporate society but was also felt to be a crime against one's brother Englishman. In the Homily of 1571, it was categorically stated that

> he that nameth rebellion, nameth not a singular and one only sin, as is theft, robbery, murder and such like; but he nameth the whole puddle and sink of all sins against God and man, against his prince, his country, his countrymen, his parents, his children, his kinsfolks, his friends and against all men universally.[82]

The state thus became the be-all and end-all of human existence and the devotion paid to it tended to make expediency the highest standard of a public act. It transcended justice, morality and the liberties of individuals, for, wrote Bishop Bonner, "in matters of state, individuals were not to be so much regarded as the whole body of the citizens."[83] Thus the judicial murders, the flagrant disregard for justice in the Tudor age are not to be judged in the light of more ordinary crimes. They were done in the name of the highest ideal known to sixteenth-century England—that of state necessity. Possibly the words of the contemporary playright, Robert Greene, best epitomize this fundamental principle when he made his villain urge James IV to murder his wife on the premise that:

> Why, Prince, it is no murder in a king,
> To end another's life to save his own:
> For you are not as common people be,

[81] Thomas Cranmer, *Miscellaneous Writings and Letters,* edited by J. E. Cox (Cambridge, 1846), 193.

[82] Quoted in John Allen, *A History of Political Thought in the Sixteenth Century* (London, 1951), p. 132 from The Homily of 1571, Sermon III, 573–574.

[83] Nicholas Sanders, "Report to Cardinal Moroni on the change in religion in 1558–9," *Catholic Record Society,* I (1904–05), 39.

Who die and perish with a few men's tears;
But if you fail, the state doth whole default,
The realm is rent in twain in such a loss.[84]

The victims of Tudor tyranny and despotism, born into a society which recognized no restraint when it came to the security of the nation, died in humbleness and obedience to the law and their sovereign because they acknowledged the necessity of doing so. Theirs was a final act of sacrifice to the principle of the inviolability of the state. The Princess Elizabeth while a prisoner at Woodstock in 1554, as she told the French ambassador many years later, had expected that even her life would be claimed by this all-encompassing ideal, and she had made up her mind to ask no request of her sister, Queen Mary, other than that a sword, not an axe, be used in her execution.[85] That the state could take her life in the name of necessity, the future Queen never doubted. When the unfortunate Lady Jane Grey heard that the Duke of Northumberland was pleading for his life, she was shocked that a man so dangerous to the nation expected to be allowed to keep his head, and she exclaimed in disgust: "What man is there living, I pray you, although he had been innocent, that would hope of life in that case, being in the field against the Queen in person as general. . . ." How could such a man, she queried, "hope for pardon whose life was odious to all men?"[86]

The fascination which this doctrine of absolute obedience exercised over the minds of the average citizen was impossible to escape, and even the more arrogant eventually succumbed to its influence. Robert Devereux, second Earl of Essex, at his trial for high treason against the Queen in 1601 scornfully addressed the jury of his peers with a degree of arrogance and disdain exceptional in Tudor trials, and exclaimed: "I do not speak to save my life, for that I see were vain: I owe God a death." When he had been found guilty and the fearful sentence pronounced, he boldly answered that he thought it fitting

[84] Robert Greene, *James the Fourth*, printed in Dyce, 211.
[85] Jean Le Laboureur, *Les Mémoires de Michel de Castelnau* (Bruxelles, 1731), I, 32.
[86] *The Chronicle of Queen Jane*, 25.

that his "poor quarters, which have done her Majesty true service in divers parts of the world, should now at the last be sacrificed and disposed of at her Majesty's pleasure."[87] The Earl clearly recognized that a final act of sacrifice was being demanded of him, but his unbridled soul refused to humble itself upon the altar of the state. However, the Earl's defiance did not last long, and in the end he died repentant and reconciled to the standards of his age. On the threshold of his passing, the Queen's favorite humbly announced: "In humility and obedience I prostrate myself to my deserved punishment."[88] The will of the nation had been upheld, the law of necessity had been administered, and Essex was executed, not so much because he was a bad man, as because he was a dangerous man. Like the Lady Jane Grey, like Thomas Cromwell and the Dukes of Buckingham and Somerset, the Earl's death was fully justified in the eyes of the state because of the peril which was implicit in his life.

If this doctrine of self-sacrifice to the will of society was such an all-pervading characteristic of Tudor life, it may justly be asked—why then the acts of treason, why the long line of executed traitors who by their defiance of constituted authority must have known that they were risking their immortal souls and denying the very core of Tudor political ideology? The answer to this brings us to the final explanation for the continuous flow of words of humility, forgiveness and obedience so characteristic of the sixteenth century confessions—the deep religious consciousness of the age and the feeling of fatalism fostered by the insecurity and uncertainty of Tudor life.

Rebellion and sedition under the Tudors were usually done in the name of God and the king. The throne as a sacred institution could do no wrong but its ministers could, and rebels almost always resorted to the subterfuge of voicing their indignation against the royal adviser. They appealed to the will of God to justify their actions and claimed that they were preserving their sovereign from the intrigues of evil councillors. In this light treason was no

[87] State Trials, I, pp. 1356, 1358.     [88] Ib., p. 1360.

longer treason, but the action of a loyal subject who had the best interests of God and crown at heart. There is an old adage that successful and fortunate treason is called virtue, a saying which the contemporary author, Sir John Harrington, transliterated into the jingle:

> Treason doth never prosper; what's the reason:
> Why, if it prosper, none dare call it treason.[89]

Possibly with this proverb in mind, rebels assumed that God was their prop and stay, and that the success of their plans was manifest proof of divine blessing. By the same standard, failure indicated that after all God had withheld his grace. Sir Thomas Wyatt warned the witnesses of his execution,

> Let every man beware how he taketh anything in hand against the higher powers. Unless God be prosperable to his purpose, it will never take good effect or success, and therefore ye may now learn at me.[90]

Inasmuch as there was no way of knowing whether God was indeed "prosperable" to a rebel's purpose except in terms of its outcome, the unsuccessful traitor tended to look upon his death as evidence of his failure to gain the support of the divine power. This, in fact, may explain the seeming contradiction of men such as Robert Aske who at their execution compliantly submit themselves to their fate and deny the very ideals on which they had staked their lives.[91] Their death must have been obvious proof to them that they had disobeyed the will of God, had violated His ordinances, and therefore justly deserved to die. Their end was evidence that after all right was on the side of the government, and having denied that right and having transgressed the laws of God, there was only one way of saving their souls from perdition. This was to confess their faults, humbly ask forgiveness and resign themselves to their just desserts. The sin which burns most fiercely in the Christian hell is pride, and for the sixteenth century treason was pride incarnate. What could be more presumptuous than to defy God, crown and commonwealth? What could

[89] Sir John Harrington, *Nugae Antique* (London, 1804), I, 385.
[90] *The Chronicle of Queen Jane,* 73.
[91] *State Papers Henry VIII,* I, No. xci, pp. 558–559.

be more deadly to the soul than to die still "puffed up with insatiable pride"? It was this fear that finally pierced the armor of the Earl of Essex's vanity, which broke his self-assurance when his chaplain persuaded him to "Give glory to God, and make confession of your fault."[92] If there was one thing of which Tudor England was convinced, it was that the convicted rebel not only deserved death as a traitor but also forfeited his soul and brought upon himself "eternal damnation ever to be in the burning fire of hell."[93] Thus a victim with the full knowledge that he had led an ungodly and sinful life was fain, as George Boleyn confessed, "to die the death of a Christian man," and consequently he usually endeavored to purge his soul by a timely confession of his faults.

In the fluid society of the sixteenth century, fortune and chance could thrust men to unimagined heights and just as quickly deprive them of their unexpected wealth and position. A few months of the royal favor could transform a man overnight from an obscure minion or adventurer into a personage of station and dignity, clothed and liveried with such gaudiness and lavishness that he rivaled in outward aspects at least peers of the most ancient lineage. As wealth and estate stemmed from the royal bounty, so they could be removed by the royal disfavor. Almost all of the leading personalities of Tudor England knew the truth of Sir Robert Nauton's description of Raleigh's precipitous career when he said that fortune had batted Sir Walter about like a tennis ball "for she tossed him up of nothing, and to and fro to greatness, and from thence down to little more than to wherein she found him, a bare gentleman."[94] In a society in which death hovered closely, ready to take a man at the very instant of his fame, in a world in which both life and riches were at the mercy of fickle fortune, men tended to regard death and disgrace as the consequence of a turn of luck or the ordinance of God. Those

[92] Thomas Birch, *Memoirs of the Reign of Queen Elizabeth* (London, 1744), II, 475–476.

[93] Public Record Office, London, *State Papers Domestic, Edward VI,* (Sp 10), VIII, No. 37, p. 66.

[94] Sir Robert Nauton, *Fragmenta Regalia: Memoirs of Elizabeth* (London, 1824), 103.

who stood upon the scaffold and spoke their last remaining words were usually convinced that divine predestination or capricious fortune, not the king or his ministers, had brought them to their fate. Sir George Boleyn took pains to warn his audience

> that from my mishap ye may learn not to set your thoughts upon the vanities of this world, and, least of all, upon the flatteries of the court, and the favors and treacheries of fortune, which only raiseth men aloft that with so much the greater force she may dash them again upon the ground. She in truth it is who is the cause that, as ye all witness, my miserable head is now to be dissevered from my neck; or rather, in greater truth, the fault is mine, and it is I who ought to be blamed for having adventured to lean on fortune, who hath proved herself fickle and false unto me, and who now maketh me as an example to you all and to the whole world.[95]

Although the inconstancy of fortune came in for her fair share of condemnation by the victims of Tudor tyranny, death was more often attributed to the ordinance of God. Sir Thomas Palmer admitted that he was going to a fate "worthily well deserved at God's hands, for I know it to be his divine ordinance,"[96] while the Duke of Norfolk in 1571 acknowledged that he was ready and willing to submit himself "to this which God hath prepared for me."[97] This constant reiteration that "It is the ordinance of God thus to die, wherewith we must be content."[98] led men to bow themselves to the unavoidable with quiet courage and fatalistic indifference, for, as Sir Thomas More remarked to Norfolk in 1533: "There [is] no more difference between your Grace and me but that I shall die today and you tomorrow."[99] Possibly the best summation of the fatalism so prevalent among the victims is found in the lines supposedly scribbled upon one of the prison walls of the Tower and attributed to Lady Jane Grey.

> To mortals' common fate thy mind resign,
> My lot today, to-morrow may be thine.[100]

---

[95] *Lettre sur l'exécution d'Anne Boleyn,* 10–11.
[96] *The Chronicle of Queen Jane,* 23.   [97] *State Trials,* I, p. 1033.
[98] Froude, V, 361. This is the Duke of Somerset speaking.
[99] Roper, 63.   [100]Nicolas, 60.

It was not the King or Parliament or even the laws of the nation that decreed a man to die, but God working his will through these earthly instruments. This may be one of the reasons why the royal character comes forth from these confessions untarnished; why men in effect pray that their murderer may have many years of life and prosperous possession of his kingdom: and why they admit to the justice of their execution, for it was not the King who had sentenced them but the design of God or the caprice of fortune.

Whether any or all of these possible explanations for the seemingly inexplicable behavior of the victims who were sacrificed upon the altar of Tudor statism are correct must remain in doubt. All that can be said with any degree of certainty is that these are possible causes some of which may have motivated individual action. More than this cannot be claimed; it is patently as hazardous for the living generation to penetrate the minds of those separated from us in time as it is to comprehend the behavior of Russian victims who are severed from us geographically.

In closing, however, one distinction should be observed. Brutal as the Tudor period may have been, it at least lacked one of the major characteristics of modern despotism. It is true that the victims were sacrificed to maintain the principle of the inviolability of crown, law and nation, a principle which could only be established if the prisoners themselves acted out the final travesty upon the scaffold and at the moment of death acknowledged the sanctity of the canon. However, the state did not demand of men their souls, and those who were led to their execution still retained their dignity as individuals. They may have bowed to the will of authority, they may have humbled themselves before the inevitable, but their courage was magnificent. There is no sense of grovelling about their final actions. Even when confronted with a traitor's death they still maintained a certain grandeur, and for this reason their closing words are all the more impressive. Possibly it is both vain and frivolous to inquire too deeply into the motives which led these men and women to die as they did, to attribute causes to actions which, in the final reckoning, are beyond

90

analysis. It may be best simply to accept their decision and say with Matthew Arnold:

> Let the long contention cease!
> Geese are swans and swans are geese.
> Let them have it how they will!
> Thou art tired: best be still.

# II

## ELIZABETHAN SCIENCE

*Patrick Cruttwell's "Physiology and Psychology in Shakespeare's Age" was first published in January,* 1951, *in the* Journal of the History of Ideas (*XII*, 75-89).

*Paul H. Kocher's essay, "Body and Soul," is taken from his book* Science and Religion in Elizabethan England, *and is Chapter* 14 *of this book.*

## PHYSIOLOGY AND PSYCHOLOGY IN SHAKESPEARE'S AGE

### By Patrick Cruttwell

> For nature crescent does not grow alone
> In thews and bulk, but as this temple waxes,
> The inward service of the mind and soul
> Grows wide withal.     (Hamlet, I.3)

The object of this paper is to describe some theories of what we should now call physiology and psychology that were current in sixteenth-century and early seventeenth-century England, to examine their appearances in the imaginative writing of the age, especially Shakespeare's, and to analyse any effects they may have had on such writing. It was a pair of quotations from Shakespeare that started me on this investigation. One is from *Lear;* the king, as he feels the approaches of madness, cries out:

> *Hysterica passio,* down, thou climbing sorrow,
> Thy element's below.

The other is from *The Winter's Tale;* Leontes, suffering the agonies of jealousy:

> I have *tremor cordis* on me; my heart dances,
> But not for joy, not joy.

The two Latin tags are quoted in such a current manner as to make it clear that Shakespeare was here using scraps of medical knowledge known both to himself and to a part at least of his audience; the questions that propose themselves are—what was this knowledge? how much of it did the educated layman know? and how did it fit in with, and influence, his general view of humanity and of life?

To answer the first of these questions I have gone to Thomas Vicary, of whose career I shall give just enough to justify my use of him as representative authority. Vicary was born c. 1490-1500. By 1528 he was one of the royal surgeons to Henry VIII, a position he held through the reigns that followed, Edward VI, Mary, and Elizabeth. In 1530 he was Master of the Barber Surgeons' Company, a position he held again more than once; and in 1548, when St. Bartholomew's Hospital, at the dissolution of the religious houses, was handed over to the government of the City of London, Vicary was appointed one of its governors. It was also in 1548 that Vicary published the book I have used here: *A Profitable Treatise of the Anatomie of Mans Body*. This is the first textbook of anatomy printed in English. The fact that its own age regarded it as authoritative is shown by its republication in 1577, after Vicary's death by the Surgeons of Bart's; the book, in fact, remained a standard text book for more than a century later. It was not, it seems, in the least original; it goes back to a fourteenth-century MS. which in turn goes back even earlier. It was not up to date; Vicary, apparently, was ignorant of the anatomical discoveries of Vesalius. It is, then, a thoroughly representative document of late medieval science.

The physiology of the Middle Ages was derived almost entirely from Galen (and he, it seems, got most of it from Hippocrates and Aristotle). That Galen's authority was still accepted, almost implicitly, in Shakespeare's time, there is plenty of evidence to show. In the "Epistle Dedicatorie" which the surgeons of Bart's prefixed to their edition of Vicary, we are told of "reason and experience which are two principal rootes of Phisicke and Surgerie, As it is graunted by Galen, in his thirde Booke, *De Methode Medendi.*" And again: "Therefore Galen truely writeth, saying That no man can worke so perfectly as aforesayde, without the knowledge of the Anatomie." Vicary himself, in his own introduction, talks of "Galen the Lanterne of all Chirurgions." And as for the laymen, there is Bishop Hall of Exeter:

> Worthie were Galen to be weighed in golde,
> Whose help doth sweetest life and health upholde.
> (Satires, Bk. II, Sat. 4)

There is Marlowe's Faustus, who says "Galen, come" when he thinks of medicine in his opening soliloquy, and there is even Falstaff claiming to have read him:

> It [the Apoplexy] hath its original from much grief, from study, and perturbation of the brain; I have read the cause of his effects in Galen; it is a kind of deafness. (2 Henry IV, I.2)

The basis of Galen's physiology was, of course, the Four Elements—Earth, Water, Fire, Air—and the Four Humours or Temperaments—Phlegmatic, Melancholy, Choleric, Sanguine. The latter are too well known to need elucidation. But the point is worth making that they were conceived of as strictly and literally physiological realities; their use as metaphors for human characters was secondary, and very closely linked, as I shall show, to the physiological basis. The humours, as Vicary tells us, are "ingendered and distributed . . . from the Spermatike matter of the Liuer"; they are thought of as liquids, spread through the body in the blood. When they were perfectly balanced, the health of man was assured. And when one or another of them was in excess, this condition was thought of as a physical disease, to be dealt with by dieting or by drugs. Choler, for instance:

| Guild. | The king, sir, is in his retirement marvellous distempered. |
| Ham. | With drink, sir? |
| Guild. | No, my Lord, rather with choler. |
| Ham. | Your wisdom should show itself more richer to signify this to his doctor; for, for me to put him to his purgation, would perhaps plunge him into far more choler. (III.2) |

Hamlet is not indulging in fanciful jesting. In a medical treatise by Andrew Boorde (of whom more hereafter), we get a list of drugs for the treatment of choler: "These thynges followyng do purge color: Fumytory, Centory, wormewod. . . ." Among Boorde's list is "Reuberbe": Webster was aware of that, for in the *Duchess of Malfi* Ferdinand calls for

> Rhubarb, oh for rhubarb
> To purge this choler! (II.5)

You could prescribe for choler; you could also diet for it. Boorde has a chapter in his *Dyetary* which "sheweth a dyete for Colorycke men"—and Shakespeare knew all about it:

> And better 'twere that both of us did fast,
> Since of ourselves, ourselves are choleric,
> Than feed it with such over-roasted flesh.
> (Tam. of Shrew, IV.1)

> And I expressly am forbid to touch it [sc. mutton]
> For it engenders choler, planteth anger. (*Ibid.*)

The humours, as Vicary tells us, are liquids conveyed in the blood from the liver; this also Shakespeare knew, since it is thus that he describes the effect of the poison that Romeo buys of the apothecary:

> Presently through all thy veins will run
> A cold and drowsy humour. (IV. 1)

Not only the liver was concerned with the humours; there was also the spleen, whose function, says Vicary, is "that the nutritiue blood should by him be made the more purer and cleane, from the drosse and thicking of melancolie, &c." And that description is closely followed in *King John:*

> Or if that surly spirit, melancholy,
> Had baked thy blood and made it heavy-thick,
> Which else runs tickling up and down the veins. . . .
>
> (III, 3)

And also the gall-bladder; it, according to Vicary, "is ordeyned to receyue the Cholerike superfluities which are ingendred in the lyuer." Falstaff had heard of that; when he, posing as a young gallant, is reproaching the Lord Chief Justice for the latter's failure to allow for young blood, he puts it thus:

> You that are old, consider not the capacity of us that are young; you measure the heat of our livers with the bitterness of your galls.          (II Hen. IV, I.2)

By which Falstaff means: Your gall has adequately performed its physiological function of "receiving the choleric superfluities," but mine (I being young and hot) has not. I therefore am passionately choleric; you are a tame and respectable old man.

From this physiological basis, the step is a very short one to thinking of humours as composing the characters of men. The step was made easier by the theory (which descends from Aristotle) that the appearance of a man's body was a clue to his character; as Vicary puts it:

> And therefore it is to be noted, that the shape of the members of the body bctokneth and iudgeth the affections and wyll of the Soule of man, as the Philosopher sayth.

King Duncan mentions that theory, only to reject it:

> There's no art
> Can find the mind's construction in the face.   (Macb. I.4)

How the physiology of humours was also a psychology,

may be seen from a few examples. There was, for instance, the notion that a hot and moist humour was indicative of lechery; as Othello says to Desdemona:

> Give me your hand; this hand is moist, my lady . . .
> This argues fruitfulness and liberal heart;
> Hot, hot and moist; . . . this hand of yours requires
> A sequester from liberty, fasting and prayer,
> Much castigation, exercise devout.          (III.4)

This notion is referred to again, in the key of joking, by the badinage of Cleopatra's maids:

> There's a palm presageth chastity, if nothing else.
> Even as the overflowing Nilus presageth famine.
> Nay, if an oily palm be not a fruitful prognostication. . . .
> (I.2)

There was also a theory that the color of the cheeks was symptomatic of the prevailing humour. Vicary describes it in detail. If the cheeks are "full, ruddy, and meddled with temperate whiteness," it shows a "sanguin and temperat" nature; if they are "white coloured, without medling of rednes," the nature is "flematike"; if "browne in colour," choleric; if "as it were blowen in colour" (which I take to be a livid yellowish pallor), then the temperament is melancholy. So, in *Troilus and Cressida,* we get:

> Princes!
> What grief hath set the jaundice on your cheeks?   (I.3)

—which is the color of melancholy; and in *Romeo and Juliet:*

> What a deal of brine
> Hath washed thy sallow cheeks for Rosaline!   (II.3)

—melancholy once more. And again, when Viola describes her imaginary sister:

> She never told her love,
> But let concealment, like a worm i' the bud,
> Feed on her damask cheek; she pined in thought,

98

> And with a green and yellow melancholy,
> She sat like patience on a monument,
> Smiling at grief, (T.N. II.4)

neither the cheek nor the green and yellow are the merely figurative expressions that modern readers take them for; they are pure physiology.

Next in importance to the humours were the spirits. These too are conveyed in the blood. The function of the arteries, according to Vicary, is to bring "from the herte to euery member, blood and spirit of lyfe." Which reminds us of Shakespeare's

> Universal plodding prisons up
> The nimble spirits in the arteries, (L.L.L., IV, 3)

and also of Marlowe's

> Your Artiers which alongst the veins convey
> The lively spirits which the heart engenders. . . .
> (2 Tamburlaine, 1. 4485)

There were three kinds of spirits, defined for us by Andrew Boorde:

> There be thre, naturall, anymal, and vytall; the naturall spyrite resteth in the head, the animall spirite doth rest in the lyuer, and the vital spirite resteth in the hert of man. (*Breuyary,* the 329 chapitre)

(Vicary seems to disagree with Boorde here, putting the animal spirit in the head and giving to the liver a "spirit nutrimental"; he also seems to add a fourth, the generative spirit, which resides in the sexual organs and is responsible for procreation.) The three organs which produced these three spirits were regarded as the essential, the master organs of the body. Shakespeare has this twice:

Liver, brain, and heart, these sovereign thrones. (T.N. I.1)

The liver, heart and brain of Britain,
By whom I grant she lives. (Cymbeline, V.5)

First, then, the liver. It, says Vicary, was ordained "because that the nutrimental blood shoulde be ingendred in him," and in this blood was the nutrimental spirit. But Shakespeare, it seems, follows Boorde here, making the liver the seat of the passions, of the appetitive part of man:

> This is the liver vein, which makes flesh a deity,
> A green goose a goddess.  (L.L.L. IV.3)

> Their love may be called appetite,
> No motion of the liver, but the palate.  (T.N. II.4)

> My knight, I will inflame thy noble liver,
> And make thee rage.  (2 Hen. IV. V.4)

Next, the heart. It is the supreme organ, "the principal of all other members" in Vicary's words. Its function, to make the vital spirit, is carefully expounded by Vicary. The heart, he says, has two ventricles; to the right ventricle comes a vein that brings the blood from the liver; of this blood some remains in the heart, to nourish it, and then:

> The residue that is left of this, is made subtill through the vertue of the hart; and then this blood is sent into a concauitie or pytte in the myddest of the Harte betweene the two Ventrikles and therein it is made hote and pured; and then it passeth into the left Ventrikle, and there is ingendred in it a spirit that is clearer, brighter, and subtiller then any corporal or bodely thing that is ingendred of the foure Elementes: For it is a thing that is a meane betweene the body and the soule.

This is the vital spirit. When the physician, in Marlowe's *Tamburlaine,* is diagnosing the hero's disease, he follows his Vicary:

> The Humidum or Calor, which some hold
> Is not a parcel of the Elements,
> But of a substance more divine and pure,
> Is almost clean extinguished and spent,
> Which being the cause of life, imports your death.
> (l. 1480 et seq.)

Thirdly, the head. Its function, to make the animal spirit, is explained by Vicary with equal care:

> In some places of the brayne the Veynes and the Arteirs goo foorth of him [i.e. the *pia mater*] and enter into the diuisions of the brayne, and there drinketh of the brayne substaunce into them, asking of the hart to them the spirite of lyfe or breath, and of the Lyuer, nutriment. And the aforesayde spirite or breath taketh a further digestion, and there it is made animal; by the elaboration of the spirite vital, is turned and made animal.

The animal spirit, which derives from *anima*—soul, was thought of as something very near to the soul.  Cf. Donne:

> As our blood labours to beget,
> Spirits, as like souls as it can . . . .  (The Ecstasy)

The head, says Vicary, "is the habitation or dwelling place of the reasonable soule of man," a theory which Shakespeare knew:
> His pure brain,
> Which some suppose the soul's frail dwelling-house.
> (K. John, V.7)

Shakespeare knew also that it was the animal spirit which kept man active and forceful; Antony, boasting that he is still young enough to fight:

> Though gray
> Do something mingle with our younger brown, yet ha' we
> A brain that nourishes our nerves, and can
> Get goal for goal of youth.  (IV.8)

Vicary's anatomy of the brain divides it into three ventricles, each of which has two parts. In the foremost ventricle are the "fyue Wittes, as Hearing, Seeing, Feeling, Smelling, and tasting." Here also is "the vertue that is called Fantasie, and he taketh al the formes or ordinances that be disposed of the fiue wittes"; "the Imaginatiue vertue," "the Cogitatiue or estimatiue vertue," and "the vertue Memoratiue" are there as well. This physiology of the mind was certainly known to Shakespeare. Take Holofernes' account of it:

101

A foolish extravagant spirit, full of forms, figures, shapes, objects, ideas, apprehensions, motions, revolutions;

(so far, "the vertue that is called Fantasie")

these are begot in the ventricle of memory, nourished in the womb of pia mater, and delivered upon the mellowing of occasion.   (L.L.L. IV.2)

Lady Macbeth, describing the effects of drink on Duncan's guards, uses the same phrasing:

That memory, the warder of the brain,
Shall be a fume, and the receipt of reason
A limbec only.   (I, 7)

(The "receipt of reason" is Vicary's "cogitatiue or estimatiue vertue.")

The moon, according to Vicary, has a profound influence over the brain, which

moueth and followeth the mouing of the Moone; for in the waxing of the Moone, the Brayne followeth vpwardes; and in the wane of the Moone, the brayne discendeth downwardes, and vanisheth in substaunce of vertue; for then the Brayne shrinketh togeather in itselfe, and is not so fully obedient to the spirit of feeling.

Or, as Shakespeare puts it, more tersely:

For thy [sc. life's] complexion shifts to strange effects,
After the moon.   (M. for M., III.1)

This, of course, explains why lunatics are lunatic:

And this is proued in menne that be lunatike or madde. . . .

So Shakespeare:

Lovers and madmen have such seething brains.   (MND, V.1)

The brain is as liable to the humours as any other part. It has to be cold and moist "that he shoulde, by his coldnes

102

and moystnes, abate and temper the exceeding heate and drought that commeth from the harte." And again:

> Wherefore (sayth Aristotle) when it happeneth that the Brayne is eyther too drye or too moyst, then can it not worke his kinde; for then is the body made colde; then are the spirites of lyfe melted and resolued away; and then foloweth feebleness of the wittes, and of al other members of the body, and at the last death.

Falstaff, expounding the virtues of sherris sack, relies on this sort of physiology of the brain:

> It ascends me into the brain; dries me there all the foolish and dull and crudy vapours which environ it. . . .
> (2 Hen. IV, IV.3)

The concept "spirit" seems to have been a maid of all work to the medieval physiologist. It is also invoked to explain the workings of the senses. Vicary explains the faculty of sight by observing that two sinews go from the eyes, and that these sinews:

> be hollowe as a reede, for two causes. The fyrst is, that the visible spirit might pass freely to the Eyes: The second is, that the forme of visible thinges might freely be presented to the common wits.

Such a theory lies behind the conceit in Donne's *Ecstasy:*

> Our eyebeams twisted, and did thread
> Our eyes upon one double string,

and "spirit of sense" is a phrase that Shakespeare uses. It is also used in Sir John Davies' *Immortality of the Soul:*

> For all those nerves, which spirits of sense do bear.

Spirits, like humours, were psychological as well as physiological. There was a theory that when a person was in a state of intense excitement, or if his character was unusually pure and simple, then the spirits shone through the bodily covering. Macbeth, assuring his hired murderers that he does not doubt their sincerity, tells them:

> Your spirits shine through you. (III.1)

103

The Queen tells Hamlet (describing his excitement at the sight of the ghost):

Forth at your eyes your spirits wildly peep.    (III.4)

Donne thus conveys the purity of the heroine of his *Anniversaries:*

> Her pure and eloquent blood
> Spoke in her cheeks, and so distinctly wrought,
> That one might almost say, her body thought.
> (Second Anniversarie, l. 244)

And Shakespeare does the same for Perdita, with the phrase "her blood looks out": that phrase, for an Elizabethan audience, was not merely a vivid and charming description of a blush; it also told them something about Perdita's character; it told them that she was a person of such exceptional purity and sincerity that her spirits "looked out" through her body.

So much for the main outline of Vicary's physiology. Before I go on to discuss some wider issues, there are one or two minor correspondences that may be mentioned. These come, not from Vicary but from Andrew Boorde. He was born c. 1490; a Carthusian monk, but not a very pious one, according to his enemies; Doctor of Physic of Montpellier (possibly). He wrote two works of popular medical knowledge: *A Compendyous Regyment or A Dyetary of Helth,* and *A Breuyary of Helth,* both written c. 1542.

The great diagnostic standby of the medieval physician was, of course, the examination of his patient's urine. Marlowe's doctor in *Tamburlaine:*

I view'd your urine, and the hypostasis [sediment]
Thick and obscure, doth make your danger great.    (l. 4474)

"Carry his water to the wisewoman," says Maria, by way of giving helpful advice on Malvolio's madness. But Boorde, it seems, was a trifle sceptical:

I do say that an vryne is a strumpet; or an harlot for

104

it will lye; and the best doctour of Phisicke of them all
may be deceyued in an vryne,            (Extrauagantes)

a phrase which appears to have been almost proverbial; it
appears in Scogin's Jest Book, and we find it again in
Webster:

> There's no more credit to be given to the face
> Than to a sick man's urine, which some call
> The physician's whore, because she cozens him.
>
> (Duchess of Malfi, I.1)

Another correspondence between Boorde and Webster
is concerned with sleep. "Immoderate slepe and sluggysh-
nes doth humecte and maketh lyght the brayne. . . . And
specyally it doth instygate and lede a man to synne"
(Dyetary, chap. 8). The villainy of one of Webster's
scoundrels is accounted for precisely thus:

> If too immoderate sleep be truly said
> To be an inward rust into the soul,
> It then doth follow want of action
> Breeds all black malcontents.   (Duch. of Mal. I.1)

That was the standard psychological explanation of the
Elizabethan villain. He was villainous because he was
"malcontent"; he was malcontent because he was frus-
trated. And this too, it would seem, had its roots in
physiology.

Boorde on the effects of wine is quite astonishingly close
to Falstaff's oration:

> It doth acuate and quicken a man's wyttes, it doth com-
> fort the hert, it doth scowre the lyuer . . . it doth reioyce
> all the powers of man, and doth nourysshe them; it doth
> ingender good blode, it doth comfort and doth nourysshe
> the brayne and all the body . . . it is full of agylyte;
> wherfore it is medsonable.   (Dyetary, chap. 10)

One of the chapters (Chap. 4) of Boorde's Dyetary
gives advice on choosing a site for a house. Avoid, he tells
us, a southern aspect; for "the south wynde doth corrupt
and doth make euyl vapours." Shakespeare had heard of
this. "All the contagions of the south light on you!" are

105

the words of Coriolanus to his fleeing soldiers; and "the
south fog rot him!" is a curse of Cloten's.

What all this amounts to, then, is a psychology that may
almost be called behaviorist: a rigorous physical determinism. But there was, of course, an essential difference
between this and modern behaviorism—the fact that
Shakespeare's age believed in the soul, in a part of man
that was wholly spiritual in nature and divine in origin.
Looking at the physical framework, and remembering also
the great part played by the influence of the stars, it is a
little difficult to see how the soul was fitted in. And, in fact,
the precise relationship between body and soul was one
of the most debated questions of the age. Donne hints at it:

> Poor soul, in this thy flesh what dost thou know?
> Thou know'st thyself so little, as thou know'st not
> How thou didst die, nor how thou wast begot.
> Thou neither know'st how thou at first came in,
> Nor how thou tookst the poison of man's sin.
>
> (Second Anniversarie)

And Sir John Davies gives us the conflicting theories:

> In judgment of her substance thus they vary,
>   And thus they vary in judgment of her seat;
> For some her chair up to the brain do carry,
>   Some thrust it down into the stomach's heat;
> Some place it in the root of life, the heart;
>   Some in the river-fountain of the veins;
> Some say, she's all in all, and all in every part,
>   Some say, she's not contained, but all contains.
>
> (Immortality of the Soul: Intro.)

(One of these theories, that which placed the soul in the
brain, was known to Shakespeare, as we have seen.) When
Davies comes to give his own opinion, his conclusions are
excessively vague; and that, I think, was true of the age
in general. As Donne indicates, the problem was regarded
as insoluble.

It was equally difficult to fit in the consequence of
having a soul the possession of free will. The age had, at
the same time, a craving for freedom and a deep need
for control; and it may be that the tension between the
two is largely responsible for the tragic attitude of Shake-

106

speare and his contemporaries. One sees the tension, for instance, in Edmund's ridiculing of astrology: "This is the excellent foppery of the world, that when we are sick in fortune, often the surfeit of our own behaviour, we make guilty of our disasters the sun, the moon, and the stars." It may be that Shakespeare agreed with Edmund's opinions, but the man who delivers them is utterly condemned. For Edmund is not only criticising a false belief, he is also throwing off a spiritual control. The medieval system of beliefs was so closely-knit that it was impossible to touch any one part of it without affecting others. The physiology, as we have seen in Vicary's remarks on the moon and the brain, was closely linked to theories of natural phenomena. Shakespeare, for instance, finds it natural to describe an earthquake in physiological terms:

> Diseased Nature oftentimes breaks forth
> In strange eruptions, oft the teeming earth
> Is with a kind of colic pinch'd and vext,
> By the imprisoning of unruly wind
> Within her womb; which for enlargement striving,
> Shakes th' old beldame earth, and topples down
> Steeples and mossgrown towers.   (I Hen. IV, III.1)

That comparison follows very closely the disease which Vicary calls "Iliaca Passio," expounded as follows in another source:

> *Iliack Passion,* a painful wringing or twisting of those Guts, when they are stopt up, or full of Wind, or troubled with sharp humours, or when the upper part of any Entrail sinks or falls in with the lower. (Kersey's Phillips's New World of Words, 1706, cited in E.E.T.S. edition of Vicary's "Anatomie.")

Physiology, again, is closely concerned with morals and ethics. Liver was seat of passion, head of reason. The brain, says Vicary, is "the gouernour or the treasurie of the fyue wittes." And reason is man's prerogative, the thing that distinguishes him from the beasts.

> O God! a beast, that wants discourse of reason
> Would have mourned longer . . . .   (Ham. I.2)

From this foundation develops the clear-cut issue of passion versus reason, the terms in which Shakespeare invariably sees the tragic situation. From countless examples only one need be given: the debate in *Troilus and Cressida,* in which Hector and Troilus discuss whether Helen should be returned to the Greeks. Hector—for reason—advises her return:

> What's merit in that reason which denies
> The yielding of her up?

Troilus—for passion—argues against it:

> Manhood and honour
> Should have hard hearts, would they but fat their thoughts
> With this crammed reason; reason and respect
> Makes lovers pale, and lustyhood deject. (II.2)

Statecraft and politics were also involved. It seems inevitable that when Shakespeare is thinking of a troubled state, he thinks of it in medical terms. Again, the examples are countless; perhaps the most striking is a crucial scene in *Coriolanus* (III, 1) in which we get in quick succession:

> And wish
> To vamp a body with a dangerous physic
> That's sure of death without it.
> Sir, those cold ways
> That seem like prudent helps, are very poisons
> When the disease is violent.
> For 'tis a sore upon us,
> You cannot tent yourself.
> He's a disease that must be cut away.
> O, he's a limb that has but a disease:
> Mortal, to cut it off; to cure it, easy.

And these are not all, in this one scene.

The age of Shakespeare, then, had still the integrated medieval view of the world and of man's place in it. One's ideas on man's body were connected with ideas on his soul and character, on his actions as a political animal, and on the universe. For imaginative literature, the consequence was that it was not only possible and easy, it was inevitable, that descriptions of men and women doing and suffering should also convey a philosophy of life. Shakespeare is not

108

really a philosopher; he had no philosophy of his own. He didn't need to have one; it was given him. He had simply to describe human life as honestly, vividly, and completely as he knew, and then, through the very terms of reference by which alone he *could* describe it, a philosophy emerges. One might contrast the position of later poets, Wordsworth and Tennyson, for instance. They have to *make* a philosophy; it costs them infinite pain and labor, and, on the whole, the effort is detrimental to their poetry.

The integrated medieval view was valuable to imaginative art in another way. The close connection between physiology and psychology—their identity, in fact—made it, again, not only possible and easy, but inevitable, for the Elizabethan poet to describe states of mind and emotion in physical terms. Take, for example, the opening of Shakespeare's 129th sonnet:

> The expense of spirit in a waste of shame
> Is lust in action.

That phrase, for the modern reader, has a poignant emotional force; but I doubt if he realises what Shakespeare precisely means. Go back to Vicary, and we learn that from the heart to the sexual organs a vein goes, bearing the "spirit generative." "Expense" is used in the sense of "expenditure" or "loss": what the phrase refers to is the loss of "spirit generative" in the act of sex. Shakespeare, in fact, sets forth, baldly and crudely, a statement of the sexual process as his age conceived it; he adds one wonderful emotional phrase—"in a waste of shame"—and thereby achieves just the effect he desires, of satiety and cold disgust.

It may be that here we have the fundamental reason for Mr. Eliot's "dissociation of sensibility"; perhaps it was caused by the loss of this complex of beliefs which made possible a close physical-psychical parallelism. Certainly, if you look at later psychology, the difference, in this respect, is striking. Locke writes a great work on the "Human Understanding" with virtually no reference to the human body: a feat which no man thinking in the medieval way could even have dreamt of. It is reasonable to suppose that the art which emerges from such an abstract psychology will itself tend to be abstract. And so it does. Take, for example, Pope's account of the mental process:

> Nature to all things fix'd the limits fit,
> And wisely curb'd proud man's pretending wit;
> As on the land while here the ocean gains,
> In other parts it leaves wide sandy plains.
> Thus in the soul while memory prevails,
> The solid pow'r of understanding fails;
> Where beams of warm imagination play,
> The memory's soft figures melt away.
>
> (Essay on Criticism, 1.52 et seq.)

Remembering Shakespeare's "begot in the ventricle of memory," we can see that Pope's concepts—wit, memory, understanding, imagination—are so many abstract counters, to be pushed about at will, with no solid framework to hold them. What has been lost is the physical presence. "The inward service of the mind and soul" has become divorced from the body.


# BODY AND SOUL

## By Paul H. Kocher


### 1

When re-editing, with a rather myopic Protestant eye, the Catholic work, *The First Booke of Christian Exercise* (1585), Edmund Bunny found its doctrine of the passions too deterministic. So he added a long marginal note to explain that "the soul doth not follow, but rather doth uze such temperature as the bodie hath."[1] A man's complexion or bodily constitution, Bunny admitted, may indeed render him particularly prone to certain types of emotional bias, but these are "neither good, nor il of themselves" and can be controlled by his will for righteousness. The contrary view leads to doubt about the immortality of the soul, for if the soul depends on the temperature of the

[1] P. 171.

110

body, and this temperature itself dies with the body, must not the soul die too? In the 1598 edition of the same book Robert Parsons, its original author, retorted angrily (and quite accurately) that neither he nor Catholics in general meant any such thing.[2] They were as anxious as any Protestant to guard the human will against a doctrine of physical determinism. For us this bit of unpleasantness has at least the value of showing how abhorrent to clergymen of both faiths was the tenet that the manners and choices of an individual's soul are automatic results of the proportions in which the humors are mingled in his body—in other words, of his complexion.[3]

This tenet was in truth hostile to the whole Christian concept of man as a spiritual being. The soul was carefully defined, we remember, as a separate, spiritual, immortal substance for which the body is merely vehicle.[4] With its faculties of reason and will, soul is placed in the flesh to rule it, not to be ruled by it. Unless by the autonomy of his will the choleric man can curb his temptations of anger, the melancholy man his despair, virtue and vice are meaningless, and all ideas of Christian warfare against the world, the flesh, and the devil merely a dream. Even the most rigorous Calvinists fought hard for the principle that the will is free in this sense.[5] What they maintained, not without paradox, was that the will thus freely choosing would choose evil because of original sin unless God gave it grace;

[2] Fol. IIv.

[3] Good summaries of the familiar Renaissance doctrine of complexion may be found in Ruth L. Anderson, *Elizabethan Psychology and Shakespeare's Plays,* Univ. of Iowa Humanistic Studies, III, no. 4 (1927); Lily B. Campbell, *Shakespeare's Tragic Heroes* (Cambridge, 1930); Timothy Bright, *A Treatise of Melancholie* (1586), pp. 4 ff.; Peter Lowe, *The Whole Course of Chirurgerie* (1597), sig. CI v. The doctrine performed for Elizabethans the extraordinary double duty of explaining both the likenesses and unlikenesses between men and the differences between health and sickness in the same man. For a description of the physiological process by which the predominant humor influenced passion see Thomas Wright, *The Passions of the Minde* (1604), pp. 37, 47; La Primaudaye, *Second Part of the French Academie* (1605), pp. 230–31.

[4] See chap. 11 ante.

[5] E.g., Perkins, *Gods Free Grace, and Mans Free Will* in *Works* (1605).

111

and that certain men were predestined to receive this grace, others not. But this is a very different matter from denying the free function, if not the very existence, of the will on the ground that the humors decided everything.

Glancing back to Chapter 10 on judicial astrology, we can now recognize the united clerical attack on that science as one campaign in this larger war against materialism. The line which divines tried to hold at all cost was that the stars may incline a man's will in this or that direction, but never compel it. Stars act upon humors; humors beget passions; passions solicit will; but the last word lies with will. Hence there can be no genuine science of astrological prediction. Similarly in the broader controversy with medical materialism divines always took the position that body may predispose but never decide the character of man. And their conclusion, analogously, was that the medical sciences have no business meddling with man's higher nature. But the wide divergence between the astrologer and the physician in this respect was that the former needed a physical determinism as the first principle of his science, whereas the doctor did not. The latter could and did retire into the exclusive study of the human body, with only the most diffident excursions into the region of the mind. One result of this necessary but jealous guardianship of the soul by all Christian churchmen may well have been to discourage systematic study of the interrelationships of body and soul, or what we know today as psychology. It will also appear in a moment that for methodological reasons the medical man was on the whole content with this cleavage of jurisdictions, and in fact encouraged it wherever advantageous to the purity of his science.

The temptations of the Elizabethan physician towards materialistic determinism may readily be illustrated from the medical books of the time. Nothing is more common in them than those familiar lists of the traits to be found in men of each of the four humoral types, a jumble of characteristics ranging from color and texture of hair, eyes, and skin to intelligence and stupidity, virtue and vice. Peter Lowe's conglomeration in *The Whole Course of Chirurgerie* (1597) is representative:

112

He of the sanguine complexion is fleshie, liberall, loving, amiable, gratious, merrie, ingenious, audacious, given to Venus game, red coloured, with divers other qualities which sheweth the domination of the blood. . . . The cholericke is hastie, prompt, & in all his affaires envious, covetous subtill, hardy, angrie, valiant, prodigall, leane, yellow coloured, and is hot and drie, & is in good health in winter. The *Flegmaticke* is fat, soft, white, sleepie, slothfull, dull of understanding, heavie, much spitting, & white coloured. . . . The *Melancholicke,* which is eyther by nature or accident of colour livide and plumbin, and solitarie, coward, timide, sad, envious, curious, avaritious, leane, weake, tardife, and so foorth. . . .[6]

Language of this kind sounds distinctly deterministic. Lowe says not that a man of the choleric type tends to be covetous, or is tempted by covetousness, but that he *is* covetous. A moral result is stated as if springing automatically from a physical condition without any intervening act of choice by the will. Similarly when Thomas Walkington in *The Optick Glasse of Humors* (1607) says of sanguine men that "they bee liberally minded; they carry a constant loving affection . . . they are very hairy,"[7] the love and liberality seem to be about as voluntary as the hairiness. The same tone carries over into the Elizabethan view, a familiar extension of the doctrine of complexion, that national temperaments are the result of geographical environment acting upon the humors of the people. Lowe, for example, can say that "the people towards the South are mealancholick, cruel, vindicatyf, always timide."[8] Others describe northerners as dull-witted, alcoholic, and so forth because the cold and moist climate increases phlegm. Not all statements of this kind are so unconditional, but as a genre they leave the strong impression that there is no such reality as the human will.

The reasons for this categorical and deterministic tone lie close at hand. Under a Galenic theory in which disease

[6] Sig. C3r. Also Levinus Lemnius, *The Touchstone of Complexions,* tr. T. Newton (1581), fols. 38v, 64v, 84r; Valentinus, *Enchiridion Medicum* (1612), pp. 15–26 and 5 ff.
[7] Fol. 59v. Also Burton, *The Anatomy of Melancholy* (1621), ed. A. R. Shilleto, (1896), I, 485–86.
[8] Sig, C2r; Walkington, fol. 15r; Ambroise Paré, *Workes,* tr. T. Johnson (1634), pp. 19–20.

is an upset of the patient's normal balance of humors, the doctor must discover both what that balance used to be and what has since happened to it. As far as he is concerned, the mental traits connected with complexion are interesting not for their own sakes but solely as useful evidence of what has been going on inside the sick man's body. The connection therefore must be rigid, unqualified, and automatic if these traits are to be of any real use to him as symptoms or causes of disease. Hence his temptation to look at human behavior from a strongly deterministic point of view. The dynamics of his science seemed to require it. But this was a direction, a pressure, not an overt policy. So far as I can tell, no published Elizabethan medical book ever claimed outright that the manners of the soul inevitably and completely follow the temperature of body.

2

Elizabethan psychology was a wild medley of these medical and religious attitudes. Well might it be. Professional psychologists as a class being yet unborn, the authors of most works on psychology were either doctors or clergymen. The following table of twelve major publications before 1641 in England, either original or translated, gives some idea of the situation:

Timothy Bright, M.D., later in holy orders, *Treatise of Melancholy* (1586)

Robert Burton, Clergyman, *Anatomy of Melancholy* (1621)

F. N. Coeffeteau, Catholic Bishop of Dardania, *Table of Humane Passions* (1621)

Sir John Davies, Lawyer and Statesman, *Nosce Teipsum* (1599)

Jacques Ferrand, French physician, *Erotomania* (1640)

Juan Huarte, Spanish physician, *Examination of Wits* (1594)

Peter de la Primaudaye, French courtier, *French Academie, Pt. II* (1605)

Andreas Laurentius, Physician to Henri IV, *Preservation of the Sight* (an analysis of melancholia) (1599)

Levinus Lemnius, (Dutch?) physician and divine, *Touchstone of Complexions* (1581)

Edward Reynoldes, Bishop of Norwich, *Treatise of the Passions and Faculties* (1640)

Thomas Walkington, Clergyman, *Optick Glasse of Humors* (1607)

Thomas Wright, Jesuit (?),[9] *Passions of the Minde* (1604)

Except for two lay outsiders, doctors and divines made up this group in about equal numbers. The doctors of course started with a medical bias. The clergy were more likely to set out to find ethical and religious meanings in their subject. But since passion was the chief instigator of the will to vice and subsequent damnation, and since passion in turn was largely the immediate product of complexion, divines writing on psychology were led deeply into physiology and a consideration of body's impact on soul. Hence the dual tenor, physical and ethical, of many of these Elizabethan treatises, often juxtaposed in radical, unresolved conflict. Like Polonius, one might distinguish many types among them, such as the physical-psychological, the psychological-ethical, the physical-psychological-ethical-theological, and so forth. But a brief look at some of the individual books is worth a world of classifications.

One of the best balanced of all these writers is La Primaudaye, whose *Second Part of the French Academie* (1605) is a kind of Renaissance *Summa Psychologica*. It assembles and gives full value to all elements bearing upon the relationship between passion and will: the concupiscent body whence passions are born; the rectification to be sought in custom, education, and religious counsel, which help the will to grow into a good habit; the power of God; and of course, fully discussed, the immediate protagonists, passion and will themselves.[10] Affirming the will's power over complexion and its minions, the passions, and calling for its direction towards virtue and salvation, La Primaudaye—Wright and Coeffeteau resemble him in this[11]—refuses determinism, eschews undue emphasis on body,

[9] Burton, I, 290 and 483, refers to "Wright the Jesuit in his Book of the Passions of the Mind," but the *DNB* denies the identification.

[10] P. 382 gives a characteristic summary.

[11] Wright, esp. Books II and III; Coeffeteau, sig. A7r.

115

and looks at psychology from a prevailingly ethical and religious point of view.

With Reynoldes' *A Treatise of the Passions* we begin to shade over into works which put more stress on the contributions of body to psychology. Where his emphasis falls may be gauged from his statement that the rational soul

> . . . depends in all its ordinarie and natural operations, upon the happie or disordered temperature of those vitall Qualities, out of whose apt and regular commixion the good estate of the Body is framed and composed. For though these Ministeriall partes have not any over-ruling, yet they have a disturbing power, to hurt and hinder the operations of the Soule: Whence wee finde, that sundry diseases of the Body doe oftentimes weaken, yea, sometimes quite extirpate the deepest impression and most fixed habits of the minde. . . .[12]

There is all the difference in the world between saying, as Reynoldes seems to say, that "body controls unless—" and saying, as La Primaudaye does, that "will controls un-less—." The same leaning is implicit in the heading of Reynolde's second chapter: "In what Cases the depend-ance of the Soule on the Body, is lessened by Faith, Cus-tome, Education, Occasion."

In *The Touchstone of Complexions* by Lemnius this trend towards body is much more marked, though it is not easy to sift anything definite out of this loose and chaotic piece. Most of the book goes to an analysis of the physi-ology of the four humors and their psychic consequences. Granted, Lemnius says in a few isolated passages, that reason can resist such emotions by the aid of God and that education and good counsel are of some use,[13] but the language used to describe how bodily qualities make men what they are is so unqualified, his obsession with the onrush of passion so frequent and strong, that we come away thinking most men to be what their bodies dictate.[14] Lemnius virtually dispossesses the will as an active force.

The same description applies to Walkington's *The Op-*

[12] P. 4.
[13] E. g. fols. 13v-14v, 60v.
[14] Fols. 25r ff., 64r ff., 128r.

116

*tick Glasse of Humors,* which assumes that moral result follows more or less inexorably from humoral condition.[15] Thus it shares the medical man's point of view, not the moralist's, and it is perhaps significant in this regard that the authors chiefly cited are Lemnius, Fernelius, Cogan, and other physicians.

Huarte's *Examination of Wits* amounts to an early book of vocational guidance, but on a very strange theory. Beginning from a belief that all knowledge is complete in a child's soul at birth but that it can reveal itself only in so far as the temperature of body is favorable,[16] Huarte comes to the bizarre conclusion that the only requisite in education is a physical regimen proper to development of the right bodily temperatures. All souls are inherently equally endowed with knowledge, but selective mating of parents and variations in their offspring's diet as he grows up will serve to provide constitutional temperatures which make available parts of this intellectual endowment suitable for this or that profession in life. Huarte's entire interest, therefore, is in body as the soul's instrument. Soul, being already perfect in knowledge, is beyond his attention except that he takes care to assert, as did Bright, Laurentius, Lemnius, and other advocates of the medical view before him, that soul in its essence can never be tainted by an adverse temperature of body. The net result is a book more divorced from genuine moral and religious considerations and more totally ridden by the idea of body than most other Elizabethan works on psychology and than not a few professedly medical treatises.

The five foregoing treatises run the gamut of Elizabethan psychology. None of the writers believed, presumably, that body really completely determines will. Some denied it in so many words. But their incorporation of the language and emphases of medical science sometimes made them sound like determinists in spite of themselves. Even divines writing on psychology might stumble into such contradiction. Nevertheless as clergymen they could make no con-

[15] Fol. 9v. The heading of Cap. 2 is the Galenic theorem, "That the soule simpathizeth with the body and followeth her crasis and temperature." Also fols. 10r, 15r, 31r, and 55v ff.
[16] Pp. 32 ff.

117

scious compromise with the principle that the manners of soul, though biased by the temperature of body, did not necessarily succumb to it.

## 3

On the contrary, the Christian position was that the current flowed the other way. Temperature of body was in some large but unspecifiable degree determined by the manners of soul, that is, by the success or failure of the individual's will in asserting itself over his passions and by the internal order or disorder which then prevailed. In this contention the Church had, to an extent we must now explore, some support from Galenic medicine.

Many medical and psychological books described how the process worked.[17] When an emotion of the soul was aroused by some experience from the outer world of sense or by some suggestion of memory from within, the heart's vital heat was thereby augmented or dismissed, depending on the happy or threatening nature of the stimulus. By this cardiac dilation or contraction, the manufacture of arterial spirits and their distribution throughout the body were changed for better or worse, and the purity and proportion of humors underwent mutation. If emotion of the same kind was repeated often enough, it altered the whole bent of the physical constitution. It might make the body ill. "These mocions of the spirit," observed the physician William Bullein in his *Bulwarke of Defence* (1562),

> . . . must be as well considered, and diligently observed of the Phisicion, in the tyme of sicknesse, as moche as any other common knowen sicknesse. For these perturbacions or painfull affeccions of the spirites, do chaunge the estate of the bodie, marveilously and sodainly.[18]

[17] Coeffeteau, p. 2: "That which is called passion, say they, is no other thing, but a motion of the sensitive appetite, caused by the apprehension or imagination of good or evill, the which is followed with a change or alteration in the body, contrary to the Lawes of Nature." Wright, pp. 32, 45; Valentinus, pp. 22–23; Lowe, sig. F4r & v; Sir Thomas Elyot, *The Castell of Helth* (1572), fols. 64v ff.
[18] Sig. Lxxiir.

From the standpoint of the Christian teacher the will must intervene to discipline such emotions before any harm set in to body or mind. Peace must bring health. And the physician, too, could not blink the need for a better mental attitude in any patient thus afflicted. But since he felt concerned with the physical, not the ethical and volitional, side of the problem, he could not afford to be drawn off very far into psychic or spiritual considerations. Emotion was only one factor in the case. He had others to weigh.

His master Galen had reduced under six heads—six so-called "non-natural things"[19]—the factors which mold, alter, or confirm the complexion at any time between birth and old age. Sir Thomas Elyot, in *The Castell of Helth* (1572), named them in their usual order: "Ayre, Meates & drinke, Slepe & watche, Meving and rest, Emptines and repletion, and Affections of the mynde."[20] All these determined the proportions of heat, cold, dryness, and moisture in the body, and so its complexion. The same tally, in this same order, was repeated by almost every Elizabethan work on medicine or psychology. Tagging along always so inconspicuously at the end, the final item, the "affections of the mynde," has for us a quiet but vast significance. It was Elizabethan medical recognition that states of soul are inevitably reflected in the matter which soul inhabits.

But this recognition seems in most cases to have been a merely verbal and perfunctory one. The great majority of medical books in the period contented themselves with a bare mention of the passions as causes of complexion and gave virtually their whole attention to the other five items:

[19] Called "non-natural" in order to distinguish them from the seven "natural" factors: elements, complexions, humors, members, powers, operations, spirits. Cf. Christopher Wirtzung, *The General Practise of Physicke,* tr. J. Monson (1605), To the Reader; Paré, p. 39. Other, more remote factors bearing upon complexion, such as heredity, the stars, and ultimately God's Providence, were given by various medical writers sometimes a good deal of stress, sometimes less, sometimes none at all.

[20] Fol. 1r. Also Valentinus, p. 15: "There are six things necessary to the nourishment and preservation of mans life, and are called not naturall. 1 The Aire. 2 Meate and Drinke. 3 Sleepe and watchfulnesse. 4 Exercise and rest. 5 Emptiness and repletion. 6 The affects of the minde."

air, food, sleep, exercise, and evacuation. For example, Phayre's *A Godly Brief Treatise of the Pestilence* (1596), discussing the six non-natural things whose abuse produces corrupt humors, allotted exactly two sentence to the passions of the mind.[21] Recipes for drinks, pomanders, and powders followed at far greater length. In all its 790 folio pages *The General Practise of Physicke* (1605), by Christopher Wirtzung, noticed the soul only twice: once briefly in the introduction, where peace of soul was listed as conducive to good health, and again in the chapter on melancholia, where fear and sadness were described as mental accompaniments of the disease. But Wirtzung in this latter chapter laid all his emphasis on diet and other physical factors as real causes of melancholia: "The cause of these melancholicke fantasies do proceede most from the nature of the meates which ingender melancholicke bloud; to wit, all Venison, but especially Hares. . . ." Consequently, the therapy must also be physical, such as the eating of "young Mutton, Kids. . . ."[22] Bathing and the hearing of music are likewise good. This last, however, was but a gracious afterthought cramped in among prescriptions for phlebotomy, syrups, purgations, and vomits. It is not that Wirtzung, a sensible man, was blind to the psychic influences in melancholia, but that he did not feel it any duty of his to treat that aspect of the disease. Hence a sharp separation of body from soul for purposes of methodology.

The best Elizabethan text on anatomy, John Banister's admirable *The Historie of Man* (1578), opened its chapter on the brain with the single statement that it is the "seate of the principall part of lyfe, by whose benefite we imagine, reason, and commit to memory," then proceeded to show its structure in detail without reference to its functions as an organ of the soul or any apportionment of the several

[21] Sig. M4v. See also Gratarolus, *Directions for Health* (1574), which of a total of 150 pages discussing the six non-natural means for preserving health gives three pages to "affections of the mind"; and Walter Cary, *Farewell to Physicke* (1583). Thomas Newton, *The Old Mans Dietarie* (1586) allows a fair proportional representation to the passions. Thomas Cogan, *The Haven of Health* (1584) leaves them out entirely.

[22] Pp. 117–61, esp. p. 131. See similarly Philip Barrough, *The Method of Phisicke* (1601).

"ventricles" to their appropriate faculties.[23] Indeed, Banister's use of the word "lyfe" rather than "soul" indicates how completely he left the whole religious aura out of the discussion. Likewise Nicholas Gyer, *The English Phlebotomy* (1592), described in Galen's highly sterilized fashion the three life powers, "the animall vertue . . . diffused from the braine, by the sinewes: The vitall force from the hart, by the arteries: The naturall strength from the Liver by the veines,"[24] without tracing them back to the animal, sensitive, and vegetal virtues of the soul, or any of its spiritual activities. Gyer was a clergyman, but he chose to follow here his classical, Arabian, and recent continental medical authorities who isolated body almost entirely from "soul," as distinguished from "life." So imperious was the medical tradition even to divines working in it.

The dominant tendency among Elizabethan doctors, then, was to minimize the soul in professional discussion, if not to exclude it altogether. Their reasons were largely methodological. Physicians had much more control and understanding of tangible diet, sleep, exercise, and so on, than of intangible perturbation, will, and reason. The latter were intrusions into the otherwise orderly, comprehensible system of the human body. Better to leave them alone.

A few more rash or, if you prefer, more advanced spirits took a different view, however. Sir Thomas Elyot in *The Castell of Helth* (1572) rated affections of the soul at least as important as air, food, sleep, and the other "nonnatural" things. A special feature of his approach was that under each passion, after picturing its consequences to body and to the moral status of the soul, he offered both moral advice and medical prescription. These Elyot regarded as inseparable:

The last of thinges called not naturall, is not the least parte to bee considered, the whiche is of affectes and passions of the minde. For if they be immoderate, they

[23] Fol. 98r. Wirtzung, p. 117, follows him in this, but Thomas Vicary, *The Englishmans Treasure* (1586), p. 17, fully discusses the inner senses of the sensitive soul, though not the passions or the rational soul, in connection with the brain structure.
[24] P. 131. *Phlebotomy* (1601) by Simon Harward, likewise a divine, imitated the same method.

do not only annoy the body and shorten the life, but also they do appaire, and sometime loose utterlye a mans estimation. And that much more is, they bringe a man from the use of reason, and sometime in the displeasure of Almighty God. Wherefore they do not only requyre the helpe of phisicke corporall, but also the counsaile of a man wise & wel learned in moral Philosophy. Wherefore they do not only requyre the helpe of phisicke corporall, but also the counsaile of a man wise & wel learned in moral Philosophy. Wherefore after that I have recited, what they be, I will briefelye declare suche counsayles as I have gathered.[25]

The moral consolation then set forth accents the need for Christian humility and forgiveness and refers often to the example of Jesus. Thus Elyot felt obliged to act as both divine and physician where most other Elizabethans were content to leave each field to a specialist.

William Bullein's *The Booke of the Use of Sicke Men and Medicines* (1562)[26] is in the same category. Perhaps the classic example of how far this tendency may go, however, is John Jones's *The Art and Science of Preserving Body and Soul in Health* (1579). This very heterogeneous book traced the steps by which the parents and nurse of a growing child can give him simultaneously a healthy body, good morals, and the theological virtues of faith, hope, and charity. Physical health, said Jones, allows the soul to govern by reason its illicit passions, whereas a sickly body makes for ungovernable passions and hence for vice. Health engenders virtue; virtue engenders health. Later chapters went over into a theological handbook outlining Protestant tenets of original sin and grace, besides discussing ethical theory. Indeed the author, able to set no narrow bounds to measures necessary for health of soul, branched out largely into exhortations on politics and the state of England generally. Medicine was almost, but not quite, squeezed out of the book by these alien elements. But to call them alien perhaps betrays our modern bent towards specialization, which bothered Jones, Elyot, and Bullein not at all.

[25] Fol. 64r & v.
[26] Printed with Bullein's *Bulwarke of Defence*.

Nevertheless their own books make the perils of their method stand out vividly. For these works are not clear expositions of medical science interrelated with clear expositions of mental science. They are badly jumbled expositions of both and successes in neither. The result, perhaps, is to confuse medicine and not to help ethics and religion. Only Elyot managed to handle the two subtly merging disciplines together with some measure of intelligibility. Yet the opposite choice—that of keeping medicine quite bare of all spiritual connections—had its own serious vices. Human habit is insidious. Perpetual dealing with body as if there were no soul too often precedes the conclusion that indeed there is none. The medical man in his desire to keep his subject within limits of verification may, if he is not constantly reminded, go down the road to materialism. And that a number did so is the unimpeachable testimony of the age. For methodology may beget philosophical system; materialism can be a rationalization of scientific method, attempted not only by the physician himself but also by thinkers who become imbued with his manner of attack. That Elizabethan psychology lay partly under this shadow has already been made clear.

From the churchman's point of view the problem of soul in medicine was much like the problems of Satan and God in medicine noticed in Chapters 6 and 13 respectively. God, Satan, and the soul were of the order of spirit, whose active preeminence in the order of matter must never be forgotten. In particular, God as the ultimate source of all health and disease must not be thrust out of the medical situation by neglect, omission, or underemphasis by either doctor or patient. Otherwise first his power and then finally his very existence might come to be denied. Less serious, though still keen in its parallel implications, seemed the going of Satan, God's agent, into medical exile. But to forget the soul as a force upon the body was as disastrous as to forget God himself. For methodological oblivion of the one would obliterate the other also.

## 4

The manners of soul do not follow the temperature of body, but the temperature of body is affected, through the passions, by the manners of soul. We have just been seeing how these two basic Christian concepts fared at the hands of Elizabethan doctors and psychologists in ordinary cases of health and disease. Rather special issues arose, however, in cases of mental disease like mania and melancholia.[27] There the patient's reason and will might sometimes be entirely submerged; causeless feelings of guilt falsely resembling the remorse of conscience might torment him; and his religious faith itself be shaken by delusions. Definition of the relative shares of body and soul in such mental illness posed for Elizabethan psychologists problems of the gravest difficulty, which have scarcely been solved even today.

Their first step always was to save the Christian premise that the soul was a separate spiritual substance. Being incorporeal, soul cannot be sick in the same sense that the body is. No physical or mental disease can touch its immortal and imputible essence. The alternative would be materialism, and a good many writers such as Bright, Laurentius, and Burton say so emphatically. In the words of Laurentius:

> And yet I would not have thee (O thou Atheist whosoever thou art) hereupon to conclude, that the soule of man suffereth anything in his essence, and thereby to become subject to corruption: it is never altered or changed, neither can it suffer any thing, it is his instrument that is evill affected.[28]

[27] Authoritative treatments of Elizabethan views on melancholia are Sanford V. Larkey's introduction to his facsimile ed. of Laurentius, *The Preservation of the Sight* (Oxford, 1938); Laurence Babb, *The Elizabethan Malady* (Lansing, Mich., 1951); Erwin Panofsky's interpretation of Dürer's 'Melancholia I' in *Albrecht Durer* (Princeton University, 1943), I, 156–71.

[28] P. 82. Also Reynoldes, p. 5; Walkington, fol. 12v; Huarte, pp. 90–92.

Melancholia and madness may invade liver, heart, and brain, but these are only physical organs of the soul, not the immaterial soul itself. Bright uses the ancient comparison of the soul to a musician, the body to his lute, which if badly tuned gives out discords though the player's skill remains always undiminished.[29] This principle, however, was meant only to guard the soul inviolate from physical change. There was no denial that by passion and by sin the soul undergoes non-corporeal changes in its internal habit and status. Only in this metaphorical sense might the soul be called sick, even in the most mental of mental diseases.

The milder forms of melancholia and mania[30] did not deprive the will of its freedom, but the severer forms did. All Elizabethans acknowledged this distinction, but nobody of course knew precisely where the dividing line came. On one side of the line, said Laurentius in his text on melancholy, lay the inclinations of natural complexion which being controllable by reason and will were the subjects of moral choice; on the other, melancholia grown to a disease and causing involuntary action not susceptible to moral judgment.[31] But he was sure that even the worst cases of corrupt or 'adusted' humor did not penetrate to the essence of the soul. They merely rendered reason and will impotent by infecting their instruments—brain, heart, and liver. Being a doctor Laurentius then went on to as-

[29] Bright, p. 38.
[30] Most diseases were regarded by Elizabethans as only mildly and temporarily coloring the patient's outlook, but those settling in the brain and causing prolonged delusions were "dotages." "We call that dotage," said Laurentius, p. 87, "when some one of the principall faculties of the minde, as imagination or reason is corrupted." In advanced stages, melancholia and mania both were abiding dotages unaccompanied by fever or physical obstruction within the brain. The difference between their symptoms was that mania brought with it rage and fury as against the fear and sadness characteristic of melancholia. Mania's causes were "choler adust and blood incensed" flowing to the brain, whereas in melancholia of the worst type the brain "is become too drie and colde," sometimes from an excess of the natural melancholy humor, sometimes from an adustion of any one of the humors into an unnatural state. See Barrough, p. 44; Burton, I, 160-61 and 193; Laurentius, p. 88.
[31] P. 81.

sume tacitly that the whole area of melancholia with which he was dealing was involuntary. No doubt in doing so he had the best of humanitarian motives for absolving the sufferer from moral blame, yet to a captious mind the thought may occur that such an expulsion of the unpredictable will also made his subject easier and more manageable. He chose that part of the field in which, if the manners of soul did not exactly follow the temperature of body, they were at least paralyzed by it.

Not so Robert Burton. To be sure Burton, like Bright before him, agreed at bottom with the prevailing medical view of melancholia as primarily a physical illness with emotional reverberations. He discussed its causes and cure in terms of the usual Galenic list of six "non-natural" factors,[32] although he expanded his analysis of the sixth item, "emotional discontents," far beyond its ordinary scope. But far from concluding that the patient's will need become the slave of his depraved humors, Burton sought instead the aid of religion to combat them. On occasion he did trip into some dangerously deterministic language. Usually, however, by arguing constantly for the psychopath's ability to do something to relieve his own misery, by urging him in chapter after chapter to make the effort, by recommending prayer, Scripture reading, and conference with godly ministers, Burton threw his emphasis to the view that most melancholics can rule their ailing bodies. They need God's grace, but he will freely give it if asked. Burton, therefore, though deeply immersed in the medical interpretation of his subject, fell into neither determinism nor religious indifference and achieved perhaps as fair a balance as in this age it was possible to achieve between the demands of medical science on one side and religion on the other. Only we may ask whether after these demands had been met anything remained in the middle for psychology per se.

Besides these problems about the effect of mental disease upon the will arose equally pressing problems about the connections between such disease and remorse of con-

[32] I, 247-87; II, 24-117 ff. For a somewhat too enthusiastic estimate of Burton's anticipations of modern psychiatry see Bergen Evans, *The Psychiatry of Robert Burton* (New York, 1944).

science. Elizabethans were well aware that feelings of guilt ordinarily accompanied melancholia. Did melancholia then produce remorse of conscience? Or vice versa? Or, worst of all, was there no real difference between the two? In the latter event, the unwary or malicious critic might easily infer that no such thing as conscience existed, that all self-conviction of guilt in the individual's mind was a mere fume of his melancholic humors. This type of materialistic confusion would destroy the moral self-criticism which was the foundation of the Christian's inner life.

Yet to the great distress of the English clergy the point of view made some headway among the irreligious and the merely muddle-headed. "Some thinke," conceded William Perkins in *The Second Treatise of the Ministerie* (1605),

> . . . that all trouble of mind is nothing but *melancholy,* and therefore thinke nothing needes but *Phisicke* and outward comforts: but . . . nothing can *properly* trouble the *mind* but sinne . . . so the *good Phisitian* of the soule, must first of all search into the cause of his sicknesse, that is his *sins,* and must take them away, which if they doe not, then al their labour is lost: for al the company, musick, recreation, wine, diet . . . cannot so much comforte the distressed soul of a sinner, as this voice *of a minister,* spoken from God upon good grounds, *thy sinnes are forgiven thee.*[33]

The issue evidently went deep into questions of repentance and absolution, and indeed implicated the entire Christian doctrine of sin. John Abernethy, Richard Greenham, and Philip Melanchthon were among the large number of other theologians who expressed their alarm.[34] Greenham, for example, censured the folly of trying to cure a guilty conscience as many do "by drinking at tavernes, by minstrelsie, in merie companie, by purging melancholy in taking phisicke."[35] Such people, he said, were treating the

[33] Pp. 36-37 in Perkins, *Works* (1605). See also his *Discourse of Conscience* in the same volume, pp. 643-660.
[34] John Abernethy, *A Christian and Heavenly Treatise* (1630), pp. 114-23; Philip Melanchthon, *De Anima* (Vitebergae, 1542), fol. 123v. Babb, pp. 51-53, cites much additional evidence.
[35] *A Sweet Comfort for an Afflicted Conscience* in *Workes* (1599), p. 245; Burton, III, 453, 458.

wrong affliction. Remorse of conscience had a spiritual cause and must have a spiritual remedy.

Some distinctions between false melancholic guilt and true remorse of conscience obviously were imperative. In making them Christian divines could fall back upon a concept of conscience which was at least as old as Aquinas. Perkins could point out, for instance, that conscience was a function of reason applying the general moral law to the individual's particular circumstances.[36] Being in the rational soul and having no specific organ in the body, conscience could not possibly be influenced by physical malaise. Its verdict of self-accusation or excuse must be right, for God placed it in man as a judge of his daily life. Melancholia, by contrast, was a distemperature of body entailing fear and sadness without real cause. An undue sense of guilt was one of its symptoms. This sense might often superficially resemble true remorse, or indeed be outwardly indistinguishable from it, but the two radically differed as to source, the one coming from the foul vapors of bodily disease, the other from the voice of the soul.

Here then was the perennial issue of materialism again in a new guise. Naturally no published Elizabethan treatise, medical or otherwise, came out in defence of the heresy. But judging from the vehemence of the clergy's attack it had a good deal of circulation. And we may suspect that its origins lay in those materialistic trends in medical science which have already been noticed amply. The one psychologist particularly bothered by the problem was Timothy Bright, who as a physician later to turn divine, saw its manysided implications and tried to work them out at great length in *A Treatise of Melancholy* (1586).

He wrote this wise and tender book to help a friend suffering, by Bright's diagnosis, from both melancholia and a guilty conscience at the same time. To equate the two, or even to think of the former as producing the latter, was in Bright's view to impeach the reality and independence of the rational soul and so to advocate atheism.[37] Pangs of

[36] *A Discourse of Conscience* in *Works* (1605), pp. 619-20. And see nn. 3 to 5 of chap. 2, ante.
[37] Epistle Dedicatorie, fols, 2v ff. and p. 38.

conscience could not come from melancholia.[38] But it was still theologically open to him to observe that the reverse might be true, that hypochrondria might come from the terrors of a smitten conscience. An acute student of human nature, Bright seized the opening eagerly. A restless conscience, he advised his friend, often so stirred the emotions of dread and despair as to cause alterations in the humors, leading to melancholia. Thus there could be a one-way traffic from conscience to mental disease but not back again. The manners of the soul could hurt, but could not be hurt by, the temperature of the body. Pursuing these two main lines of analysis, Bright then divided the *Treatise* into parts, one directed to his friend's melancholia, the other to the prick of conscience—one medical, the other theological.

To the medical analysis he gave most of his space, approximately the first thirty-one chapters, treating the causes, symptoms, and cure of melancholia on a Galenic, physical basis. But Bright conceived of this melancholia as not merely coexisting with remorse of consicence in his unfortunate friend but as complicating it. Melancholia distorts consolation offered to the conscience by clergymen, for this must come from the outer world through senses and imagination already depraved. Moreover, Satan takes advantage of despondency to suggest that damnation is inevitable; he encourages curious searching by the mind, panders to self-doubt, and misinterprets for the worst the doctrine of predestination.[39] Hence Bright, feeling impelled to offer his friend religious as well as medical comfort, was led far into theology. Chapter 36 became a consolation to the afflicted conscience on purely religious grounds such as might have been written by Perkins, Hume, Abernethy, or any other theologian. Bright's later entry into holy orders is clearly foreshadowed here. Yet he reverted at the end to a medical note. The four final chapters prescribed treatments for melancholia ranging from recreation and soothing objects of thought to diet, bloodletting, medication, and purges. All these were shown to reduce the humors to normalcy and, by thus removing or abating

[38] Chaps. 32-35, esp. 34.
[39] Pp. 198 ff.

129

physical impediments, to make conscience accessible to religious aid. In sum, wherever *A Treatise of Melancholy* was not religious it was medical. Between these two great alternatives Elizabethan psychiatry saw its parts distributed and lost all independence of being.

Finally there was, parallel to the foregoing questions about the power of mental disease over will and conscience, the question about its power over religious faith. Doctors did not fail to notice that psychopaths often developed strange aberrations in belief. In *The Method of Phisick* (1596) Philip Barrough observed that "Many of them do alwaies laugh and many do weepe, & some thinke themselves inspired with the holy Ghost, & do prophecy upon things to come."[40] Andrew Boorde in *The Breviary of Healthe* (1552) was curious about others who thought themselves God, or were convinced that they were damned.[41] Then might not all the varieties of religious experience depend on such and such variations in the mixture and quality of humors? Some sixteenth-century Englishmen evidently thought so. Bright considered them so numerous and consequential that he opened *A Treatise of Melancholy* by stigmatizing them emphatically, though without naming any names. Some, he charged, have judged

> . . . more basely of the soule, then agreeth with pietie or nature, & have accompted all maner affection thereof, to be subject to the physicians hand, not considering herein any thing divine, and above the ordinarie events, and naturall course of things: but have esteemed the vertues them selves, yea religion, no other thing but as the body hath ben tempered, and on the other side, vice, prophanenesse, & neglect of religion and honestie, to have bene nought else but a fault of humour.[42]

Interestingly enough, he then traced their attitude back to an argument based on the power of medicine to cure frenzies, madness, and melancholy. In one sense, Bright's whole book was aimed at refuting this disastrous error.

[40] P. 46. See also Babb, pp. 47 ff.
[41] Fol. 78r.
[42] Epistle Dedicatorie, fol. iii v; also pp. 187, 193-95.

Certainly here, in this frontal assault upon faith, the dangers latent in what I have broadly called the medical or biological attitude converged and came out into the open. How many people engaged in this assault, and who they were, we do not know. Probably the doctors themselves were less to blame than the free-thinkers who seized and carried to extremes their doctrine of methodological expedience. At any rate, as in related questions of conscience and will, so in this question of faith the Christian answer was clear. The communion of faith is directly from the rational soul to God, without participation of the flesh. The manners of the rational soul do not follow the distemperature of body.

Looking back over the whole field, we may see rather clearly why the Elizabethan clergy and a number of the physicians themselves feared the materialistic and deterministic tendencies of the medical sciences as a group. Most medical works had attained a practical disregard of the soul not merely in its religious and ethical connotations but also in its emotional and cognitive effects on body. Being at a loss to know what to do with incomprehensible spirit, and finding it methodologically expendable in their study of the system of matter, many physicians acted as if it were not there. Psychologists, of course, were in much less danger of forgetting the soul, but they were unlucky victims of the great Elizabethan dualism. Of the two constituents of psychology, matter and spirit, one seemed to belong to the medical sciences, the other to ethics and religion. It is altogether fascinating to watch psychologists veering from one to the other, trying to hold together a topic which persisted in flying apart into halves separated by a metaphysical vacuum. What they needed for a stable subject was a new entity, soul-in-body, distinct from either soul or body, and a resolve to find the laws peculiar to its working. Failing this, most psychologists gravitated towards what seemed the easier certainties and solidities of medical science. Inevitably they took from it some tinge of determinism, some taste of materialism, which they reconciled as best they could with the higher insights of religion or overlaid with not always consistent protestations of piety. A few like Bright, Burton, and Wright digressed far into

131

questions of holiness and virtue or set down the medical and religious points of view side by side not worrying too much about a possible dichotomy. Seen all together, Elizabethan works on psychology are a phantasmagoria of imperceptibly shifting points of view, so tenuous, intershading, and perplexed that I have been able to give only a simplified outline of them here.

# III

## ELIZABETHAN CREDULITY AND BELIEF IN THE OCCULT

*Both Madeleine Doran's essay, "On Eliza-bethan 'Credulity,' " and Walter I. Trattner's sketch of Dr. John Dee, "God and Expansion in Elizabethan England," were first published in the* Journal of the History of Ideas, *the one in April,* 1940 (*I,* 151-176), *the other in Jan-March,* 1964(*XXV,* 17-34).

## ON ELIZABETHAN "CREDULITY" WITH SOME QUESTIONS CONCERNING THE USE OF THE MARVELOUS IN LITERATURE

### By Madeleine Doran

Although this paper is for the most part necessarily declarative in form, it is wholly interrogative in spirit. It is intended to raise questions both historical and critical. The historical question is concerned with Renaissance attitudes of mind towards marvels in the realm of natural history. The critical question follows from it: Given certain attitudes towards strange features of the world, how will these attitudes affect the response of reader and audience towards literature that makes reference to these wonders? An attempt will be made to assess the differences in the quality of response of Elizabethan and modern readers to such characteristic features of Elizabethan literature.

Elizabethan "unnatural natural history" has been the subject of many inquiries, but it is not at all in the patron-izing spirit of the antiquarian collector of quaint lore that

I wish to approach the subject. It is rather insofar as one can recapture that, the spirit, of the cultured and adult Elizabethan, who saw his world through his own eyes, not ours.

1

The lion, as all know, is a royal beast. The "greatnesse and roughnesse of his Necke betokeneth a magnanimious and liberall mind." He is so proud in his nature that he disdains to touch again food he has once left, so just that he proportions his revenge exactly to the injury done him —for a slight hurt only biting a little, not killing,—so grateful that he remembers every kindness done him (as in the case of Androcles), so merciful that, "except in ex-tremitie of famine," he will spare a man prostrate in petition before him, so magnanimous that he kills only men and spares weak women and children. He never stoops to guile, but, fighting in the open, faces his enemy with a "scornfull grinning." In a word, he is the noblest of all animals.[1] His shrewdness is shown by the manner in which he outwits the unicorn, one of the deadliest of his natural enemies. The unicorn is a fierce beast, untameable except by a virgin; his voice is horrible to hear, "strained aboue measure"; he is known, according to some authorities, but not to all, for his chastity; and on his head he bears a precious horn, the powder of which has the wonderful virtue "of dissoluing and speedy expelling of all venome or poison whatsoeuer."[2] The manner of combat between the lion and the unicorn is this:

as soone as euer a Lyon seeth a Vnicorne, he runneth to a tree for succor, that so when the Vnicorne maketh

---

[1] The account given here is from Edward Topsell's *Historie of Foure-Footed Beastes* (London, 1607), pp. 456-487. If anyone thinks the modern lion has degenerated from the nobility of his Elizabethan ancestor, let him read Martin Johnson's *Safari* (New York, 1928), especially pp. 260-278; the keynote of the chapter is a statement quoted from a big game hunter: "The lion is a sportsman and a gentleman."

[2] On the unicorn, see Topsell, *Beasts,* pp. 711-721.

134

force at him, hee may not onely auoide his horne, but also destroy him; for the Vnicorne in the swiftnesse of his course runneth against the tree, wherein his sharpe horne sticketh fast, then when the Lyon seeth the Vnicorne fastned by the horne without all danger, he fauleth vpon him and killeth him.[3]

The same method is adopted by hunters, but, one gathers, rarely with success. Topsell says that his horn "cannot be taken from the Beast being aliue, forasmuch as he canot possible [sic] be taken in any deceit."

Elizabethan natural history is largely composed of creatures like lions and unicorns. Like the unicorn, many beasts are fabulous; like the lion with no joints in his neck or the elephant with none in his legs, many of the real ones are unlike their modern descendants; and all, fabulous or real, from the courteous and devout elephant to the savage and hypocritically tearful crocodile, from the pious phoenix doing obsequies to its parent to the ill-meaning siren luring the unwary seaman to his undoing—all are, like the lion, possessed of human virtues and vices, and therefore have for mankind a lesson. Topsell suggests that God preserved the animals in the Ark "for that a man might gaine out of them much deuine knowledge, such as is imprinted in them by nature." He continues:[4]

And for the knowledge of man, many and most excellent rules for publicke and priuate affaires, both for preseruing a good Conscience and auoiding an euill daunger, are gathered from Beasts: . . .
Were not this a good perswasion against murder to see all beasts so to maintaine their natures, that they kill not their owne kind? Who is so vnnaturall and unthankefull to his parents, but by reading how the young *Storkes* and *Wood-peckers* do in their parents olde age feed and nourish them, will not repent, amend his folly, and bee more naturall? What man is so void of compassion, that hearing the bounty of the *Bone-breaker Birde* to the

[3] *Ibid.,* p. 719. For numerous other examples, see G. Boas, *The Happy Beast,* especially Chap. V. *Cf.* also the incident of the unicorn and the jeweler in Chapman's *Bussy d'Ambois,* II, i, 117-23 in the edition by Frederick F. Boas, 1905.
[4] Topsell, *Beasts,* A4, A5.

young *Eagles,* will not become more liberall? Where is there such a sluggard and drone, that considereth the labours, paines, and trauels of the Emmet, Little-bee, Field-mouse, Squirrel, and such other that will not learne for shame to be more industrious, and set his fingers to worke? Why should any man liuing fall to do euill against his Conscience, or at the temptation of the Deuill, seeing a Lyon will neuer yeeld: *Mori scit vinci nescit;* and seeing the little *Wren* doth fight with an *Eagle,* contending for Soueraignty? woulde it not make all men to reuerence a good King set ouer them by God? Seeing the Bees seeke out their King if he loose himselfe, and by a most sagacious smelling-sence, neuer cease till he be found out, and then beare him vpon their bodies if he be not able to fly, but if he die they all forsake him. And what King is not inuited to clemency, and dehorted from tyranny, seeing the king of Bees hath a sting, but neuer vseth the same?

How great is the loue and faithfulnesse of Dogges, the meeknesse of Elephants, the modesty or shamefastnesse of the adulterous Lyonesse, the neatnesse and politure of the Cat and Peacocke, the iustice of the Bee which gathereth from all flowers that which serueth their turne, and yet destroyeth not the flower. The care of the *Nightingale* to make her voice plesant, the chastity of the Turtle, the Canonicall voice and watchfulnesse of a Cocke, and to conclude the vtility of a Sheepe: All these and ten thousand more I could recite, to shew what the knowledge of the nature of brutish creatures doth worke or teach the minds of men, . . .

This, then, is the animal world the Elizabethans knew. How credulous are we to call them for holding such a picture? There is a tendency to make and to remember handy generalizations about an age, and one of the most current is that the Elizabethans were a credulous people. In what follows I propose, first, to examine the validity of the term "credulity" as applied to naturalists like Conrad Gesner and John Caius; and secondly, to raise questions concerning the bearing of scientific credulity or incredulity on the response of cultivated Elizabethans to the marvelous in their literature. I use "Elizabethan" to include the early Jacobean as well as the strictly Elizabethan period.

The natural historians occupy a middle position between, on the one hand, the best of the mathematicians and astronomers, and, on the other hand, the popular encyclopedists and the makers of epitomes or "varieties" of curious and interesting lore. Conrad Gesner, a Swiss, one of the principal naturalists of the sixteenth century, was both an encyclopedist in the medieval tradition and an observer in his own right. He looks in both directions; he represents the age both as it had been and as it was coming to be. And the same is for the most part true of English naturalists like Caius, Turner, Moffett, and Gerard. Gesner's zoological books were published in Latin in the fifties.[5] It is with Edward Topsell's translation of part of Gesner—*The History of Four-Footed Beasts,* 1607, and *The History of Serpents,* 1608, that I shall be chiefly concerned.[6] Since Topsell often varies from Gesner, I shall try to assign particular statements to their originator, but since the relationship is complicated, I do not claim always to be successful.[7] To analyze the defects of Elizabethan science is but to limp after Bacon. My concern, however, is not primarily with its fruitfulness or barrenness, with its potentialities, or lack of them, for further advance; nor is it with its merely curious differences from ours. It is rather with the state of mind of those who could find it acceptable and consider it science.[8]

The problem of truth is an urgent one for both Gesner and Topsell. In his second epistle to the reader, Gesner says,

---

[5] *Historia Animalium,* Zürich, 1551–58.

[6] *The Four-Footed Beasts* is taken from the *Hist. Anim.,* Lib. I: *De Quadrupedis Viviparis;* the *Serpents* is from Lib. V: *De Serpentium Natura,* and also from the *Historiae Insectorum Libellus, qui est de Scorpione,* Zürich, 1587. My references to *De Quadrupedis Viviparis* are from the Frankfurt edition of 1603.

[7] In his address "To the Learned Reader," Topsell says that he has had to change Gesner's words, method, form and matter in some things; for whereas Gesner had collected all that had ever been written on every beast in order to make a dictionary for the private use of learned men, he, Topsell, intended to show to every plain and honest man in his own vulgar tongue the wonderful works of God in every beast.

[8] On this whole question see Hardin Craig, *The Enchanted Glass,* (New York, 1936), Chap. III, esp. pp. 64–68.

Those things truely which I thought were false or any way absurd, I either altogether omitted them, or so placed as I may conuict them: or if at any time I haue not done it, it was either thorough lacke of knowledge, or for some other cause.[9]

He says he will always give the authority for his information, and he does not promise his own in all cases. Topsell, in his own separate preface, expresses a similar determination to keep to the truth when he is able to judge of it:

The second thing in this discourse which I haue promised to affirme, is the truth of the Hystory of Creatures, for the marke of a good writer is to follow truth and not deceiuable Fables. And in this kind I haue passed the straightest [*i.e.*, straitest?] passage, because the relation of most thinges in this Booke are taken out of Heathen writers, such as peraduenture are many times superstitiously credulous, and haue added of their owne verie many rash inuentions, without reason, authority, or probability, as if they had been hyred to sell such Fables.[10]

He declares that he has not related all that is said of these beasts, but only what is said by many, unless it is clear enough to need no more than a single testimony, or unless it has only one witness, in which case he attributes it to that authority, "not giuing the Reader any warant from me to beleeue it." In the text occurs this passage, typical of many:

in this and all other honest discourses of any part of Phylosophy, the onely marke wherat euerie good student and professor ought to ayme, must be veritie and not tales:[11]

and the statement is often repeated that we must not believe anything "against reason." Yet both Gesner and Topsell give credence to much of the traditional lore about strange creatures, and about the even stranger behavior of

[9] Topsell, *Beasts*, ¶6ʳ–6ᵛ; Gesner, *De Quad*, bʳ.
[10] Topsell, *Beasts*, A5ᵛ.
[11] *Ibid.*, p. 47.

authentic beasts. There is clearly here a problem in mental attitude for us to try to comprehend. Since they think of themselves as regarding their knowledge rationally, since they are conscious of credulity in others and disclaim it in themselves, and since, most important of all, they accept cautiously or reject altogether things they consider strange, we have no right to convict them of gullibility on the mere difference of their beliefs from ours. We must attempt, first, to understand what to them is normal and what strange, in other words, what their standard of reasonable judgment is.

The differences between modern science and Renaissance science—or, more specifically, natural history—may for convenience be treated under three heads: body of data, process of verification, and frame of reference.

In the first place, modern science, partly through geographical exploration and partly through the aid of instruments extending the range of observation, has at its disposal a much larger collection of verified data. The point needs no elaboration, but it is worth noting that where a Renaissance scientist had opportunity for firsthand experience, he could be very accurate. Witness Gerard's meticulous descriptions of plants. His indignant denial of the legendary character of the mandrake is based on his own observation:[12]

> There haue been many ridiculous tales brought vp of this plant, whether of olde wiues or some runnagate surgeons or phisickmongers, I know not, (a title bad enough for them:) but sure some one or moe that sought to make themselues famous in skill full aboue others were the first brochers of that errour I spake of [*i.e.,* that the roots always resembled the legs of a man]. They adde further, that it is neuer or verie seldome to be founde growing naturally but vnder a gallows, where the matter that hath fallen from the dead bodie, hath giuen it the shape of a man: and the matter of a woman, the substaunce of a female plant; with many other such

[12] *The Herball or General Historie of Plantes* (London, 1597), pp. 280–82. William Turner had made a similar denial in his *Herbal* ("lately ouersene, corrected and enlarged," Cologne, 1568), pp. 45ᵛ–47.

doltish dreames. They fable further and affirm, that he who woulde take vp a plant thereof must tie a dogge thereunto to pull it vp, which will giue a great shrike at the digging vp; otherwise if a man should do it, he should certainly die in short space after: besides many fables of louing matters, too full of scurrilitie to set foorth in print, which I forbeare to speak of: all which dreames and olde wiues tales, you shall from henceforth cast out of your bookes and memorie; knowing this that they are all and euery part of them false and most vntrue; For I my selfe and my seruaunts also haue digged vp, planted, and replanted verie many: & yet neuer could either perceiue shape of man or woman, but sometimes one straight roote, sometimes two, and often sixe or seauen braunches comming from the maine great roote; euen as nature list to bestowe vpon it as to other plants.

He says that idle drones have carved the roots of briony into the shapes of men and women, and that this practice has confirmed the error among simple and unlearned people, who take these roots to be the true mandrakes. As for the virtues of the plant,

*Dioscorides* doth particularly set downe many faculties heere of, of which notwithstanding there be none proper vnto it, sauing those that depende vpon the drowsie and sleeping power thereof, which qualitie consisteth more in the roote then in any other part.

Witness also John Caius' account of English dogs, which has little in it, aside from a moral tale or two, of the marvelous. Notice his caution and yet his open-mindedness, a truly scientific attitude, with respect to the dog called Piscator or Fisher. He addresses Gesner on the subject:[13]

The Dogge called the fisher, whereof Hector Boethus writeth, which seeketh for fishe by smelling among rockes & stones, assuredly, I knowe none of that kinde in

[13] *Of English Dogges . . . newly drawne into Englishe by Abraham Fleming* (London, 1576), p. 18. Fleming's translation appears in Arber's *English Garner* (London, 1895), Vol. III, pp. 225–68; also in *The Works of John Caius,* edited by E. S. Roberts, Cambridge University Press, 1912.

England, neither haue I receaued by reporte that there is any suche, albeit I haue bene diligent & busie in demaunding the question as well of fishermen, as also of huntesmen in that behalfe being carefull and earnest to learne and vnderstand of them if any such were, except you hold opinion that the beauer or Otter is a fishe (as many haue beleeued) & according to their beliefe affirmed, and as the birde *Pupine,* is thought to be a fishe and so accounted. But that kinde of dogge which followeth the fishe to apprehend and take it (if there bee any of that disposition and property) whether they do this for the game of hunting, or for the heate of hunger, as other Dogges do. . . When I am fully resolued and disburthened of this doubt I wil send you certificate in writing.

However, knowledge of exotic animals and plants had to depend for the most part either on the accounts of the ancients or on travellers' tales. The European zoological collections appear to have been slenderly stocked, and the English one in the Tower, as described by travellers in the nineties, was a sorry affair: six lions and lionesses, two of them said to be over a hundred years old, and a lean, ugly wolf, supposed to be the only one in England.[14] About the same time a showman had an elephant for exhibition, and in 1623 King James owned an elephant and a small herd of camels, which were put to graze in St. James's Park.[15] Apparently the first extensive collection in England of museum specimens for the study of natural history was that begun by John Tradescant in the later years of James I's reign.[16]

[14] See "Journal of the Duke of Würtemberg, 1602" translated in W. B. Rye, *England as Seen by Foreigners in the Days of Eliza-beth and James the First* (London, 1865), pp. 19–20; also *Thomas Platter's Travels in England, 1599,* translated and edited by Clare Williams (London, 1937), p. 163.

[15] See Johnson, *Every Man Out of his Humour,* IV, vi, 59–61 (Herford and Simpson's edition); Donne, *Satires,* i, 80–82; and Samuel Chew, *The Crescent and the Rose* (New York, 1937), pp. 18–19.

[16] On the Tradescants and their collection, see Chap. IX, "The Ashmolean Museum," in R. T. Gunther, *Early Science in Oxford,* Vol. III (Oxford, 1925).

In the second place, the process of verification, as modern scientists understand it, was not widely understood. The question of authority may be considered here. Let us not too complacently throw stones at the Renaissance man for believing what Aristotle, Theophrastus, Dioscorides, Pliny, Aelian or Galen had said. We too believe what our scientists tell us—with unwavering faith. We must, of course, let the specialist's authority count for something, if we are to get on; each man cannot verify every truth of nature for himself, and it would be stupid of him to try. The true difference between our relation to authority and the Elizabethans' is not that we do not accept it and that they did, but that we accept it for the most part with better reason—or should I say, with more likelihood of its being well-founded, since the layman tends to accept it without much thought for the reason. Our scientific authorities are heirs to a meticulous and elaborate technique of verification, and we accept what they say because we suppose them (rightly or wrongly) to have applied this technique. For the Elizabethans, without an established technique of controlled experiment or a clear understanding of procedure by hypothesis and test, acceptance must often rest on the reputed wisdom and honesty of the authority who had made the report. Who could, then, doubt lightly what the wisest of the ancients had said? A faith in ordinary travellers' tales would be less excusable, but, in point of fact, we do not know how much credence these were given by educated people. Professor Chew, in his recent book on English travellers in Islam during the Renaissance, *The Crescent and the Rose,* collects a number of references from the late sixteenth and early seventeenth centuries showing mistrust of travellers' stories. The remark of Mercury in Jonson's *Cynthia's Revels* is a fair sample: a traveller "will lie cheaper than any beggar, and louder than most clocks."[17]

Perhaps a growing critical sense is illustrated by the difference between the attitude towards Pliny of Gesner and Topsell and of Sir Thomas Browne. The older men do not hesitate to reject the authority of Pliny if they consider a modern report more trustworthy. As an instance,

[17] II, iii, 99–100.

they reject the notion of the bear cub's being licked into shape (despite the authority of Pliny, Solinus, Aelian, Orus, Oppianus, and Ovid), for the truth is "most euidently otherwise, as by the eye witnes of *Ioachimus Rheticus* and other, is disproued."[18] Rheticus was a contemporary scientist who had some correspondence with Gesner. But the untrustworthiness of Pliny and the other authorities in this instance did not lead Gesner and Topsell to suspect their accuracy in general, or at least—for they do say that the ancients often fabled—it did not lead them to apply their suspicion actively to reports for which they had no modern denial. Sir Thomas Browne, however, devotes a whole chapter in the *Pseudodoxia Epidemica* to the relative trustworthiness of authorities, and he clearly sees that those who, like Pliny, were merely transcribing the reports of others, had no claim to authority in themselves. He calls Pliny "the greatest Collector or Rhapsodist of the Latines," and says,

> there is scarce a popular error passant in our days, which is not either directly expressed, or diductively contained in this Work; which being in the hands of most men, hath proved a powerful occasion of their propagation. Wherein notwithstanding the credulity of the Reader is more condemnable than the curiosity of the Author: for commonly he nameth the Authors from whom he received those accounts, and writes but as he reads, as in his Preface to Vespasian he acknowledgeth.[19]

Verification would also rest for the Elizabethan on experience, if not often on purposive experiment. Why should a man doubt the existence of a unicorn if he could see, and even handle, its horn? In 1599 Thomas Platter, a Swiss traveller, saw two in England, one in the collection of treasures at Hampton Court, and one, which he was told had been sent to Henry VIII from Arabia, in a similar collection at Windsor. The one at Hampton Court had been filed down to obtain medicinal powder. The one at Windsor weighed twenty pounds and was one foot taller than

[18] Topsell, *Beasts,* p. 37; Gesner, *De Quad.,* p. 944.
[19] Book I, chap. viii. In the *Works,* edited by Geoffrey Keynes (London 1928), Vol. II, pp. 59–60.

Platter; he could almost compass its circumference with one thumb and forefinger. At a Mr. Cope's collection of exotic objects in London, he saw, not a unicorn's horn, but a unicorn's tail.[20] Gesner inquired very carefully into reports of unicorns' horns and made a census of those extant; he says that in Europe there were "twenty of these hornes pure, and so many broken."[21] Of most of them he gives detailed descriptions, some in the form of letters he had received in reply to inquiries. One in Poland was found along with a skeleton of great bones, "bigger in quantity than a horse."[22] Unlike most of the horns, which were as tall as a man, straight, and "wreathed about with diuers sphires,"[23] this one was smooth and curved almost to half a circle. His informant argues that those found in Poland could hardly come from elephants, since they were never found in pairs, but always single.

Somewhat later, the visitor to London might have seen in Tradescant's Ark in the South Lambeth Road, along with hundreds of other curiosities, the following wonders: a griffin's beak or head, "Barnacles, four sorts" (meaning, of course, barnacle geese, since they are listed under birds), "A natural Dragon, above two inches long," a monoceros' horn, a sea-horse's head and teeth, a remora, the hand of a mermaid, and "Two feathers of the Phoenix tayle." All of these but the mermaid's hand appear in the catalogue made by the younger Tradescant in 1656, before the collection passed into the hands of Elias Ashmole, and became the foundation of the Ashmolean Museum at Oxford. As late as 1675, there was exhibited among other rarities in the Anatomy School at Oxford a siren's hand; a catalogue of 1709 lists a sea-horse's head, a unicorn's horn, and the thigh bone of a giant.[24] Tradescant's sea-horse's head, for

---

[20] Platter, pp. 171ff., 204–205, 215.
[21] Topsell, *Beasts,* p. 716; Gesner, *De Quad.,* p. 694.
[22] Topsell, p. 717; Gesner, p. 695.
[23] Topsell, p. 715; Gesner, p. 691—"rectum & spiris contortum."
[24] For the account of the Tradescant collection in 1634, see Gunther, III, 283–284; for the catalogue of 1656, see Appendix A in the same volume; for catalogues of the Anatomy School collections, pp. 252–279.

that matter, may still be seen in the Ashmolean collection at Oxford. It is in reality the skull of a walrus.[25]

It is obvious from the naming of these fragments that the Elizabethans had achieved no reliable system of classification. This brings us to a consideration of the third point of difference between Renaissance and modern science, and that is the matter of the frame of reference. What does Topsell mean when he says we must believe nothing "against reason"? What were his rational standards of judgment, apart from experience and authority?

We believe, rationally enough, in many things we have never ourselves sensuously perceived as fact. We have a basis of judgment in things directly known and we admit as possible things not directly experienced but reported by others if they violate no principle to which the world more directly known to us seems to conform. Extensive labors of careful scientific observation over a long period of time have given us a large and highly articulated equipment of facts and principles to use as criteria of probability. In biology, for instance, the detailed classification of living forms and the evolutionary conception of their relationships have permeated, even if in vague ways, the knowledge of the man of ordinary education, sufficiently to make him consider a satyr, a dragon, or a griffin, as described by Gesner, impossible monstrosities. But the modern classification of living forms on the basis of structure and function showed only faint beginnings in the sixteenth century; it is principally the work of Linnaeus and his successors in the eighteenth. The finer points of Aristotle's classification appear to have been lost sight of or were not well enough understood to be applied; enough examples of hesitating or arbitrary classification from Gesner or Caius could be assembled to show that most natural scientists of the Renaissance had in mind no very clear principles.[26] One suspects that the concept of the final cause and the ethical view of nature, the latter a heritage of Plato and the Neoplatonists, fostered through centuries of allegorical application in fable, *exemplum,* and emblem, had replaced

[25] Photograph in Gunther, III, opposite p. 344; described on p. 346.
[26] See the quotation from Caius already given, where he is not sure that the beaver and the otter may not be fish.

physical principles as the standard of judgment about what is probably to be found in the natural world.

The ethical view of nature has been illustrated in the account I have given of the lion and the unicorn, and may be found in any book of natural history one chooses to examine. A pleasant example is Thomas Moffett's treatise in ottava rima on *The Silkewormes, and their Flies* (1599), wherein he asserts that of all creatures the silk-fly, pure white in color, faithful to one mate, and in the worm stage hard-working and simple in its diet, has the least degenerated, through the fall of our first parents, from its original blessed condition. Another example is Charles Butler's *Feminine Monarchie* (1609),[27] which, together with the most detailed observations on the appearance, habits, and care of bees, has plenty to say of their industry, their sagacity, their skill, and their loyalty to prince and commonwealth. The principle of the final cause is well illustrated in the excerpt I have given from Topsell's preface. Compare also this passage from Bartholomew:

Also beasts are ordained, not onelye for meate of the bodye, but also for remedie of euills, and also for many manner of medicines. All kinds of beastes, wilde and tame, going and creeping, is made and ordayned for the best vse of mankinde, as *Plinius* and *Iohn Damascenus* meaneth. But some beastes are ordained for mans meate, as Sheepe, Harts, and other such: and some serue for the seruice of mankinde, as Horses, Asses, Oxen and Camells, & other such: and some for mans mirth, as Apes, Marmosets, and Popiniayes: and some be made for exercitation of man, for man should know his own infirmitie, and the might of God, and therefore are made flyes and lice: and Lyons and Tygers and Beares be made, that man may by the first know his owne infirmitie, and be afeard of the second, and haue succour by calling of Gods name. Also some beasts are made to releeue & helpe the neede of many maner infirmityes of

[27] Yet Butler makes a special disclaimer of repeating fables; the sub-title of his book is *A Treatise concerning Bees, and the Due Ordering of Them: Wherein the truth, found out by experience and diligent observation, discovereth the idle and fond conceipts, which many have written anent this subject.*

mankinde, as y^e flesh of y^e adder *Vipera* to make Triacle . . .[28]

Bacon saw that science would be at a stay until it threw overboard final causes:

> For to say . . . that the clouds are for watering of the earth; or that the solidness of the earth is for the station and mansion of living creatures and the like, is well inquired and collected in metaphysique, but in physique they are impertinent. Nay, they are indeed but *remorae* and hindrances to stay and slug the ship from further sailing, and have brought this to pass, that the search for physical causes hath been neglected and passed in silence.[29]

If you had found a use for a beast, then you had found its place in the world, and need inquire no further into the matter. Without any clear concept of species, or accurate knowledge of the process of generation and of the workings of heredity, there is no reason why an Elizabethan should have found anything inherently incredible in the griffin with its lion's body and its eagle's head and wings, in the satyr with its human or apelike trunk and goat's legs, or in any such monstrous combination. On the basis of structure and habit alone, we ought ourselves to find the penguin, the whale, the bat, and the duck-billed platypus incredible, but evolutionary principles of relationship and adaptation provide for us a sufficient explanation. So far as a creature like the unicorn is concerned, it is not at all less probable, even on modern standards of structure, than the antlered hart, the trunked elephant, or the humped camel. For myself, I find the unicorn much less improbable than the giraffe.

But all this is negative. The Elizabethans had certain positive principles of reference by which they could judge of the probability of things not known at first hand. One is the principle of sympathies and antipathies. It is basic

[28] *Batman vppon Bartholeme, his Booke De Proprietatibus Rerum* (London, 1582), p. 338.
[29] *The Advancement of Learning,* Everyman's Library edition, p. 97.

to the medieval and Renaissance pharmacopœia; and it underlies such expressions as "for every ill there is a remedy," "like cures like," a certain animal hates another "by kind":

> . . . for God in nature hath likewise ordained some bodies, whereby the Scorpion should be, and is dryuen away, scarred [sic], and destroyed.
>   First of all therefore men, which are the cheefe, and head of all liuing creatures, do by naturall instinct, kill and destroy Scorpions, and therefore *Galen* wryteth thus, Let vs (saith he) kill Scorpions, Spyders and Vipers, not because they are euill in themselues, but because it is ingrafted in vs by nature, to loue that which is good vnto vs, but to hate and auert from that which is euill vnto vs, *Non considerantes genitum ne ita sit an secus,* not considering whether it were so bred or not.[30]

If the universe operated on a system of secret attractions and repulsions, as it seemed from observation to do, what was improbable in the curing of warts by the wart-stone? in the breeding of scorpions in the brain of a man who smells basil, since the herb itself when crushed corrupts into scorpions? Or what unlikely in the serpent's avoiding the shadow of the ash-tree, naturally deadly to him? in the lion's fear of the crowing cock? in the elephant's terror of the voice of swine? in the loadstone's loss of virtue when rubbed with garlic? in the taming of a wild bull by tying him to a fig tree, or of a wild ox by putting a halter of wool about his neck? As with the proverbial method of catching birds, there would be some difficulty in putting the latter experiments to the proof.

An allied principle is that of analogy. In the sea there is a beast correspondent to every one on land; man is a little image of the great world, and so on. Topsell's position with regard to the "buffe" (*Tarandos*), a Scythian ruminant of some sort, will serve not only to illustrate this principle, but also to show the author's deliberation before giving credit to a report on the face of it improbable. The buffe is reported by Pliny and others to change his hue

---

[30] Topsell, *Serpents,* p. 227; Gesner, *De Scorpione.*

when he is frightened to match his surroundings, becoming green among green boughs, like rocks among rocks, and so forth. Topsell agrees that the report seems incredible, but he is led to subscribe to it by two considerations: first, by analogy with the effect of emotion on the countenance of men—

> because we see that the face of men and beasts thorough feare, ioy, anger, and other passions, doe quickly change; from ruddy to white, from blacke to pale, and from pale to ruddy againe. Now as this beast hath the head of a Hart, so also hath it the feare of a Hart, but in a higher degree; and therefore by secret operation it may easily alter the colour of their haire, as a passion in a reasonable man, may alter the colour of his face;

and second, by analogy with the polypus-fish and the chameleon, which change color with their surroundings. To the objection that unlike these creatures the buffe has hair and that it is impossible for the hair to receive any tincture from the passions, Topsell answers that nature can multiply and diminish her power, and that if she can make the feathers of birds and the scales of fishes of different colors, she "may and doth as forcibly worke in the haires of a *buffe,* as in the skinne of a *Chamæleon;* adding so much more force to transmute them, by how much farther off they stand from the blood."[31] His acceptance of the reported phenomenon has been made on entirely rational grounds in accordance with his principles respecting the operation of nature.

Besides the principles of sympathy and antipathy, besides his own analogous experience, the Elizabethan scientist has also, for reference, the myths and fables of the ancients. These his Christian doctrine, if nothing else, forbids him to accept literally. But he treats them as if they had allegorical reference to actual facts of experience, and therefore, if one but pierces the fable, one has credible evidence of the truth. Gesner's treatment of the satyr is a

---

[31] Topsell, *Beasts,* pp. 55–57; see Gesner, *De Quad.,* pp. 140–141, but he merely states the report and the objections without arguing the matter.

case in point.[32] One view he takes of it is that it is a real animal, a kind of rarely seen ape, that has occasioned men to think it a devil; and poets, painters, and the rest have therefore described it with horns on its head and feet like goats, "whereas Satires haue neither of both." He treats them at length, their countries, their habits, and stories concerning them. In like manner the Sphinx or Sphinga is classified as an ape and described according to Pliny and Calisthius. An elaborate naturalistic explanation is then given of the Greek story of the riddle of the Sphinx.

When we attempt to account for the monsters believed in by former ages—the Elizabethan, for instance—do we not say that they probably often had a basis in fact, but that they assumed strange shapes and habits under the influence of imagination? Tradescant's walrus' skull, for instance, was metamorphosed into the skull of a sea-horse. How does Topsell's approach to the strange creatures of myth differ in this respect from ours except, on his part, in a far less trustworthy body of knowledge and principle to which to refer the marvelous for comparison?

A further point of reference for the Elizabethan scientist is the active presence of supernatural beings in the world. For instance, although Topsell thinks with Gesner that what are generally called satyrs are apes, he says it may be that devils have appeared to men in the likeness of satyrs as they have in other forms.

> It is certaine, that the deuils do many waies delude men in the likenes of the Satyres, for when the drunken feasts of *Baccus* were yearly celebrated in *Parnassus,* there were many sightes of Satyres, and voyces, and sounding of cymbals heard.[33]

Once grant the possibility of the active agency of the supernatural, and the bases of credibility, as we know them, are radically changed. The Scriptures alone made it clear that the presence in man's world of supernatural beings was not only possible, but actual. Did not Satan appear to Eve in

[32] Topsell, *Beasts,* pp. 12–15; Gesner, *De Quad.,* p. 862 *ff.*
[33] Topsell, *Beasts,* p. 14; see Gesner, *De Quad.,* p. 863, but he appears to have no statement quite like this.

the likeness of a serpent?[34] The realm of the monstrous therefore remained open in a way in which it does not to most of us and belief might range, with apparent reason, over an enormously wider area.

Scriptural warrant went, of course, for things natural as well as things supernatural. Because of the ninety-first Psalm, *Super Aspidem et Basiliscum ambulabis,* it was impossible for Sir Thomas Browne to deny the existence in Biblical times of the basilisk; he could only deny its monstrous modern relative, the cockatrice, "a Hieroglyphicall fansie," as he calls it, quite different from the ancient basilisk, which he holds to have been a proper kind of serpent.[35] And Topsell's argument for the existence of the unicorn is impregnably buttressed by the ninety-second Psalm, the thirty-ninth chapter of Job, and many other Scriptural references. Topsell waxes indignant over those who, despite abundant proof, doubt the existence of the unicorn because of the too-wonderful powers of his horn:

Now our discourse of the Vnicorne is of none of these beasts, for there is not any vertue attributed to their hornes [rhinoceros, the fish Monoceros, one-horned kine, rams, birds, etc.], and therefore the vulgar sort of infidell people which scarcely beleeue any hearbe but such as they see in their owne Gardens, or any beast but such as is in their own flocks, or any knowledge but such as is bred in their owne braines, or any birds which are not hatched in their owne Nests, haue neuer made question of these, but of the true Vnicorne, whereof ther were more proofes in the world, because of the noblenesse of his horn, they haue euer bin in

[34] But the literal truth of *Genesis,* iii, 1–6, 13–15, was sometimes questioned. See, for instance, John Deacon's and John Walker's *Dialogicall Discourses of Spirits and Divels* (London, 1601), pp. 107–117, where, in a controversy over some notorious modern cases of alleged demoniac possession, they deny Satan's power to assume a material body; they interpret the Scriptural passage in two not clearly reconciled ways: (1) that "serpent" is to be understood in a purely metaphorical sense as applying to Satan, not to the beast, and (2) that Satan merely induced the actual serpent to speak, without being in his body.
[35] *Pseudodoxia Epidemica,* Book III, chap. vii; Keynes' edition, Vol. II, pp. 199–204.

doubt: by which distraction, it appeareth vnto me that there is some secret enemy in the inward degenerate nature of man, which continually blindeth the eies of God his people, from beholding and beleeuing the greatnesse of God his workes.[36]

It is what seems possible in a given world that is credible. Modern science, working outwards from within, has developed its laws hand in hand with observation; they form an evolving and adjustable structure. It has learned to put its faith in the solid core of verified brute fact rather than in the envelope of provisional principle.[37] Principle always remains strictly relevant to fact, because both are treated from the same physical point of view; hence what is possible is limited with a definiteness it could not have been for the Elizabethans. Renaissance science, on the other hand, in so far as it was medieval and not looking towards modern ways, suffered from lack of relevance between fact and theory. Within a rigid enclosing framework of theological, metaphysical, and moral principles, it was inaccurate and confused in detail. Whatever apparently physical principles there were, such as sympathy, antipathy, analogy, were largely magical in character, although perhaps not recognized as such. The possible was therefore limited only by man's ingenuity in finding an explanation for a reported phenomenon in some generally irrelevant principle. The latitude was wide.

2

When we come to consider the bearings of all this on Elizabethan literature, we enter on highly speculative

[36] Topsell, *Beasts*, p. 712; no corresponding passage in Gesner.
[37] *Cf.* William James's interesting comment in *The Will to Believe* (in *The Will to Believe and Other Essays in Popular Philosophy*, New York, 1897, p. 21) on science's "so-called method of verification": "she has fallen so deeply in love with the method that one may even say she has ceased to care for truth by itself at all. It is only truth as technically verified that interests her. The truth of truths might come in merely affirmative form, and she would decline to touch it."

ground. I am making the tentative assumption (by analogy with modern times) that the educated Elizabethan would have somewhat the same attitude towards fact and marvel, if not the same technical knowledge, as the scientist—at least as the scientist whose work, like Gesner's or Turner's or Gerard's, was available in English and somewhat popular in presentation. We may, for instance, consider Raleigh, although he had perhaps too much special interest in science to be a typical example. With reference to theological wonder and miracle, he is often thought of as skeptical, in his own day as atheistical. Yet in the midst of his sober and accurately recorded experiences in Guiana, we find him giving credence to a report of a race of men like Othello's, with heads beneath their shoulders. He accepts them because of the number of witnesses both Indian and Spanish to their existence.[38]

Next unto *Arui* there are two riuers *Atoica* and *Caora,* and on that braunch which is called *Caora* are a nation of people, whose heades appeare not aboue their shoulders, which though it may be thought a meere fable, yet for mine owne part I am resolued it is true, because euery child in the prouinces of *Arromaia* and *Canuri* affirme the same. They are called *Ewaipanoma:* they are reported to haue their eyes in their shoulders, and their mouthes in the middle of their breasts, & that a long train of haire groweth backward betwen their shoulders. The sonne of *Topiawari,* which I brought with mee into England, tolde mee that they are the most mightie men of all the lande, and vse bowes, arrowes, and clubs thrice as bigge as any of *Guiana,* or of the *Orenoqueponi,* and that one of the *Iwarawakeri* tooke a prisoner of them the yeare before our arriual there, and brought him into the borders of *Arromaia,* his fathers Countrey. And farther when I seemed to doubt of it, hee tolde me that it was no wonder among them, but that they were as great a nation, and as common, as any other in all the prouinces, and had of late years slaine manie hundreds of his fathers people, and of other nations their neighbors, but it was not my chaunce to heare of them til I was come away, and if I had but spoken one word of it

[38] *The Discoveries of the Large, Rich, and Bewtiful Empyre of Guiana* (London, 1596), pp. 69–71.

while I was there I might haue brought one of them with me to put the matter out of doubt. Such a nation was written of by Maundeuile, whose reports were held for fables many yeares,—and yet since the East *Indies* were discouered, wee finde his relations true of such thinges as heeretofore were helde incredible: whether it be true or no the matter is not greate, neither can there be any profit in the imagination, for mine own part I saw them not, but I am resolued that so many people did not all combine, or forethinke to make the report.

When he came to Cumana in the West Indies, a Spaniard who had been in the interior up the Orinoco told him he had seen many of these creatures. The last sentence in the paragraph quoted is the significant one. Like Gesner and Topsell in so many things, Raleigh has a suspicion of the fabulous, but like them, on credible witness he gives in.

The validity of the premise that the attitude of educated men would be conditioned by the scientists of the day is suggested by a number of recent studies of Elizabethan learning, such as Professor Hardin Craig's *Enchanted Glass,*[39] Louis B. Wright's *Middle-Class Culture in Elizabethan England,*[40] Francis Johnson's *Astronomical Thought in Renaissance England,*[41] and other studies, such as Mr. Oliver Willard is making on the circulation of Elizabethan books, will enable us to evaluate the assumption further. For the moment, let us make it, and see what follows for our present purpose, or rather, what questions it raises.

Shakespeare's plays have many meanings: to make an over-simplified statement, they had a meaning for him himself; they have a meaning for us as members of our own age, and another as separate individuals; they had a meaning to his own audience, and a different meaning to differ-

[39] New York: Oxford University Press, 1936.
[40] Chapel Hill: University of North Carolina Press, 1935.
[41] Baltimore: Johns Hopkins Press, 1937. For a somewhat later period, see Professor Marjorie Nicolson's series of studies on the effect of the telescope and the microscope on the literary imagination: *Mod. Phil., XXXII* (1935), 233–260; *Studies in Phil.,* XXXII (1935), 428–462; *Jour. Engl. Lit. Hist.,* II (1935), 1–32; *Smith College Studies in Mod. Lang.,* Vol. XVI, No. 4 (July, 1935), and Vol. XVII, No. 2 (Jan., 1936).

ent cultural levels of his audience. I wish to consider the meaning of one element in Elizabethan literature, and on one level—that is, the meaning to the educated Elizabethan of the use of the marvelous in the literature of his own day. And I have seen a way of approaching it by means of the scientists themselves, since, in order for us, as moderns, to entertain imaginatively the Elizabethan's response to this element in his literature, we must first of all see the phenomenal world through his eyes, so far as that is possible, instead of through our eyes; and to do so means knowing what for him would be fact and what marvel.

The marvelous is always out on the periphery of knowledge. As Joyce's old man in *The Portrait of the Artist as a Young Man* says, "Ah, there must be terrible queer creatures at the latter end of the world." Perhaps one difference between the Renaissance and the modern world is that that periphery, at least as regards natural history, was for them spatial, whereas for us it is largely temporal. Strange creatures inhabited for them the fringes of the known world: it is the far-travelled Othello who talks of "Anthropophagi, and men whose heads do grow beneath their shoulders"; it is Ortelius' map of Iceland that bears the most monsters. Modern exploration has not only covered the entire earth with a fine net; it has brought back photographic testimony for all the rest of us to see. We are given a chance to make personal verification. Perhaps that is why the marvelous, for us, has largely receded from the realms of natural history (except as shown in circus sideshows); it still occupies the heavens for many people (not merely the believer in astrology, but the reader of Eddington and Jeans), and for still more it occupies the occult realm of psychic phenomena. In the realm of natural history, it is chiefly the past and the future that have held, and may hold, the wonderful. The remote geologic past, with its monstrous and now extinct creatures, holds for us, despite scientific warrant for their actual existence (or perhaps because of it), the wonder which is the authentic mark of the marvelous. The future suggests possibilities, through the very advance of scientific knowledge, which may make biological forms, including man, very different from what they are now; a book such as Huxley's *Brave*

155

*New World* gives us the genuine experience of the marvelous because its picture of the world is both strange and seemingly possible—hence terrible.

The distinguishing feature of the marvelous would seem to arise, then, not from the failure of conformity to actual fact of the marvelous thing; the marvelous is not simply something not true which is believed in. It is the unaccountable thing which *may* be true, and sometimes is (as in the case of visions and of biological monstrosities). In so far as one gives it any degree of belief, one feels in some degree the fear and the wonder that the unaccountable gives.

I suggest, tentatively, that one may distinguish three levels of response to the marvelous.

(1) The highest level is complete acceptance. This is not the same in effect as the acceptance of commonplace facts, since the facts are marvelous "facts." The phenomena are thought extraordinary or supernatural, and yet for some reason demand assent. For many, but not necessarily all, of Shakespeare's audience, ghosts and witches would have been in this category. For some modern people, as I have already suggested, the "facts" of contemporary science are marvelous on this level. An authentic thrill comes to many from the thought of the great interstellar spaces of the modern astronomer's universe; to some it comes from the "mysteries" of the chemist's or physicist's laboratory or of a radio receiving set.

(2) The second, or intermediate level, is the entertainment of the possibility without actual belief; it often arises from a conflict between a rational attitude of scepticism and an emotional willingness to believe. This is the attitude today of many "enlightened" people towards psychic phenomena such as telepathy, or towards common superstitions. Often a humorous entertainment of such ideas, or indulgence in such practices, meant to imply disbelief, really masks a willingness to believe, or at least a troubling capacity to be moved by a sense of their possibility or efficacy. This is the attitude of people who laugh when they knock on wood or comment on a black cat's crossing the path. For some in Shakespeare's audience, ghosts would have been in this category instead of in the first; many of the stranger features of natural history, if we may judge

156

by scientists' awareness of their being called in question, would have been here.

(3) The third level is the complete rejection of the potential actuality of the phenomenon in question, yet a willingness for reasons of convention or of symbolism to entertain the fiction imaginatively. One might use in this connection Coleridge's term of "negative faith."[42] Clearly, this state of mind not only applies to references to the contemporaneous marvelous, which may be accepted by one element of readers or audience, and rejected by others except on this imaginative level; but also, and especially, it applies to references to the marvelous of a past age—for the Elizabethans, particularly to classical mythology; for us, to classical myth of course, and to Biblical myth, but also to medieval and Elizabethan myth, whether found in the literature of those times or employed again in ours. The unicorn, for instance, is a beast that dies hard. For centuries the use of classical mythology in poetry has depended on this sort of response. The higher the literary culture of the audience, the more effective the use of the marvelous in this purely literary sense will be; whereas on the other two levels, the less literate education, at least of a speculative kind, the better.

The possibility of response to Elizabethan literature on the first, and perhaps even the second level, has for most of us, I imagine, disappeared. Instead, our response to the outmoded features of the Elizabethan world is generally of two kinds: either we accept them seriously for the time being, as we do the ghost in *Hamlet,* with a conventional suspension of disbelief,[43] or we smile at their "quaintness," as we are likely to do at Ulysses' elephant, which "hath joints, but none for courtesy" and whose "legs are legs for necessity, not for flexure."[44] But for the Elizabethan, there

---

[42] *Biographia Literaria,* Everyman's Library edition, p. 242.

[43] The response of Sir Oliver Lodge or Sir Arthur Conan Doyle would perhaps have been compounded of the first and third levels —belief in the supernatural *possibility* of a spirit's communication with his son along with purely literary acceptance of Shakespeare's *method* of exhibiting it. Perhaps I under-estimate the number of modern people who are moved by the ghost in *Hamlet* on the first or second level.

[44] *Troilus and Cressida,* II, iii, 113–115 in the Globe edition.

157

was possibility of response on all three levels, and this, I think, would have given his own contemporary literature a richness of texture of a certain sort that is lost to us.

But first we need to exclude what would be for him the merely factual, non-marvelous things that are no longer facts for us, and hence are likely to seem naïve or amusing. It is not easy for us to know just what these were, or at just what time hitherto accepted facts would be moving, for different cultural levels, into the realm of myth. This is where the historian of science can help us, and a more searching examination than I have made should reveal much. It seems clear, for instance, that the general idea of spontaneous generation—of bees from the putrifying flesh of oxen, hornets from horses, fleas from dust, moths from cloth, toads from earth, snails from rain, and so on— was entertained as a purely factual notion; it had ordinarily no more coloring of the marvelous about it than any other little understood operation of nature. "Rottenness and putrefaction is the mother of many creatures and herbs."[45] But when Antony and Lepidus discuss, along with the pyramids and the nature of the crocodile, the peculiar property of Nile mud—

> Your serpent of Egypt is bred now of your mud by the operation of your sun: so is your crocodile—[46]

we catch the note of wonder at a strange thing in a strange land.

Our specific question, then, is at which of these three levels the response of a cultivated Elizabethan would be to a given literary instance of the marvelous. The ghosts in *Hamlet* and *Macbeth* and the witches in *Macbeth* are the classic cases. It is in the realm of astrology and the supernatural that the matter of belief is most crucial, because phenomena from these realms may be used dramatically, as actual characters, or as motive forces. The ghost in *Hamlet* not only appears on the stage, but also precipitates the entire tragic crisis in the mind of Hamlet; the stars in *Romeo and Juliet* are not merely evocative stage-

[45] Topsell, *Beasts*.
[46] *Antony and Cleopatra*, II, vii, 29–31.

setting for the balcony scenes, they are an inauspicious fate, to fear, to defy, and to submit to. The frequency with which astrological and supernatural phenomena occur in Elizabethan drama suggests that the dramatists expected a response on the first or second level, that is, the level of complete belief, or the level of emotional willingness to entertain belief. From those of us who must respond to *Hamlet* and *Macbeth* entirely on the third level, the level of mere suspension of our normal disbelief, something of the full horror of these plays must always be withheld.

The realm of plant and animal lore which we have been examining appears in literature abundantly enough, but for the most part only in metaphor. The question is at once raised whether, regardless of his state of belief or disbelief, a reader or spectator would be conscious in response to mere metaphor of the qualitative differences I have been describing. I cannot answer the question. But I shall make a few suggestions which may lead to partial answers.

The prominence of the metaphor might have some significance in this respect, and, if it did, our question would have more importance for lyric than for dramatic poetry, where metaphor is less centrally placed for attention. I am not sure, however, that the quality of such a poem as Shakespeare's *Phoenix and the Turtle* is greatly different if we believe in the phoenix, if we desire to believe in it, or if we disbelieve in it, since the idea of perfect love, not the phoenix itself, is the important thing.

> So between them love did shine,
> That the turtle saw his right
> Flaming in the phoenix' sight:
> Either was the other's mine.

On the other hand, for the understanding of Donne's "Go and catch a falling star," it does matter in what state of belief we are in with regard to mandrakes or mermaids, for if we believe in them too thoroughly we shall miss the point of the poem, that a constant woman is as strange as they.

Shakespeare sometimes gives the question of belief in strange creatures prominence in dramatic poetry, but in the instances I have noticed he does so by means of direct reference, not by means of metaphor. In *The Tempest,* for instance, where he wishes the audience to give assent to the strange occurrences on the island, he makes Sebastian say:

> Now I will believe
> That there are unicorns; that in Arabia
> There is one tree, the phoenix' throne; one phoenix
> At this hour reigning there.

And Antonio replies,

> I'll believe both;
> And what does else want credit, come to me,
> And I'll be sworn 'tis true; travellers ne'er did lie,
> Though fools at home condemn them.[47]

The technique is effective. It is a technique for moving disbelievers from the third to the second level, from mere imaginative to emotional assent. The wavering of faith might well have been convinced, and the skeptics moved to doubt their skepticism.

Another point to make, one that I have already suggested, is that a number of references to phenomena on different levels of a reader's or spectator's belief, even though they were not called into conscious focus, might have given a piece of literature a value for a contemporary quite lost to us, for whom response is generally all on one level. What I have in mind may be illustrated from the *Faerie Queene*. There, of course, the whole poem may be taken as a metaphor. For the most part its strange creatures are frankly imaginative creations and would have been understood as such by the educated readers of the poem. But the creatures that Guyon meets in his voyage to the Bower of Bliss are not in the same category with the serpent Error or the Blatant Beast.

> Eftsoones they saw an hideous hoast arrayd,
> Of huge Sea monsters, such as liuing sence dismayed.
>
> Most ugly shapes, and horrible aspects,
> Such as Dame Nature selfe mote feare to see,
> Or shame, that euer should so fowle defects

---

[47] III, iii, 21–27.

From her most cunning hand escaped bee;
All dreadful pourtraicts of deformtiee:
Spring-headed *Hydraes,* and sea-shouldring Whales,
Great whirlpooles, which all fishes make to flee,
Bright Scolopendraes, arm'd with siluer scales,
Mighty *Monoceros,* with immeasured tayles.

The dreadful Fish, that hath deseru'd the name
Of Death, and like him lookes in dreadfull hew,
The griesly Wasserman, that makes his game
The flying ships with swiftnesse to pursew,
The horrible Sea-satyre, that doth shew
His fearefull face in time of greatest storme,
Huge *Ziffius,* whom Mariners eschew
No lesse then rockes, (as trauellers informe,)
And greedy *Rosmarines* with visages deforme.

All these, and thousand thousands many more,
And more deformed Monsters thousand fold,
With dreadfull noise, and hollow rombling rore,
Came rushing in the fomy waues enrold,
Which seem'd to fly for fearc them to behold:
Ne wonder, if these did the knight appall;
For all that here on earth we dreadful hold,
Be but as bugs to fearen babes withall,
Compared to the creatures in the seas entrall.[48]

These are not Spenser's own imaginative fictions. They
are the beasts and fishes described by Olaus Magnus,[49]
the strange inhabitants of the northern seas, drawings of
some of which Spenser's readers might have seen on
Ortelius' map of Iceland.[50] In an unpublished paper to

[48] II, xii, 22–25.
[49] *Historia de Gentibus Septentrionalibus,* Rome, 1555.
[50] *Theatrum Orbis Terrarum* (Antwerp, [1595]), fol. 103; also in
English translaticn, *The Theatre of the Whole World* (London,
1606), fol. 103. The letter-press contains a description of the
animals drawn on the map: various kinds of whales, a *Hyena* or
sea-hog, sea-cows (drawn pretty much like cows), sea-horses (with
manes, webbed fore-feet, fish-tails), a *Rosmarus* (walrus; the description says he goes on the bottom of the sea on four feet, and
that he sleeps tw'ive hours together by hanging by his teeth from
a rock), a *Ziphius* (description says a swordfish, *Xiphius,* may be
intended, but the drawing is of a round-headed creature, with no
sword-like snout), and a huge creature like a ray or skate.
The Latin editions of 1570, 1603, and 1624 contain no separate
map of Iceland and no such account of marine monsters.

which the author has given me permission to refer, Professor Merritt Hughes makes the point that Spenser's moral purpose here is to show the danger of giving free rein to the imagination. The point seems to me a sound one. From that point of view it makes no difference, perhaps, whether the animals are real or fictional; in any case they run a monstrous riot in the mind. But if we regard the effect of the passage from the aesthetic rather than from the moral point of view, it seems to me to be significant that these are the creatures of the book of travel and the geography and not of the poet's mind. For us, since the names are mostly unfamiliar, they are probably the same in effect as if they were purely fanciful; they are just more of Spenser's monsters. But for the Elizabethan they would not have been the same; they were "the queer creatures at the latter end of the world" that might or might not exist, and hence this passage would have given him a sensation of the marvelous on the first or second level, unlike the merely negative faith with which he would be entertaining the other fictions of the poem. The impact of the lines would be very different from that of many other, and to us equally fictional, passages.

# GOD AND EXPANSION IN ELIZABETHAN ENGLAND: JOHN DEE, 1527-1583

## By Walter I. Trattner

Despite the more than three hundred fifty years that have passed since his death, John Dee still largely remains an enigma. Misunderstood by many of his contemporaries, and called by his later interpreters everything from a "charlatan" and "conjurer of evil spirits," to "the leading pioneer in the English Geographical Renaissance" and a man far "too advanced in speculative thought for his own age to understand,"[1] no two authorities paint the same picture of this strange Elizabethan.

Dr. John Dee,[2] a tall, thin man with a long pointed beard and a mysterious manner, presents an interesting problem for the historian. A prolific writer (and almost all of the writings are extant), as well as a man of varied activities, the events of Dee's life are well known. Yet, no satisfactory account of his important life has ever been written. Indeed, even his most sympathetic commentators do not seem to have understood fully this enthusiastic sixteenth-century seeker of wisdom and lover of the secrets of God and nature.

The fascination of his psychic projections has led Dee's biographers to ignore his solid achievements in the science, history, and geography (among other things) of his day. In addition, assuming that there were two John Dees, (1) the utilitarian scientist interested in the practical application of speculative thought, and (2) the evil practitioner of occultism, there has been an inability to see the one true Dee. John Dee was a lover of divine wisdom, a dreamer, and a thinker, living in an age which was becoming increasingly dominated by the middle-class utilitarian ideal. Dee was an intellectually honest, sincere, and pious Christian torn between the passing old and rising new order. He was, in other words, an Elizabethan.

A discussion of two related phases of his many activi-

---

[1] Many writers have called Dee both a "charlatan" and a "conjurer of evil spirits." Two notable examples are: Louis B. Wright, *Middle-Class Culture in Elizabethan England* (Ithaca, 1958) and William Alexander Ayton, *The Life of John Dee,* translated from the Latin by Dr. Thomas Smith (London, Theosophical Publishing Society, 1908). The term "English Geographical Renaissance" (which is used throughout the paper) belongs to E. G. R. Taylor, *Tudor Geography, 1485–1583* (London, 1930). Dee was called a man too advanced for his own age to understand by his most sympathetic biographer: Charlotte Fell-Smith, *John Dee, 1527–1608* (London, 1909).

[2] Although called "Dr." John Dee by many of his contemporaries, as well as using the title himself, Dee was not a "Dr." He had not earned any degree beyond the M.A. The chances are that the title "Doctor," so inseparable from his name, was merely bestowed in its original complimentary sense when it had become self-evident that he indeed was *doctus,* or learned.

ties not only helps one to better understand John Dee, but it also sheds further light on sixteenth-century England. Dee's rôle in the Elizabethan Geographical Renaissance has not been appreciated fully by his biographers and deserves elucidation.

Secondly, and related, an understanding of why, at the height of Dee's, and England's, overseas operations in 1583 Dee seemingly gave up his interest in those affairs that occupied so much of his time during the previous thirty years helps explain some of the motivations behind the many geographical explorations which played so important a rôle in that turbulent era. In that year John Dee suddenly migrated to the Continent and although he returned six years later, he was never again involved in exploration or colonizing expeditions. Unlike his biographers, I believe that this was a perfectly understandable development. To ask the misleading question about Dee, "How come a man endowed with his gifts and moral attributes could have lapsed into such madness [i.e., his spiritual concerns] as that which he raged?"[3] is to completely misunderstand John Dee and his age.

It was into the tempestuous and transitional world of the early 16th century[4] that John Dee was born in London on July 13, 1527.[5] Born into a family of moderate means, young Dee received the "usual" religious upbringing. He was educated at Cambridge and later became a Fellow of the newly established St. John's College. Inflamed by a love of learning even as a youth, Dee ardently studied mathematics and astronomy above all other subjects, taking countless observations of the heavens.

In May 1547, his twentieth year, Dee's thirst for knowl-

[3] Ayton, *Life of John Dee*, 95.
[4] For a good account of the "Intellectual Conditions and Characteristics of the Sixteenth Century" see L. Thorndike, *A History of Magic and Experimental Science* (8 vols., New York, 1931), V, Ch. I. Also, P. H. Kocher, *Science and Religion in Elizabethan England* (San Marino, California, 1953); E. M. W. Tillyard, *The Elizabethan World Picture* (London, 1948); and Wright, *op. cit.*
[5] Almost all of the biographical material on Dee's life has been taken from the following three biographies: Ayton, *op. cit.*; Fell-Smith, *op. cit.*; and G. M. Hort, *Dr. John Dee, Elizabethan Mystic and Astrologer* (London, 1922).

edge carried him to the Low countries where, studying at the University of Louvain, called by Rashdall "one of the earliest and, for a time, by far the most famous homes of the New Learning in Europe," [6] he formed close friendships with scientists and philosophers of world fame. Among them, his relations with the famous Girardus Mercator seem to have been the most fruitful and significant.[7] Dee also became acquainted with the great Flemish mathematician, cartographer and cosmographer Gemma Phrysius, whose first globe, accompanied by a published text on the principles of astronomy and geography, had been brought out in 1530.

No doubt it was also at Louvain that Dee's interests in alchemy and occult matters were fed and strengthened, for that great university was still under the spell of the famous spiritualist and alchemist Henricus Agrippa, whose great work, *De Occulta Philosophia* was published in 1531.[8] Before returning to his native land in 1551, Dee travelled to Paris where he remained for many months and successfully delivered the first series of public lectures ever given on Euclid there. Assuredly, Dee's sojourn to and stay in that French city was of utmost importance for his later life, for one must remember that at this time Paris was not only a leading center of astronomy and astrology, but also of the mysterious and the occult.[9] Young Dee already had acquired international fame as a mathematician, and after his Euclidian lectures he was offered an ap-

[6] Hastings Rashdall, *The Universities of Europe in the Middle Ages,* ed. by F. M. Powicke and A. B. Emden (3 vols. Glasgow: Oxford University Press, 1958), II, 226–27.

[7] Mercator was the originator of a method of cosmographical projection in which latitude and longitude are indicated by straight lines to serve the purposes of navigation and steering by compass. Cf. Hort, *Dr. John Dee,* 17. The great Portuguese mathematician and cosmographer Pedro Nuñez, as well as the famous mathematician from Louvain, Anthony Gogava, befriended and apparently influenced Dee.

[8] Agrippa's defense of the practice of magic as one of the lawful ways by which a man can attain a knowledge of God and Nature made a lasting impression on Dee. Cf. Hort, *Dr. John Dee,* 17. For an excellent discussion of Agrippa's thought, see Thorndike, *op. cit.,* V, Ch. 8.

[9] Thorndike, . .*op. cit.,* V, Ch. 14.

pointment as a Royal Mathematician with an annual salary of 200 (French) crowns; he decided, instead, to return home. But the seeds implanted during these years at Louvain and Paris bore much fruit. As a result of the acquaintances made there, Dee maintained a lively correspondence with professors and doctors at almost every university of note upon the Continent.[10]

Dee's return to England was of great significance for he brought with him two large globes, as well as a number of astronomical instruments of Mercator's making. And, writes a leading student of geography, "the importance of these instruments, leading as they did to improvements in astronomico-geographical observations cannot be overestimated."[11] Shortly after arriving back in England, Dee presented two astronomical treatises to King Edward VI, one explaining the use of the celestial globe and the other, the movements of the heavenly bodies. In 1553 the already famous scholar produced, among other things, two works on *The Cause of Floods and Ebbs* and *The Philosophical and Political Occasions and Names of the Heavenly Asterisms*. Both of these were written at the request of the Duchess of Northumberland, whose patronage had already been bestowed on Dee.

While most thoughtful Elizabethans accepted the study of science, they continued to have gnawing fears about its possible consequences. The student of nature might always go above the stars and find no Christian God. Consequently, scientists, including Dee, made every effort to show that natural philosophy served religion well and humbly; the dedications, prefaces, and even the texts of their scientific publications carried explicit reassurance on this cardinal point.

In addition to his mathematical and astronomical inter-

[10] Dee named especially his correspondents at the Universities of "Orleans, Collen, Haedelberg, Strasburg, Verona, Padoa, Ferrara, Bononia, Urbine, Roma," and "in many other . . . cities, and towns of Christendome." John Dee, "The Compendious Rehearsall of John Dee," 8. Reprinted in *Autobiographical Tracts of Dr. John Dee*, ed. by James Crossley, *Chetham Miscellanies* (Vol. I. London: Chetham Society, 1851). Hereafter cited as *Autobiographical Tracts*.
[11] Taylor, *Tudor Geography*, 83.

166

ests, John Dee's studies also followed the pursuit of occult knowledge. Many people were already beginning to see in Dee no mere scientist, but a conjurer and magician of doubtful reputation. The occult tradition, going back to Neo-Platonism, unlike traditional Christianity, held that some of the most important forces in the world of nature come not from the elements, but from the hidden virtues transmitted to all physical objects by the stars from the intellectual world, which in turn emanated from God. It, therefore, tended to blur the difference between matter and spirit. Moreover, the Christian denial that there existed any ambiguous or neutral spirits between the two popular un-bodied spiritual agents of God—angels and devils—was anathema to those of the Neo-Platonic persuasion. It was this belief in multitudinous orders of creatures in the ethe-real regions and a desire to explore nature with the super-natural yet not demonic spirits that later was to cause tragedy of John Dee.

The growing popular concern over Dee's occult activi-ties is understandable. In 1552 Jerome Cardan, the famous physician of Padua, visited England and lodged at the home of Sir John Cheke, where Dee frequently saw and talked with him.[12] Cardan was then in his prime; an occultist, surrounded by all the mysterious glamor of Padua, the supposed school of necromantic art, with an intense belief in his own powers, and a keen commanding intellect. Dee was considerably younger than Cardan, and may well have looked up to him as his master. The range of their discus-sions may be guessed at when we remember the super-normal powers that Cardan claimed to possess and exercise at will. He could, he declared, project his soul out of his body. He had a peculiar kind of clairvoyant vision, prac-ticed divination, and dreamed prophetic dreams. Also of importance is the fact that Cardan believed himself to be accompanied by a guardian angel, which gave him counsel and assisted him in his undertakings.[13] His companionship must have given Dee stimulus and inspiration, for from this time on Dee continually pursued occult knowledge.

[12] Hort, *Dr. John Dee,* 22–23.
[13] For a thorough discussion of Cardan's thought see Thorndike, *op. cit.,* V, 363–83.

Meanwhile, with the death of Edward VI, Queen Mary took favorably to Dee, and upon invitation Dee drew up the new monarch's horoscope. Soon, however, he consolingly turned to Mary's younger sister and connivingly entered into correspondence with the Princess Elizabeth in her semi-captivity at Woodstock. Recalling this at a later date Dee reminded the Queen that "Before her Majesties coming to the crowne, I did shew my dutifull good will in some travailes for her Majesties behalfe, to the comfort of her Majesties fauourers then, and some of her principall servantes, at Woodstock. . . ." [14] Dee allayed Elizabeth's fears by predicting her fortune from the stars. When discovered and reported, however, Dee was easily charged with both treason—using magic against the Queen's life —and heresy. Although near the flames and imprisoned for a while, he was eventually acquitted of both charges and released.[15] The implications of the charge, however, were never to wear off.

When set at liberty again, Dee occupied himself for a while with projects for founding a State National Library of books and manuscripts which were being rapidly destroyed with the pillaging and destruction of monasteries. In January 1556, he presented to the Queen *A Supplication For The Recovery And Preservation Of Ancient Writers And Monuments* both in England and throughout the Continent. Dee concluded this remarkable document with a generous offer of his services to the realm:

> . . . by furder device of your said suppliant, John Dee (God granting him his life and health), all the famous and worthy monuments that are in the notablest Librarys beyond the see (as in Vaticana at Rome, S. Marci at Venice, and the like at Bononia, Florence, Vienna, &c.) shall be procured unto the said Library of our soveraign Lady and Queen, the charges thereof (beside the journeying) to stand in the copying them out, and the carryage into this realm only. And as according all other excellent authors printed, that they likewise be gotten in

[14] I. D'Israeli, *Amenities of Literature* (2 vols., New York, 1841), I, 300.
[15] John Dee, *Autobiographical Tracts,* 20.

wonderfull abundance, their carriage only into this realme to be chargeable.[16]

The death of Queen Mary in 1558 brought her younger sister to the throne. And Elizabeth, remembering the sage whose prophecies had illuminated her dark hours, at once summoned Dee to the court to calculate a favorable day for her coronation. Dee named January 14, 1559, and from that time on the scholar, settling at Mortlake on the Thames, remained in favor. Over the next few decades Dee was continually busied one way or another at the fancy of the Queen who not only made frequent demands upon him for personal services, but also often visited his home and famous library—the largest in all of England.[17]

It was at this time that John Dee turned much of his ceaseless energy to geographical concerns. In this connection two things must be pointed out. First, in the sixteenth century the world location of England had been completely altered. From her slumbers on a remote margin of the Old World, Englishmen now awakened to find themselves on the very threshold of a new one. Secondly, scientific geography has its roots in astronomy—in a knowledge of the shape and size of the earth, of its apparent motion relative to the heavenly bodies—knowledge which allows accurate fixing of position by astronomical means; hence, the debt of geography to astrology, based on just such astronomical knowledge was great. The cosmographer was, in fact, in the first instance a mathematician and an astronomer, so that geographical literature was sought within many astronomical and mathematical works.[18]

Geography owes a large debt to Roger Bacon for his general teaching (as well as specific works) concerning the importance of applied mathematics and the experimen-

[16] Hort, *Dr. John Dee,* 27; Fell-Smith, *John Dee,* 15. A copy of this document can be found in Dee's *Autobiographical Tracts,* 46–49.
[17] Dee's library was internationally known, and his more than 4,000 volumes and manuscripts was without a doubt the largest collection in all of England. For a list of the Manuscripts he possessed see "The Lists of Manuscripts Formerly Owned by Dr. John Dee," with a preface and identified by M. R. James. *Supplements to the Transactions of the Bibliographical Society, 1921–1926* (Supplement 1, London, 1926).
[18] Taylor, *Tudor Geography,* 2.

169

tal approach to science. Bacon profoundly influenced many of the pioneers of the English Geographical Renaissance, including John Dee.[19] In the words of the leading historian of English geography of the Elizabethan era, after the publication of a new edition of Cabot's world map in 1549, "a new chapter in English geographical thought and practice opened." And that new chapter was, on the practical side, the beginning of the English search for Cathay; on the theoretical side, a story in which John Dee is one of the leading figures.[20]

Keeping in mind the opportunities and stimuli which Dee's personal connections afforded him in his approach to geography, it is no wonder that his interest turned to the seas. His training and Continental travels gave him further opportunities, which he did not neglect, both to confer with the learned and to acquire a fine library of foreign books. No man in all of England was better qualified for the office of technical adviser for various overseas voyages than was the skilled mathematician, astronomer, and astrologer John Dee, with his friendships throughout the Continent and within the Elizabethan Court.

It is known that Dee's advice was sought in 1553 by Sebastian Cabot when he undertook to organize the first Northeast expedition, thus beginning in earnest an era of English expansion.[21] And when the Duke of Northumberland also turned to the promotion of the discovery of Cathay by way of the Northeast (a venture which from the promise it held of new markets for English woolens had gained the support of the great London merchants), it was again Dee who was asked to put his skills at the new company's disposal. In 1559 Dee made his services available to the Muscovy Company. He instructed those heading the voyage (Stephen and William Burroughs) in vari-

[19] The largest number of books and manuscripts written by any one author among Dee's 4,000 works were those by Bacon. It should perhaps also be noted that Dee possessed many of Robert Grosseteste's works.
[20] Taylor, op. cit., 19.
[21] George Bruner Parks, Richard Hakluyt and the English Voyages, edited with an introduction by James A. Williamson. American Geographical Society Publication. No. 10 (New York, 1930), 10.

ous mathematical and technical skills. And although the Muscovy Company's discovery of a route to Persia and new trade led in the early 1560's to its practical abandonment of the search for Cathay, others like Jenkinson, Sir Humphrey Gilbert, and John Dee kept Cathay before the public mind.

Dee, however, did not abandon his "other" studies. Remember that sometime in the early 1550's Dee wrote two astronomico-geographical treatises for the Duchess of Northumberland. He also published a number of treatises on subjects apparently remote from geography. The most important of these was his *Hieroglyphic Monad Explained Mathematically, Cabalistically, and Anagogically,* written in the Neo-Platonic tradition with additional cabalistic embroideries. In this work, published in 1564 and dedicated to Maximilian, King of Hungary, Dee expressed his belief in the hidden sympathies and antipathies of things, the transmission of the force of the super celestial intellectual world to earth through the stars and planets, and the existence of spiritual beings of a high order not quite synonymous with the angels of Christianity. In addition, it is not surprising that in the text he expressed the belief that the letters of the alphabet embody great mysteries, that medicine is contained in the monad, and that people should raise cabalistic eyes to the sky. Dee indulged in much number mysticism and depiction of characters in the usual Neo-Platonic manner, holding that through the knowledge of superior numbers, one penetrates into the inner mysteries.[22] After proclaiming that such mysteries were not for the vulgar, Dee closed the treatise with a request to the printer to print only a limited amount of copies of the work to be judiciously distributed to the initiated.

In 1570, however, Dee wrote one of his most significant works. In the form of a Preface to Henry Billingsly's *English Translation of Euclid,*[23] he composed a magnificent

[22] Edward W. Strong, *Procedures and Metaphysics* (Berkeley, 1936), 197.

[23] According to Samuel Eliot Morison this book, along with Dee's Preface, was required reading for all upperclassmen at Harvard College in the seventeenth century. S. E. Morison, *Harvard College in the 17th Century* (2 vols., Cambridge, Mass., 1936), I, 147.

171

exposition of the relationship and application of mathematics (especially arithmetic and geometry) to the practice of skilled arts and crafts. It was, in fact, a plea for the scientific method, and it obviously owed much to the great schoolman, Roger Bacon, of whom Dee was so devout a disciple.

Apart from its autobiographical details, the most important sections of the Preface were those dealing with mathematics as the esssential foundation for the practice of surveying, navigation, cosmography, and hydrography. The twofold aspect of mathematics, as a pure and an applied science, was constantly on Dee's mind. And the discussion of navigation, and its obvious grounding in mathematics gave Dee an opportunity to remind his countrymen of their duties and privileges in the matters of discovery. In a passage which foreshadowed his later masterpiece, Dee asserted to his fellow Englishmen in a good Christian manner that

> In navigation none ought to have greater care to be skilful than our English pilots. And perchance some would more attempt, and other some willingly would be aiding, if they wist certainly what privilege God had endued this island with, by reason of situation most commodious for navigation to places most famous and rich. . . . I say . . . some one or other should listen to the matter: and by good advice and by discreet circumspection, by little and little win to the knowledge of that trade and voyage; which now I should be sorry (through carelessness, want of skill and courage) should remain unknown and unheard of. Thereof verily might we grow commodity to this land chiefly, and to the rest of the Christian Commonwealth, far passing all riches and earthly treasure.[24]

The final phrase on "riches" and "treasure" is a reference to that secret hope which really lay behind all Dee's efforts, the hope of a revelation of occult mysteries in the East.

In 1573, Dee's friend, the expansionist Edward Dyer, was restored to the Queen's favor, while another favorite, Christopher Hatton, was also rising to a position of impor-

[24] Quoted in Taylor, *Tudor Geography*, 105.

tance. By now Dee obviously already had begun to dream of England as mistress of a Northern empire based on a command of the seas. And it was through the influence of these two men, both of whom had their hearts set on the discovery of Cathay, that Dee urged his expansionist schemes. In 1577 it was "To The Right Worshipfull, [*sic*] discrete, and singular fauorer, of all good Artes, and sciences, M. Christopher Hatton, Esquier: Captain of her Maiesties Garde, and Ientleman of her privy Chamber,"[25] that Dee dedicated the first volume (*A Pety Navy Royall*) of his *magnum opus, General and Rare Memorials Pertayning to the Perfect Arte of Navigation.*[26] This work, *A Pety Navy Royall,* addressed to all those who "carefully desire the prosperous state of the Common Wealth, of this Brytish Kingdom, and the Politicall SECVRITIES thereof," does not bear directly on discovery. But it has as its object the setting forth of the advantages of having a navy of vessels in permanent commission and the means whereby such a scheme could be financed. Such a fleet was, of course, a pre-requisite of the policy of expansion which Dee was advocating, namely that of establishing a British maritime Empire. And while many have dismissed Dee as a fanatic and a megalomaniac, his picture (on the front piece of the work in 1577) of Queen Elizabeth at the helm of the Christian ship of Europe, had in it an element of the prophetic.

Mingling what has become the traditional elements of expansion with God and patriotism, Dee urged the importance of establishing a *Pety Navy Royall* of "three score tall ships or more, but in no case fewer," of 80 to 200 tons burden[27] to be thoroughly equipped and manned "as a comfort and safeguard to the Realme."[28] He shows the

[25] Dee, *A Pety Navy Royall* (London, 1577), 4. A microfilm copy of this work can be found in the University of Wisconsin Library Rare Book Room. University Microfilm No. 12113 (Case 63, Carton 378).

[26] *The General and Rare Memorials Portraying to the Perfect Arts of Navigation* was a four volume work. Hatton was to bring the work to the notice of the Privy Council, while Dyer, who appears to have borne the charges for its printing, was to bring the work to the attention of the Queen.

[27] Dee, *Pety Navy Royal,* 3.      [28] *Ibid.,* 4.

173

security this navy would give to English merchants: "I report me to all English Marchants . . . of how great value to them, and Consequently, to the Publik-Weale, of this Kingdom, such a securitie were? Whereby, both outward, and homeward (continually) their Marchantlike Ships (Many or few, great or small) may, in our Seas, and somewhat farder, pas quietly vnpilled, vnspoyled and vntaken, by Pyrates, or others. . . ."[29] This navy would also "decipher our coasts," sound channels and harbors, and observe tides. Thousands of soldiers, he says, "will thus be hardened and well broke to the rage and disturbance of the sea, so that in time of need we shall not be forced to use all fresh water soldyers" ready at hand.[30]

Dee then touched on the question of unemployment: "hundreds of lustry handsome men will this way be very well occupied and have needful maintenance, which are now idle or want sustenance, or both."[31] Quoting the ancient advocate of sea strength, Pericles, Dee reminded his audience that "These skilful sea-soldyers will be more traynable to martiall exploits, more quick-eyed and nimble than the landsmen."[32] Not only will the *Pety Navy Royall* look after pirates, but it also would protect England's valuable fisheries with the result that "many a hundred thousand pounds yerely Revenue, might grow to the Crown of England, more than (now) doth."[33]

Coming to the financial side, he asserts that every natural born subject of the "Brytish Impire" will willingly contribute towards this "perpetuale benevolence for sea security" the hundredth penny of his rents and revenues, and the five-hundredth penny of his valuation.[34] Dee would end the carrying off of English gunpowder and saltpeter from the realm. "Good God," he cried, "who Knoweth not what provise is made and kept in other Common Weales

---

[29] *Ibid.*     [30] *Ibid.,* 5.     [31] *Ibid.*     [32] *Ibid.,* 10.

[33] Dee said the "Flemish" herring fisheries were worth £490,000 a year, but were conducted almost entirely off the English coast, and Englishmen then have to buy their own commodity from strangers. It might be mentioned that an Act similar to the one advocated by Dee at this time was passed by James I in 1609, a year after Dee's death. It required foreign fishing vessels to obtain a license (at a fee) to fish in English waters.

[34] Dee, *Pety Navy Royall,* 10.

against armour carrying out of their limits?"[35] He deplores the wholesale destruction of English forests and timber (which is needed for ships) to keep the iron works going.[36]

The question of the limits of sea jurisdiction was also carefully discussed by John Dee. At that time it was commonly held that the diversity of natural products between one country and another was divinely appointed to promote intercourse between nations, and hence that God intended the seas to be free to all.[37] Dee, however, declared for a "closed sea."[38] He held that closed waters extend for 100 miles from a nation's shore, or in the case of narrow seas (less than 200 miles across) to a point midway between the home and foreign coasts. By laying claim for England to the shores and islands conquered by the former British Kings, Arthur and Madoc, and hence to a stretch of sea for a hundred miles around each of these, Dee was able to establish fairly well a rightful jurisdiction across the North Atlantic and Arctic Oceans (the recent discoveries of Stephen Burroughs having extended British rights toward the Northeast)

Dee devoted a final chapter to the history of "that Peaceable and Proudest Saxon, King Edgar," whose "yerely chief sommer pastymes [were] . . . sayling round about his whole Isle" guarded with "hys grand nauy of 4,000 sayls, at the least."[39] Then he asks, "Shall we . . . not Iudge it, some parte of wisdome, to Imitate carefully, in some little Proportion . . . the prosperous Pastymes of Peaceable King Edgar, that Saxonicall Alexander" who "so Highly, and Faithfully [served] . . . the glory of God . . . ?"[40]

Dee then concludes by asserting that England must attain this "incredible politicall mystery"—the supremacy of the seas.[41] England must be "Lords of the Seas" in order

[35] *Ibid.*, 15.    [36] *Ibid.*, 16ff.

[37] R. and R. Hakluyt, *The Original Writings of the Two Richard Hakluyts*, 2 vols., introduction and notes by E. G. R. Taylor (London: Hakluyt Society, 1935), I, 11, footnote.    [38] Dee, *Pety Navy Royall*, 27ff.

[39] *Ibid.*, 56.    [40] *Ibid.*, 57.

[41] It is no more coincidence that throughout the entire work Dee repeatedly uses the term "political." Coming mainly from Machiavelli, although from other sources as well, "Politik" in the sixteenth century implied the mystical and the mysterious; the dark and reserved domain for only the initiated few.

that its "wits and travayles" may be employed at home for the enriching of the Kingdom, that "our commodities (with due store reserve) may be carried abroad," and that peace and justice may reign,[42] for, as he earlier stated, "It is an olde Proverb, A Sword Keepeth Peace."[43]

Enough has been said of this book to show that, among other things, it was a remarkable contribution towards the history of the naval and fishing industries of Great Britain. Dee's treatise voiced the ideals of many sixteenth-century Englishmen, and twelve years later with the defeat of the Armada they were to be realized.[44] A. L. Rowse, in his *Elizabethans and America* recently wrote: "Strange to say —and everything about Dee is strange—the megalomaniac proved prophetically right: perhaps he was not a clairvoyant for nothing after all."[45]

In spite of John Cabot's early failure, in 1497, to reach Cathay by sailing west and north from England, the belief in a Northwest Passage around America persisted for many years. Englishmen sent voyage after voyage in this profitless and discouraging quest. The most recent examples of the search for the Northwest Passage were the three voyages of Martin Frobisher in 1576, 1577, and 1578. Dee was intimately involved in these attempts, dealing with the expedition both as a promoter and an official geographer. As a promoter he had subscribed some money to Frobisher but although a shareholder in the venture, George Parks is quite correct in maintaining that Dee's "economic interest was in all likelihood a result and not a cause of his intellectual interest; he was probably adviser first and investor

[42] Dee, *Pety Navy Royall*, 59.    [43] *Ibid.*, 15.
[44] The second volume to *The General and Rare Memorials Pertayning to the Perfect Arte of Navigation*, called *The Perfect Arte of Navigation*, was too long to be rescued from manuscript, where it still lies. Apparently the third volume was kept a mystery by Dee, while the last volume, on *Famous and Rich Discoveries*, likewise remained in manuscript form. The purpose of the fourth volume was to show how the English might bring back the riches of the East, not merely spices and material wealth, but the secrets of true wisdom. See, Parks, *Richard Hakluyt*, 48. In his *Autobiographical Tracts* Dee wrote: "And so great is the volume thereof, [*General and Rare Memorials*] that, to have it fairely and distinctly printed, with all the appertenances it would be in bulk greater than the English Bible, of the greatest volume. . . ," 61.
[45] A. L. Rowse, *The Elizabethans and America* (London,1959), 18.

176

second."[46] As early as 1576, even before the writing of his *General and Rare Memorials* Dee had been called upon to give lectures in the art of navigation to Frobisher's company.[47]

At about this same time (1577-1580) Francis Drake was making his successful voyage around the world. There is strong evidence that Dee was also in the counsels of those responsible for that venture. The promoters of Drake's voyage included the Earl of Leicester, Walsingham, a Court Secretary and leader of the colonial party, Hatton, and Dyer, all of whom were close acquaintances of Dee. And the earliest entries in Dee's *Private Diary* refer to visits from Drake's friends and backers at precisely this time.[48]

By the year 1577 the active, restless brain of Humphrey Gilbert was at work on the problem of the exploration and colonization of America, and it is perhaps more than a coincidence that Gilbert called on Dee the day before he affixed his signature to the document entitled: "How her Majesty May Annoy the King of Spain." On November 6th, 1577, Dee recorded, "Sir Umfrey Gilbert cam to me at Mortlak."[49] Shortly thereafter Gilbert was awarded a patent for his colonizing scheme in the New World. Only about three weeks later Dee was summoned to the Court to explain to both the Queen and Secretary Walsingham (who was behind both Drake's and Gilbert's voyages) her title to the land to be colonized.

While most Englishmen justified England's right to land in the New World on John Cabot's 1497 voyage, Dee declared the Queen's title rested on discoveries first made under King Arthur, then Madoc and later by the British merchant-explorer Thorne (1494) as well as Cabot three

---

[46] Parks, *Richard Hakluyt*, 47.

[47] Frobisher sailed up Hudson Bay, which he believed to be the route to the East. When it was believed that he found gold in some black and glistening rocks, his voyage tended for some time to divert attention away from a search for the East. See J. E. Gillespie, *A History of Geographical Discovery, 1400–1800* (New York, 1933), 80.

[48] Dee, John, *The Private Diary of Doctor John Dee,* edited by James Orchard Halliwell (London: The Camden Society, 1842), 4.

[49] *Ibid.,* 3.

years after. And it was on this priority that Gilbert's patent rested. To accompany his views on the matter Dee also drew up a map of Atlantis (the New World)[50] as well as several tracts on the "hydrographic description of the Atlantis." Dee thought that the term generally used at that time for America, "West Indies," was misleading; he preferred the term "Atlantis," even over "America."[51] In all probability Dee took the term "Atlantis" from Plato's *Timaeus* which opens with the tale of the old Athenian State that fought for its own and others' freedom against the people of Atlantis until the earthquake ended the old Athenian race, and the Atlantean continent was swallowed in the sea. John Dee owned copies of many of Plato's works, including the *Timaeus*.[52]

In 1579, as his *Diary* mentions, Dee was already in touch with Adrian Gilbert and John Davis,[53] the two men later associated with the Northwest Passage attempts of 1585-1587. In June 1580, he was in touch with the two men again, while in August of the same year Dee obtained from Humphrey Gilbert a grant to what essentially amounted to the royalties of discovery of all the land north of the fiftieth latitude (the abandoned Frobisher region).[54] Queen Elizabeth graciously commanded Dee to attend her Court more often[55] and he was not slow to avail himself of the invitation. On October 3, 1580, he brought her further proof of her *Titles to Foreign Lands,* written by his hand on two parchment rolls. A week later the Queen called at his Mortlake estate and "withall told me," he inscribed in his *Diary,* "that the Lord Threasorer [Burghley] had greatly commended my doings for her title, which he had to examyn, which title in two rolls he had brought home two howrs before; . . . ."[56]

---

[50] According to Parks, serious English cartography began with the map of America drawn by Dee for the Queen in 1580. See Parks, *Richard Hakluyt,* 184.

[51] Hence, "Atlanticall" meant pertaining not to the Atlantic Ocean, but to Atlantis (i.e., America). See Taylor, *Tudor Geography,* 99; Rowse, *Elizabethans,* 18.

[52] See James, *op. cit.;* Fell-Smith, *John Dee,* 244.  [53] Dee, *Private Diary,* 7.

[54] *Ibid.,* 8.  [55] Dee, *Autobiographical Tracts,* 18.

[56] *Ibid.,* 22; Dee, *Private Diary,* 9.

In 1581 Dee's thought centered upon America and apparently he wrote a great volume in Latin on the propagation of the Christian Faith among the Infidels of Atlantis.[57] A year later Dee involved himself with Richard Hakluyt in an entirely new plan for reaching Cathay. At the same time another of Gilbert's chief backers, Sir George Peckham, came to see Dee and inquire into the English title to North American lands. In addition the "young [sea captain] Mr. Hawkins, who had byn with Sir Francis Drake, cam to . . . Mortlak."[58] The following year, 1583, however, saw Dee far more actively involved in overseas exploits than previously.

Early in 1583 the definite formulation of Adrian Gilbert's plans to search for a Northwest Passage, based on Dee's technical advice, came to a head. A clear picture of numerous meetings held both at Dee's home and elsewhere is preserved in his *Diary*. On January 23, 1583 "the Ryght Honorable Mr. Secretary Walsingham cam to my howse, where by good lok he found Mr. Awdrian Gilbert, and so talk was begonne of Northwest Straights discovery."[59] And on January 24th, 1583, Dee, "Mr. Awdrian Gilbert, and John Davis went by appointment to Mr. Secretary to Mr. Beale his howse, where only we four were secret, and we made Mr. Secretarie privie of the N. W. passage, and all charts and rutters agreed uppon in generall."[60] Once again, on March 6th, 1583, Dee recorded that "I, and Mr. Adrian Gilbert and John Davis, did mete with Mr. Alderman Barnes [one of the most influential Directors of the Muscovy Company]. Mr. Townson [a London merchant who was often associated with discoveries] and Mr. Yong [?] and Mr. Hudson [Thomas Hudson, father of Henry, and one of the founders of the Muscovy Company], about the N. W. voyage."[61] One of the results of this project was the license granted to Adrian Gilbert and John Davis to explore and plant colonies in the Northern part of Atlantis (observe Dee's influence in the name).

[57] I could find no references to this work in any of Dee's own writings, nor in any of the secondary works consulted except Parks, *Richard Hakluyt*, 48–49, and Taylor, *Tudor Geography*, 135.
[58] Dee, *Private Diary*, 11,     [59] *Ibid.*, 18.     [60] *Ibid.*     [61] *Ibid.*, 19.

Dee lived for 25 years after 1583, the date of the last extract from his *Diary,* and he continued to make notes of important events as they occurred. Yet we find no further allusion in his journal to any of the other expeditions that ensued, nor do we find any further reference made to those who were engaged in them.

Besides immersing himself in geographical pursuits, Dee, over the years, had continued to nourish his interests in astrology and alchemy. In addition, for some time he had engaged in séances with a series of mediums to call up spirits from whom he hoped to learn the secrets of God and nature; those very secrets he sought from his geographical exploits. During the previous year Dee made the acquaintance of a young man, Edward Kelley, who, in Dee's mind, had marked mediumistic powers. Daily crystal-gazing séances again were resumed and Dee believed himself to be conversing with Neo-Platonic angelic spirits. In May 1583, Dee was introduced to the Polish Prince, Laski, then on a visit to England.[62] Laski, too, was a disciple of the occult and when he visited Dee at Mortlake, Laski, Dee, and Kelley spent the entire night prying into hidden mysteries. Shortly thereafter, on September 21, 1583, Dee and Kelley, along with their families, left England in favor of the Continent. It was now that Dee abandoned his geographical activities for others that, perhaps he believed, would bring him more quickly to his ultimate goal.

If the actual attainment of the goal is a measure of success, then John Dee, notable mathematician, philosopher, astronomer, and keen student of geography and discovery was a failure. Nevertheless, it was such failures, both on the practical and theoretical side, that paved the way for the successes and clearer knowledge of the following decades. In claiming for Dee an important place in the history of sixteenth-century English geography it is sufficient to state that he was the teacher, technical instructor, friend, and adviser to most of the English mathematicians, astronomers, and geographers of his day. His pupils include such illustrious men as Richard Chancellor, Stephen and William Burroughs, Anthony Jenkinson, Martin Frobisher,

[62] *Ibid.,* 20.

Christopher Hall, Humphrey Gilbert, Adrian Gilbert, John Davis, Walter Raleigh, and Francis Drake, as well as Thomas Digges, Sir Edward Dyer, and Sir Philip Sidney. For his unceasing efforts in instructing mariners and scientists in their attempts to unveil hidden corners of the earth, John Dee is entitled to an honored place in the history of geography.[63]

Prior to 1583 John Dee appeared as a man of learning and a Court favorite—astronomer, mathematician, a brilliant lecturer and a diligent prober in chemical and alchemical secrets. He had written on navigation, history, logic, travel, geometry, astrology, and a host of other subjects. He had essayed to found a national library and he was contemplating a great work upon the reformation of the calendar. Had he remained in England, Dee doubtless would have taken a conspicuous part in later geographical ventures. It was in the critical year of 1583, however, that this man engaged in respectable popular efforts turned aside earthly wisdom in favor of the spiritual, and thereby came into disrepute in the eyes of so many of his contemporaries. Increasingly, reports were spread that Dee was initiated into the magical arts, helped by demons, and the label of "sorcerer" and "conjurer" of evil spirits became permanent. He was to die in poverty in 1608.

Dee did not abandon his geographical interests, as Rowse suggests, because having "no terrestrial preferment, nothing to live by . . . [he] at last . . . accepted better prospects from the Continent and went off to raise the spirits. . . ."[64] John Dee was an Elizabethan, and like many of his contemporaries he was part Medieval and part Renaissance. In true Renaissance style, Dee was a devotee of the new learning, but the sole object of that learning for Dee was the attainment of the older ideal of divine wisdom. Geographical exploration for Dee had not been a matter of material rewards. Beyond a concern for enough money to support himself and his family Dee was not primarily interested in financial matters, for if he had been, he would

[63] This honored position was universally conceded to Dee by his British contemporaries. See Francis R. Johnson, *Astronomical Thought in Renaissance England* (Baltimore, 1937), 139–140 (footnote).    [64] Rowse, *Elizabethans,* 21.

181

not have refused the yearly stipend of 200 French crowns offered him in Paris. A revealing paragraph from Dee's *Autobiographical Tracts* further bears this point out and is worth quoting.

> To be most briefe . . . as concerning my forraine credit, . . . I might have served five Christian Emporers; namely, Charles the Fifth, Ferdinand, Maximilian, this Rudulph, and this present Moschovite: of every one their stipends directly or indirectly offered, amounting greater each, then other: as from 500 dollars yearely stipend to a 1000, 2000, 3000; and lastly, by a Messenger from this Russian or Moschovite Emporer, purposely sent, unto me at Trebona castle . . . of my coming to his court at Moskow . . . there to enjoy at his Imperial handes £2000 sterling yearely stipende; . . . .[65]

Once again, if Dee was interested in financial betterment would he not have accepted any one of these positions rather than die in poverty, as he did?

For Dee, rather, overseas exploration was part of the search for something deeper; it was a probing for the heart of all knowledge, for the Infinite, for the Unknowable. Signs of this already were clearly visible in his *Pety Navy Royall* when Dee declared the reasons that he "doth wish and advise part of the publik threasory to be bestowed upon some two or three honest men who should be skilful in Forreyn languages." For "within the next few years," Dee continued, "in farder Cuntries great Affayres are by some of our Country-Men to be handled: If God continue his Gracious Direction and Ayde thereto, as he hath very comfortably begun: and that, *by means not yet published.*[66] For more than thirty years Dee had sought true wisdom in spirits, books, men, and distant new lands—always, however, unsuccessfully. If concentrated geographical activities failed, perhaps the shew-stone and angels would bring him to his goal.

To Dee the spirits he called upon were angels; he could not believe that he had broken the ideas of Christianity.

---

[65] Dee, *Autobiographical Tracts,* 8–9.
[66] Dee, *Pety Navy Royall,* 62.

But by the popular verdict of Elizabethan Christianity they must be devils; angels would have no such commerce with men. The case, therefore, for Dee's contemporaries was one in which the scientist abandoned his profession to resort to the supernatural. For Dee, however, that distinction was meaningless, for as he repeatedly said throughout all his life, *all* knowledge served God. In order to pursue that knowledge as he now saw fit, Dee was forced to turn once again to the Continent.

Beginning with Prince Laski's visit in May 1583, the accounts of his doings with spirits were minutely written down by Dee. They later were printed and published under the title of *"A True and Faithfull Relation of What Passed for many Years Between Dr. John Dee and Some Spirits."*[67] This illuminating work which throws a great deal of light on the reason behind Dee's psychical activities suggests that Dee's ultimate aims in both his geographical and spiritual exploits were one and the same. Especially revealing is Dee's confession[68] that he

> began and declared by long course of study for forty years, alwayes, by degrees going forward, and desirous of the best, and pure truths in all manner of studies, wherein I had passed, and that I passed as many as were commonly known and more than are commonly heard of. But that at length I perceived onely God (and by his good Angels) could satisfie my desire; which was to understand the natures of all creatures, and the best manner how to use them to his divine honor and glory. . . . And herein I had dealed sundry wayes: And at length had found the mercies of God such as to send me the instruction of Michael, Gabriel, Raphael, and Uriel, and divers other his good and faithful Messengers. . . .

Dee, the astrologer, had always been in close touch with psychic phenomena. The old idea of access to certain stores of wisdom which God had withheld from man, but

[67] Dee, John, *A True and Faithful Relation of What Passed for many Years Between Dr. John Dee and Some Spirits,* with a Preface by Meric Casaubon (London: D. Maxwell, 1659). Hereafter cited as *Some Spirits.*
[68] *Ibid.,* 239.

presumably gave to spiritual creatures of a higher order, had long attracted him. In addition, this profoundly pious man was convinced that God desired to hide nothing from the faithful seeker. This was confirmed for Dee by the sacred words of the angel Gabriel who uttered to him: "If thou remain my servant, and do the works that are righteous, I will put Solomon behind thee, and his riches under they feet."[69] Therefore man, with God's aid, may establish a real communication with the spirtual world through the calling of good spirits.[70] Once convinced of his mediumistic powers, God's wish to enlighten him through His angels became a reality for Dee. In fact, the voice of another of the divine messengers even had told him to "pluck up . . . thy heart and be merry" and "pine not thy Soul away with inward groanings," for "I will open unto thee the Secrets of Nature and the riches of the world" and "I will disclose unto you such things, as shall be wonderfull, and of exceeding profit."[71] It is, then, no wonder that Dee unhesitatingly left the island empire in favor of the Continent to seek and receive the true wisdom needed to fashion him according to his Maker. In John Dee's own words, all his endeavors, material and spiritual alike, only sought to "highly please, the eternall and almighty God, in executing for him the verity of his mercifull promises, generally made to all his sincere worshippers."[72]

English science in the sixteenth century was, on the whole, practical and experimental. Most leading scholars were not interested in abstract theory, except in so far as it was necessary for determining fundamental principles. They had a clear vision of the practical utility of science for the relief of man's estate. A few, on the other hand, were infused with the older medieval attitude and sought knowledge for its revelation of the truths of God. For Dee,

[69] *Ibid.*, 167.    [70] Dee wrote that the angel Uriel related the following to him: "For the spirit of God is twofold: working by information, and influence Celestial through the grant of God his good will, in the ministery of his Angels to the information of such as are his faithful and chosen. And another thing is to be inspired, from God himself, in his holy spirit, immediately comforting and knitting Wisdom together with you, beyond the power that is given unto his Angels. I have spoken unto you a sound and true doctrine, and have given you not fleshly but Celestial counsel: Apply your self unto it, as the Spirit of God leadeth you." *Ibid.*, 361.
[71] *Ibid.*, 49.    [72] Dee, *Autobiographical Tracts*, 42.

however, the two traditions did not conflict; rather, they were in harmony and indeed complemented each other. John Dee should be recognized as a particular variant of the proto-typical Elizabethan marriage of science, pseudo-science, and religion in the search for that divine unity which lay like a pattern behind the façade of nature.

# IV

## INTELLECTUAL FERMENT IN THE ELIZABETHAN AGE

*The first selection, Theodore Spencer's "Man in Nature: The Renaissance Conflict," was originally given as one in a series of lectures under the auspices of the Lowell Institute of Boston. As originally published, it is Chapter 2 in Spencer's book,* Shakespeare and the Nature of Man *(New York, 1942).*

*The second selection, Geoffrey Bush's "The Order and Continuance of Nature," is Chapter 1 from his book,* Shakespeare and the Natural Condition *(Cambridge, Mass., 1956). It also was originally one of a series of lectures given under the auspices of the Lowell Institute.*

# MAN IN NATURE: THE RENAISSANCE CONFLICT

## By Theodore Spencer

### 1

I have so far emphasized as strongly as I could the essential unity of the three inter-related hierarchies which made up the optimistic sixteenth-century picture of man's nature.* Each one of them reflected the order of Nature's rule, and to think of one was almost automatically to think of the others. No one expressed this fact better than Shakespeare: Ulysses' famous speech on order, in *Troilus and Cressida,* sums up nearly everything the Elizabethans felt about the matter. Ulysses is explaining why the Greeks have been so unsuccessful in their war against Troy. The trouble is, he says, that "the specialty of rule [the particular function of government] hath been neglected," and there has not been enough order in the administration of the Greek army. He first draws a parallel with the heavens, then with civil law, then with the four elements, then with natural and moral law, and finally with psychological law. Everything is inter-related and seen as part of the same scheme, obeying the same rules:

> The heavens themselves, the planets, and this centre
> Observe degree, priority, and place,
> Insisture, course, proportion, season, form,
> Office, and custom, in all line of order:

* In Chapter I of his book, "Man in Nature: The Optimistic Theory."

And therefore is the glorious planet Sol
In noble eminence enthron'd and spher'd
Amidst the other; whose med'cinable eye
Corrects the ill aspects of planets evil
And posts, like the commandment of a king,
Sans check, to good and bad: but when the planets
In evil mixture to disorder wander,
What plagues, and what portents, what mutiny,
What raging of the sea, shaking of earth,
Commotion in the winds, frights, changes, horrors,
Divert and crack, rend and deracinate
The unity and married calm of states
Quite from their fixure! O! when degree is shak'd,
Which is the ladder to all high designs,
The enterprise is sick. How could communities,
Degrees in schools, and brotherhoods in cities,
Peaceful commerce from dividable shores,
The primogenitive and due of birth,
Prerogative of age, crowns, sceptres, laurels,
But by degree, stand in authentic place?
Take but degree away, untune that string,
And, hark! what discord follows; each thing meets
In mere oppugnancy: the bounded waters
Should lift their bosoms higher than the shores,
And make a sop of all this solid globe:
Strength should be lord of imbecility,
And the rude son should strike his father dead:
Force should be right; or rather, right and wrong—
Between whose endless jar justice resides—
Should lose their names, and so should justice too.
Then everything includes itself in power,
Power into will, will into appetite;
And appetite, a universal wolf,
So doubly seconded with will and power,
Must make perforce a universal prey,
And last eat up himself.

I hope to show later how important the speech is in the dramatic structure of Shakespeare's play; what I am now concerned with is to demonstrate how Shakespeare, in characteristic Elizabethan fashion, when considering the order of the state, illustrates it—as did so many of his contemporaries—by the order of the heavens, and—at the end—by the order in the faculties of man.

189

But that order, as Shakespeare so eloquently describes, could all too easily collapse. There is a further, and important, corollary to the unity of the inter-related hierarchies; not merely, as in Ulysses' speech, can the downfall of one of them be *illustrated* by the downfall of the others, it can actually *cause* that downfall. As Richard Hooker says,

> "Let any principal thing, as the sun, the moon, any one of the heavens or elements, but once cease or fail, or swerve, and who doth not easily conceive that the sequel thereof would be ruin both in itself and whatsoever dependeth on it"?[1]

And what if man, "who was principally ordained for God's service, as all other creatures for man"—what if man, "being *nexus et naturae vinculum*," should break "his own bonds"? Would it not follow, as Godfrey Goodman states, "that all the rest of the creatures, which were bound and knit together in man, should likewise be inordinate, and overflow their own banks"?[2] It would; in fact it had, and the results had been disastrous for both man and the other creatures depending on him.

For to man, as a result of Adam's sin, was left only a small glimmer of the reason which had been his original birthright. His fall had been intellectual as well as moral, and though reason, since it was a natural gift, could not be entirely destroyed, yet of its original vigor, as Calvin says, "being partly weakened and partly corrupted, a shapeless ruin is all that remains." Though there are still some sparks which show that man is a rational animal and hence differs from brutes, yet

> "this light is so smothered by clouds of darkness that it cannot shine forth to any good effect. In like manner, the will, because inseparable from the nature of man, did not perish, but was so enslaved by depraved lusts as to be incapable of one righteous desire."[3]

[1] *Laws of Eccl. Pol.*, I, ix, 1.
[2] Godfrey Goodman, *The Fall of Man*, 1616, p. 17.
[3] *Institutes*, trans. H. Beveridge, Edinburgh, 1845, bk. II, ch. ii, sec. 12.

Man, instead of fitting into the order of Nature, now turns it upside down; the body rules the soul, instead of the soul's ruling the body; man is like good wine miserably turned to vinegar;[4] reason in virtually paralyzed, and

> Unhallowed sense, drown'd in that damnèd juice
> (Sin's cider) from Eve's fatal Apple bruis'd,
> Being deadly drunk, makes still the worser choice,
> Wherein (like Sow in mire) it doth rejoice.[5]

Consequently something occurs in the functioning of man's powers which can best be described as a short circuit. Ideally speaking, before a man performs an act of any kind, an elaborate process takes place. Through the working of the animal spirits, the outward senses perceive an object, an impression of it is conveyed to the imagination, the imagination refers this impression to the affections as pleasing or displeasing, reason debates the matter and presents its verdict to the will, the Queen of the soul, who finally dictates back to the sensitive appetite (the function which desires), telling it to act or to refrain from action, according as the object is seen as good or evil.[6] This was the way Adam invariably behaved before Eve gave him the apple, and consequently his actions were invariably rational and orderly. But once he had disobeyed God's command, Adam, and all his descendants after him, could follow this practice only with the greatest difficulty. The higher powers, reason and will, had become so feeble that, as I have said, a short circuit occurred which usually left them out, and what happened was that action was dictated by imagination, a power which was lawless, and much lower than reason—one shared, in fact, by the beasts. Hence man is enslaved by passions, which are "sensual

---

[4] Ramón Sabunde, *Natural Theology* (Montaigne's trans.), chs. 223, 231.
[5] John Davies of Hereford, *Microcosmos,* in *Works,* ed. Grosart, 1878, I, 23.
[6] For a full account of this process see Ruth L. Anderson, *Elizabethan Psychology and Shakespeare's Plays,* Iowa City, 1927, pp. 23–24.

motions of our appetitive faculty" aroused through imagination.[7] La Primaudaye says,

> Amongst the innumerable evils, which the desire of pleasure and fear of grief, engraven in the most secret parts of our soul by our first corruption, bring to man, this is the greatest and most pernicious, that they make sensible things more evident and plain unto him than things intelligible, and constrain the understanding to judge more by passion than by reason.[8]

This "transgressing the Law of his Nature," in Hooker's phrase, has drawn all "manner of harm after it:" it has brought "tribulation and anguish unto every soul that doeth evil," since man is the only creature subject to reward and punishment.[9] It has also corrupted the rest of creation, for when Adam fell, Nature fell too, and though, according to Danaeus, man's transgression could not take away the essential qualities of things, it produced,

> "as it were a sickness in the natural powers . . . and disagreement among things for lack of order. . . . In so much, that the strength and plentifulness of the earth, and of all other things, decreaseth daily, and are nothing now in respect as God first created them, which cometh to pass by reason of man's transgression."[10]

If man had not fallen, Nature would have been friendly to him, but as it is, serpents and poisons attack him in punishment and revenge, and, says Robert Burton, things are so changed since the fall of our first parent Adam, that the earth is

accursed, the influence of stars altered, the four ele-

[7] Thomas Wright, *The Passions of the Mind in General*, 1604, p. 8. For a good account of the Elizabethan view of the passions, see Lily B. Campbell, *Shakespeare's Tragic Heroes*, Cambridge, 1930. I cannot, however, completely follow Miss Campbell in her description of how Shakespeare used the passions for drama, since it seems to me likely that he was interested in doing more than the writing of case-histories.

[8] *French Academy*, trans. 1618, bk. i, ch. 3, p. 12.

[9] Hooker, *op. cit.*, I, ix, 1. Hooker is quoting *Rom.*, ii, 9.

[10] *Wonderful Workmanship of the World*, trans. T. T., 1578, ch. 41.

ments, beasts, birds, plants are now ready to offend us. . . . The heavens threaten us with their comets, stars, planets, with their great conjunctions, eclipses, oppositions . . . and such unfriendly aspects; the air with his meteors, thunder and lightning, intemperate heat and cold, mighty winds, tempests, unseasonable weather; from which proceed dearth, famine, plague, and all sorts of epidemical diseases, consuming infinite myriads of men.[11]

Furthermore the earth, on which man, this disgraced and unhappy creature, lives, could be regarded—and often *was* regarded—not as the center and most important part of the universe, but, to use Professor Lovejoy's words, as "the place farthest removed from the Empyrean, the bottom of the creation, to which its dregs and baser elements sank."[12] It could be seen, in the more Elizabethan language of the playwright John Marston, as "the only grave and Golgotha wherein all things that live must rot; 'tis but the draught wherein the heavenly bodies discharge their corruption; the very muckhill on which the sublunary orbs cast their excrements."[13] Viewed in "the light of our natural reason," as the gloomy Goodman viewed it, the entire system of Nature was running hopelessly down. "When I consider the diseases of these times, together with all the signs, tokens and symptoms: Alas, alas, I fear a relapse, I fear a relapse," he cries. Nature is incurably corrupted, the elements are engaged in civil war; human art, like a cobbler or tinker, can only "piece up the walls and repair the ruins of nature"; all the faculties of man are "in an uproar"; man's miseries are greater than his joys, any animal is happier than a man; there is no human occupation that is not full of suffering; our laws take our corruption for granted; "the whole world is turned bankrupt"—corruption even infests the material heavens (have not "perspective glasses" recently discovered spots in the moon?). In the light of all this Goodman could reach only one conclusion: the Last Judgment was about to take place. "When the hangings and

---

[11] *Anatomy of Melancholy*, Part I, sect. i, memb. i, subs. i.
[12] A. O. Lovejoy, *The Great Chain of Being*, Cambridge (Mass.), 1936, pp. 101–102.
[13] *The Malcontent*, iv, 2.

furniture are taken down," he says, "it is a token that the king and the court are removing"; nature now beginning to decay, it is clear enough, "according to natural reason," that the end of the world is at hand.[14]

Burton and Goodman, to be sure, were writing in the early seventeenth century (one in 1621 and the other in 1616), at a time when pessimism about man's situation had reached a kind of climax. But what they said was only a re-iteration, in unusually strong language, of an opinion that the sixteenth century had continually had in mind. The miseries of the human situation, so frequently emphasized in medieval literature, were never forgotten by the writers of the Renaissance. Underneath the gilt brocade of the prince was the corruptible flesh, and many courtiers who talked of how their souls could be united with the angels through Platonic love had their bones racked with syphilis. Both experience and doctrine re-inforced the familiar fact of man's general wretchedness. For example George Gascoigne—one of the most typical of all Elizabethans—published in 1576 a book which he called *The Drum of Dooms Day, Wherein the frailties and miseries of man's life are lively portrayed and learnedly set forth,* and which describes with energy and detail the sordidness and suffering which man is forced to endure from birth to death. The first part of it was a translation, Gascoigne tells us, of an old Latin book he had found (it had no title page, so he did not know the author's name) as, with a guilty conscience for his misspent life, he "was tossing and re-tossing in his small library." The original author, as a matter of fact, was Pope Innocent III, who had written the work about the year 1200, under the title of *De Contemptu Mundi.* But its being more than 350 years old would not have troubled Gascoigne; no matter when it was set down, an account of the wretchedness of man's condition was always profitable for "the reformation of manners," and should be published "for a general commodity." It was still true, as Innocent's text said, that both the universal and human worlds

do now wax old. That is to say macrocosmos and

[14] *The Fall of Man,* pp. 383 ff.

micrososmos, the greater world and the lesser world. And the longer that life doth linger in either of them, so much the worse is nature in each of them troubled and vexed.[15]

2

Thus in the inherited, the universally accepted, Christian view of man and his universe there was a basic conflict between man's dignity and his wretchedness. Every Elizabethan would have agreed with Sir John Davies who says, in his *Nosce Teipsum* (1599),—the poem is one of the finest of all the accounts of traditional psychology:—

> I know my body's of so frail a kind,
>   As force without, fevers within can kill;
> I know the heavenly nature of my mind,
>   But 'tis corrupted both in wit and will.

> I know my Soul hath power to know all things,
>   Yet is she blind and ignorant in all;
> I know I am one of Nature's little kings,
>   Yet to the least and vilest things am thrall.

> I know my life's a pain and but a span,
>   I know my Sense is mock'd with everything;
> And to conclude, I know myself a MAN,
>   Which is a proud, and yet a wretched thing.

But the conflict, as Davies suggests, was also a complement. For instance, Pierre Boaistuau, in 1577 (the work was translated into English in 1603), wrote a treatise called *Le Théâtre du Monde, où il est fait un ample discours des misères humaines,* which is immediately followed, bound in the same volume, by *un brief discours sur l'excellence et dignité de l'homme.* The two views were opposite sides of the same coin, for man's wretched condition did not at all decrease his immense importance to the universe.

[15] George Gascoigne, *Works, Cambridge,* 1910, ii, 213, 234.

He was, in fact, so necessary that God himself, after man's fall, had taken on man's shape in order to set things right again. Through the incarnation of Christ man could be restored to his original position in a Paradise regained.

The basic conflict, therefore, no matter how deep it went and no matter how many aspects it presented, could—by the doctrines of grace and redemption—theoretically be solved. But there was another conflict, more particular to the sixteenth century—and, since it was new, perhaps more intellectually and emotionally disturbing—for which a solution was more difficult. The conflict was this: belief in each one of the interrelated orders—cosmological, natural, and political—which as we have seen were the frame, the basic pattern of all Elizabethan thinking, was being punctured by a doubt. Copernicus had questioned the cosmological order, Montaigne had questioned the natural order, Machiavelli had questioned the political order. The consequences were enormous.

Upon the structure of the Ptolemaic system, with the earth in the center, everything had been built; the order of creation, the influence of the heavens on man, the parallels between the universe and the state, the theory of the macrocosm and the microcosm. But when the sun was put at the center, and the earth set between Mars and Venus as a mobile and subsidiary planet, the whole elaborate structure, with all its interdependencies, so easy to visualize, so convenient for metaphor and allusion, lost its meaning. "If the celestial spheres," said Hooker, "should forget their wonted motions, and by irregular volubility turn themselves any way . . . what would become of man himself, whom all these things do now serve?"[16]

We must, however, as Miss Marjorie Nicolson and others have shown,[17] be on guard against over-emphasizing the effects of the Copernican theory on the popular mind. It was confronted at first, considering its implications, with remarkably little opposition. For though Luther and Mel-

[16] Quoted J. B. Black, *The Reign of Elizabeth,* Oxford, 1936, p. 261.
[17] Marjorie Nicolson, 'The 'New Astronomy' and English Literary Imagination," *Studies in Philology,* XXXII (1935), 428–462; "The Telescope and Imagination," *Modern Philology,* XXXII (1935), 233–260.

anchthon attacked his views (they contradicted certain phrases of Scripture), perhaps because Copernicus' book was published in 1543 by the cautious Osiander with an apologetic preface and the word "hypothesis" on the title page, the Roman church took no official steps against it until 1616, when, because Galileo supported it, it was finally put on the Index. Even then the censure was mild; it could be read if nine sentences were changed so that they were turned from statements of fact into matters of conjecture.

The reason for this mildness is clear enough.[18] For the Copernican system could be looked at in two ways: as a mathematical theory and as a description of physical fact. Being simpler than the elaborate Ptolemaic system, it was welcomed by mathematicians as an easier means of making astronomical calculations, and it was well known as a hypothesis by the English reading public before the end of the sixteenth century. But it was not until Galileo perfected the telescope that the hypothesis could be proved to be a true description of reality. Only in 1610, with the publication of Galileo's *Siderius Nuncius,* which announced the discovery of four new planets, and various other phenomena, such as the true cause of the Milky Way, the irregular surface of the moon, and many new stars, was it clear that the old system was seriously upset. On the day the book was published, Sir Henry Wotton, the English ambassador at Venice, sent a copy of it to King James, as "the strangest piece of news that he hath ever yet received from any part of the world." Galileo, says Wotton, "hath first overthrown all former astronomy—for we must have a new sphere to save the appearances—and next all astrology."[19]

Wotton's phrase about the new sphere shows that he was still thinking in terms of the Ptolemaic system and that he saw how disastrous to its familiar pattern the new discoveries were. His friend John Donne, who always saw the implications of everything, went further, and in his *First*

[18] See Francis R. Johnson, *Astronomical Thought in Renaissance England,* Baltimore, 1937.
[19] Quoted Marjorie Nicolson, "The 'New Astronomy' and English Literary Imagination," *loc. cit.*

*Anniversary* (1611) described how the destruction of the old cosmology brought ruin to the related orders of the state and the individual as well. Nature's three domains were so closely connected that to destroy one was to destroy all. The "new philosophy," he said, "calls *all* in doubt"—the element of fire has been put out; the world, now that so many new worlds have been discovered, is, as everybody admits, crumbled to atoms; order in the state and the family is gone, and everybody thinks himself a unique individual, with no relation to anything else.

> 'Tis all in pieces, all coherence gone,
> All just supply, and all relation.
> Prince, subject, father, son, are things forgot,
> For every man alone thinks he hath got
> To be a phoenix, and that then can be
> None of that kind of which he is but he.[20]

Galileo's discoveries, of course, came too late to have any influence on Shakespeare. But they were merely a culmination of a kind of astronomical uneasiness and excitement, the kind of uneasiness and excitement which makes new explorations and destroys old concepts, which was part of the temper of the late sixteenth century, and which was to haunt the century following. Giordano Bruno, a believer in Copernicus, and a man filled with an almost visionary enthusiasm about his own new picture of the world, had spent two years in England in the early 1580's, and though his influence seems impossible to trace, he must have left some impression on the distinguished Englishmen, like Sir Philip Sidney, with whom he conversed. There were both technical treatises and semi-popular handbooks which described the new theories—one of them, Thomas Digges' *Perfect Description of the Celestial Orbs* (1576), went through six editions before 1600.[21] The disruptive effect of Galileo's discoveries had been prepared for, even

[20] Ll. 205 ff. Donne's *Anniversaries* are extremely interesting as an example of how the familiar ideas of the decay of the world could be used as poetic material. There is nothing new in any of the ideas which Donne expresses; what is new is the relation they bear to each other after Donne's wit has fused them together.
[21] See Francis R. Johnson, *op. cit.*, and below, p. 97, note 2.

though, in most minds, the Ptolemaic heavens still rolled about the stationary earth and shed their influence on men's lives.

## 3

But if the Copernican theory did not at once seem to be as destructive of the cosmological hierarchy as it later became, there can be no question about the force with which the natural hierarchy was attacked. In his "Apology for Raymond Sebond" Montaigne gave the accepted view of the second of Nature's domains such a series of blows that it was almost entirely demolished; one by one the cards were knocked down until the whole house lay flat on the ground. Not that he was entirely original; there had been earlier theoretical attacks, particularly in Italy, on the familiar psychological structure. Bernardino Telesio, for example, in his *De Rerum Natura,* had made sense the basis of all knowledge, had stated that the difference between the knowledge possible to man and the knowledge possible to animals was merely a difference of degree and not a difference of kind, and that what we call reason is but a refinement of sense, so that "the perceptive faculty, which seems to be proper to the human soul and is called rational, we think has manifestly been bestowed upon the souls of all other animals."[22] This is radical doctrine, and it is an expression of what was a general feeling among the advanced thinkers of the time: the old rigid order no longer gave a satisfactory explanation of nature, just as the Ptolemaic cosmology no longer gave a satisfactory picture of the heavens. But no one expressed this so strongly, or in such popular terms, as Montaigne. In fact his demolition of the old scheme was so thorough, and its implications so far-reaching, that we must describe it in some detail.

In 1569 Montaigne published his translation of

[22] *De Rerum Natura,* viii, ch. 15. The first two parts of this work were published in 1565 and 1570; the third part, from which my quotation is taken, did not appear until 1586, several years after Montaigne had written the *Apology*. But the thesis is clear throughout. I cannot find any evidence that the work was known to Montaigne.

Sabunde's *Natural Theology*. Sabunde had written the work about a hundred and thirty years earlier, and it had been so much admired by Montaigne's father that he had asked his son to turn its bad Latin into French. Thus the translation was an act of filial piety, and in no way a reflection of Montaigne's own interests. For what Sabunde had to say was sympathetic to the older generation, the earlier and more optimistic generation, of the sixteenth century, and nothing shows more clearly the close dependence of the Renaissance on the ideas of the Middle Ages than the fact that a work like the *Natural Theology* [144.], a product of late scholasticism, should have appealed so strongly to the father of Montaigne. What Sabunde sets out to do is to show that man can know himself by understanding the book of Nature which God has made for him; he can achieve this understanding by the use of his reason (Sabunde is so optimistic about man's capacity for achieving knowledge, even of God, through unaided reason, as to be almost heretical); the use of his reason shows man that he is the most important creature in the orderly ranks of creation—in fact it would be difficult to find a work more typical of the conventional picture of man's central place in the universe than the *Natural Theology* of Sabunde.

But Montaigne's pretended defense of it smashes the whole structure to pieces. Stimulated by his recent reading of skeptical philosophy, and irritated, perhaps, by the boredom of translating the naif and monotonous ideas of Sabunde, he proceeds to demolish Sabunde by launching an elaborate attack on the arrogance and vanity of man. Although on the surface he seems to be repeating merely the traditional platitudes about the misery of the human condition, Montaigne in fact goes very much deeper, and strikes at the entire inherited concept of what it means to be a human being. His purpose in writing the essay, he says, is to make people "sensible of the inanity, the vanity and insignificance of man; to wrest out of their fists the miserable weapons of their reason; to make them bow the head and bite the dust under the authority and reverence of the divine majesty."[23] How sincere Montaigne was in

[23] *Essays,* ii, 2, trans. E. J. Trechmann, Oxford, 1927, I, 439–440.

wanting to exalt the divine majesty, we shall probably never know; but there can be no doubt that he took a lively and ironic delight in describing the insignificance of man.

Let us then for the nonce consider man alone, without outside assistance, armed only with his own weapons, and destitute of the divine grace and knowledge, which comprise all his honor, his strength and the foundation of his being. Let us see how he will hold out in this fine equipment. Let him explain to me, by the force of his reason, on what foundation he has built those great advantages he thinks he has over the other creatures. What has induced him to believe that that wonderful motion of the heavenly vault, the eternal light of those torches rolling so proudly over his head, the awe-inspiring agitations of that infinite sea, were established, and endure through so many centuries, for his service and convenience? Is it possible to imagine anything more ridiculous than that this miserable and puny creature, who is not so much as master of himself, exposed to shocks on all sides, should call himself Master and Emperor of the universe, of which it is not in his power to know the smallest part, much less to command it?[24]

Montaigne continues,

The frailest and most vulnerable of all creatures is man, and at the same time the most arrogant. He sees and feels himself lodged here in the mud and filth of the world, nailed and riveted to the worst, the deadest and most stagnant part of the universe, at the lowest story of the house and the most remote from the vault of heaven, with the animals of the worst condition of the three; and he goes and sets himself in imagination above the circle of the moon, and brings heaven under his feet.[25]

In order, therefore, to see man as he really is and to crush his unjustified presumption, Montaigne begins by

[24] *Ibid.*, p. 441.
[25] *Ibid.*, p. 443. The three orders of animals are those on the earth, those in the water, and those in the air. Montaigne's argument is that since man lives on the lowest element, earth, he is in the worst condition.

201

making a detailed comparison between man and animals. This, to be sure, was nothing new; plenty of people, from the Greeks down, had pointed out that Nature looked after animals better than she looked after men, and that the animal condition was happier than the human.[26] But they had done so, at least in Christian writings, in order to make man more aware of his inner potentialities, and to show, through a description of his physical wretchedness, that he could rise above anything he might share with the animals into a state of rational or spiritual blessedness. A typical and popular work of this kind is the *Circe* of Giovanni-Battista Gelli (1549). Gelli tells us that when Ulysses was on Circe's island, Circe made an agreement with him. She would restore to his human shape any one of Ulysses' followers whom she had transformed into an animal, on one condition: Ulysses must persuade him that he will be better off as a man than as a beast. This seems to Ulysses an easy task, but, to his astonishment and chagrin, he finds, after talking with an oyster, a serpent, a hare, a goat, a hind, a lion, a horse, a dog and an ox, that not one of them will think for a moment of giving up his happy animal state to resume the miseries of the human condition. Not until Ulysses meets an elephant, who had been a philosopher before his transformation, does he find anyone who is willing to risk the change. The elephant, however, makes up for all the rest; Ulysses convinces him of the glories of being rational, and the former elephant, now a man once more, ends the book by chanting a hymn of praise to the Creator who has formed the world for man, the glorious possessor of reason, and the only sensible being who can understand the God who made him.

Such is the conclusion of Renaissance humanism. But such is not the conclusion of Montaigne. To Montaigne— the Montaigne of the *Apology*—man himself is only another animal, "he is subjected to the same obligation as the

[26] See George Boas and A. O. Lovejoy, *Primitivism and Related Ideas, Baltimore,* 1935. The two stock passages in classical literature which describe the superiority of the animal and which were most quoted in the sixteenth century were Plutarch's essay, the "Gryllus," and the opening of the seventh book of Pliny's *Natural History*.

other creatures of his order, and is of a very mediocre condition, without any real and essential prerogative and pre-eminence."[27] "I could easily make out a case for my general contention," he says, "that there is a greater difference between many a man and many another man, than between many a man and many an animal."[28] And he gives example after example of the intelligence, rationality, and high moral qualities of animals; they have ways of communicating with one another that we cannot understand; they share with us a kind of religion (as he proves by an example taken from the behavior of elephants), and, since they do so much that we cannot comprehend, it is clear not merely that they are our equals, but that there is "some pre-eminent faculty in them which is hidden from us."[29] In moral virtues they are particularly superior; unlike man, the animals do not make war on each other; they are both more faithful and more magnanimous than human beings. And, finally, to pursue, in Montaigne's words, "a little further this equality and correspondence between men and animals, the privilege that our soul glories in," the privilege hitherto attributed to man's soul alone, of abstracting from sensible phenomena their essential characteristics, "in order to make them conform to her [the soul's] own immortal and spiritual condition . . . this same privilege, I say, seems very evidently to be shared by the beasts."[30]

[27] *Essays,* I, 451.
[28] *Ibid.,* p. 458. This is going one step farther than Plutarch, on whose essay (*Moralia,* trans. Goodwin, v, 218), "That Brute Beasts make Use of Reason," Montaigne considerably depends. Plutarch had merely said, "I do not believe there is such a difference between beast and beast, in point of understanding and memory, as between man and man."
[29] *Ibid.,* p. 462.
[30] *Ibid.,* p. 475. Montaigne over-reaches himself here. As an examination of the text will show, he cannot give any examples of the way animals "abstract"—the particular function of reason—except those which an orthodox sixteenth-century psychologist would have attributed to the function of imagination: "For when we see a horse," he says, trying to support his argument, "accustomed to trumpets and battles and the rattle of musketry, shaking and trembling in his sleep while stretched on his litter, as if he were in the fray, it is certain that in his soul he imagines the beat of the

203

From the orthodox view, nothing could be more destructive than this. The orthodox view was that because man was able to abstract from sensible objects their essential forms, he could therefore rise to a knowledge of forms in general and hence to a knowledge of God, which was the goal of his existence. But Montaigne implies that animals could do the same thing. It is surprising that when the authorities in Rome examined the *Essais* in 1581, they said nothing about this point, but limited themselves to suggesting minor alterations: the *Essais* were not put on the Index until 1676. For St. Thomas Aquinas, who, only eighteen years before, at the Council of Trent, had been made the patron of Catholic theology, had said that if man, "who is led by faith to God as his last end, through ignoring the natures of things, and consequently the order of his place in the universe, thinks himself to be beneath certain creatures above whom he is placed," thereby derogating the natural dignity of his position, he is worthy of the same punishment that the Scriptures promise to heretics.[31] Yet this was just what Montaigne had alleged; he had said that there was no real difference between man and the other animals, and he thereby knocked man out of his crucial position in the natural hierarchy. If he was right, the whole traditional structure, so elaborately expounded by Sabunde, fell in ruins.

Once he has established this point to his satisfaction, it is easy for Montaigne to develop further his theme of man's ignorance and feebleness, and, as he says, to "strip him to his shirt." At his best, as exemplified by the philosophers, man can only come to the conclusion that he knows nothing. In the first place he knows nothing of God, and his presumption in thinking that God is made like him and that his affairs are the center of God's interest is entirely unfounded:

---

drum without noise, an army without body and without arms." This, however, cannot be called "abstraction"— it is merely the functioning of imagination or memory, faculties which belong to any creature with, like an animal, a sensitive soul. But the fact that Montaigne could not find a good illustration to prove his point does not matter; what does matter is that he wanted to make the point.

[31] *Summa contra Gentiles;* II, iii.

Therefore it was that Xenophanes wittily remarked, that if the animals create any gods, . . . as it is likely they do, they will certainly frame them in their own image, and glorify themselves as we do. For why should not a gosling say thus: "All things in the world concentrate upon me; the earth serves me to walk upon, the sun to give me light, the stars to communicate to me their influence; the winds benefit me in this way, the waters in that. There is nothing the vault of heaven looks upon so favorably as myself. I am the darling of Nature. Does not man keep me, house me, and wait upon me? For me he sows and grinds. If he eats me, so he does his fellow-man; and so do I the worms that kill and eat him."[32]

In the same fashion Montaigne ridicules the familiar arguments about man's knowledge of Nature. We presume to understand the architecture of the heavens by attributing to them "our own material, clumsy, terrestrial contrivances," and we have divided the Microcosmos, "this poor creature man," into a fantastic set of "offices and vocations" which bear no more relation to the facts than do our attempts to describe the movements of the planets. And if we know nothing of Nature, neither do we know anything about Reason and the soul. Only revelation can give us any knowledge, and as for the soul's being immortal,

let us ingenuously confess that God alone, and faith, have told us so; for it is not a lesson we have learned of Nature or of our reason. . . . Whoever will consider man without flattery, will see in him neither efficacy nor faculty that savors of anything but death and earth.[33]

Nor do we know anything of our bodies, nor of our desires. There are no standards—nothing is universally agreed upon. "Those people amuse me who, to give some certainty to laws, say that there are some that are fixed, perpetual and immutable, which they call laws of Nature," for, says Montaigne, there is not one of these laws "that is not rejected and disowned, not by one nation, but by many."[34] There may be laws of Nature in other creatures, "but in us they have vanished, this fine human reason of

[32] *Essays*, I, 533.
[33] *Ibid.*, p. 556.
[34] Vol. II, p. 26.

ours thrusting itself into everything, commanding and domineering, confusing and distorting the face of things, in its vanity and inconsistency."[35]

And, in conclusion, since nothing can be known of God or of the world or of the soul, since experience everywhere refutes any possibility of the existence of universal standards of belief or behavior, what of the senses? The rational soul of man has been proved completely useless; has he not at least a sensitive soul, like the other animals, on which he can rely? Certainly not, Montaigne answers. In the first place our senses are insufficient—we have too few of them.

> We have built up a truth through the consultation and concurrence of our five senses; but it would perhaps need the agreement and contribution of eight or ten to perceive it with certainty, and in its essence.[36]

And the five we have are notoriously inferior to those of other animals, being deceptive in every possible way. Therefore since "nothing comes to us that is not altered and falsified by our senses," any knowledge of reality is hopeless. "To judge the appearances we receive of things, we should need a judicatory instrument; to verify this instrument, we should need demonstration; to rectify this demonstration we should need an instrument: so here we are arguing in a circle."[37] "Finally," he adds, "there is no permanent existence, either of our being or that of the objects. And we, and our judgment, and all mortal things, incessantly go flowing and rolling on." And he ends his long skeptical orgy by saying that since man can do nothing by himself he must, if he is to rise from his miserable condition, abandon and renounce all his own powers by putting himself into the hands of God.

Thus Montaigne, by destroying the psychological order, destroys everything else; a human being who is indistinguishable from animals is not a human being who can comprehend the order of the universe or discover any Laws of Nature in society. Once more, in Donne's words, " 'Tis all in pieces, all coherence gone."

[35] *Ibid.*, p. 27.
[36] *Ibid.*, p. 38.
[37] *Ibid.*, p. 49.

The ideas of Machiavelli, which were more practical and less speculative than those of the new astronomers or of Montaigne, naturally received more attention. Equally subversive of all the old ideas of order and law, they had an immediate application to man's life in society which made their author seem a far more formidable menace. The reasons for this can perhaps best be realized by comparing *The Prince* and the *Discourses on Livy* with the *De Officiis* of Cicero, just as the effect of the Copernican system can best be seen by comparing it with the Ptolemaic, and the views of Montaigne in the *Apology* can most clearly be understood by contrasting them with those of the work he was apparently setting out to defend. For the *De Officiis* represents the official sixteenth century doctrine concerning the behavior of man as a governor. It was universally read; apart from many editions in Latin, there were at least eleven editions of the work in English between 1534 and 1616, and no sixteenth-century treatise on government was without some indebtedness to it.

According to Cicero, if a man is to control his fellow men and himself, justice is the essential virtue, and moral right is the basis of action.

> When the Stoics speak of the supreme good as "living conformably to nature," they mean, as I take it, something like this: that we are always to be in accord with virtue, and from all other things that may be in harmony with nature to choose only such as are not incompatible with virtue.[38]

"It is," he observes, "no mean manifestation of Nature and Reason that man is the only animal that has a feeling for order, for propriety, for moderation in word and deed. And so no other animal has a sense of beauty, loveliness, harmony in the visible world."[39] It is man's business to

---

[38] *De Officiis*, III, iii, 13, trans. Walter Miller, Loeb Classics.
[39] I, iv, 14.

develop this capacity through cultivation of the moral virtues, and so lead a tempered and rational life. All medieval thought, when describing a ruler, said the same thing; it was the basis of political theory, and like the other inherited views of man's nature, by presenting an ideal picture for him to live up to, it made man, and especially the prince, a responsible and moral being.

But Machiavelli took exactly the opposite view. He was fundamentally practical. He thought of the state, in the words of J. W. Allen, "as a morally isolated thing."[40] He regarded human history divorced from revelation, and human nature divorced from grace; he looked at man, as Bacon said, not as he should be, but as he is, and he found that man was naturally evil and that the best way to govern him for his own good was by fear and by force. Even in details Machiavelli directly contradicts the traditional view, as represented by Cicero. Cicero had written:

> There are two ways of settling a dispute: first, by discussion; second by physical force; and since the former is characteristic of man, the latter of the brute, we must resort to force only in case we may not avail ourselves of discussion.

And again:

> While wrong may be done . . . in either of two ways, that is, by force or by fraud, both are bestial: fraud seems to belong to the cunning fox, force to the lion; both are wholly unworthy of man, but fraud is the more contemptible.[41]

But Machiavelli, with Cicero's words obviously in mind, has very different things to say. In the famous eighteenth chapter of *The Prince* he writes as follows:

> You must know, then, that there are two methods of fighting, the one by law, the other by force: the first method is that of men, the second of beasts; but as the first method is often insufficient, one must have recourse to the second. It is therefore necessary for a prince to

[40] *History of Political Thought in the Sixteenth Century,* New York, 1928, p. 477.
[41] *De Officiis,* I, xi, 34; I, xiii, 41.

know well how to use both the beast and the man . . .
the one without the other is not durable.

A prince, "being thus obliged to know well how to
act as a beast, must imitate the fox and the lion, for
the lion cannot protect himself from traps, and the fox
cannot defend himself from wolves. One must therefore
be a fox to recognize traps, and a lion to frighten wolves
. . . therefore a prudent ruler ought not to keep faith
when by doing so it would be against his interest. . . .
If men were all good, this precept would not be a good
one, but as they are bad, and would not observe their
faith with you, so you are not bound to keep faith with
them.[42]

To Machiavelli any concept of universal justice, of the
Laws of Nature or of Nations, is quite irrelevant. Instead
of thinking of human government as a reflection of the
government of God, he suggests, as we have seen, that his
prince take on the characteristics of animals, and where
Montaigne had thought of man as incapable of knowledge,
since he is intellectually ignorant, Machiavelli takes it for
granted that he is incapable of good action, since he is
morally evil. "Whoever desires to found a state and give
it laws," he says in the *Discourses*, "must start with
assuming that all men are bad and ever ready to display
their vicious nature, whenever they may find occasion for
it."[43]

It was because Machiavelli based his instructions on
views like these that he so outraged sixteenth-century
sensibilities. Not realizing that he had, after all, a desirable
end in view—the unification of Italy—and perverting his
views and character into a figure of diabolic significance,
the later sixteenth century regarded him with mixed feelings of fascination and horror. Though for about half a
generation after *The Prince* was written in 1513 (it was
printed in 1532), its views attracted no very remarkable
degree of attention, once they were seriously considered,
the storm broke with what now seems extraordinary violence. No term of abuse was too strong for Machiavelli's
principles, works and character. The Jesuits of Ingoldstadt

[42] Trans. L. Ricci, Modern Library ed., New York, 1940, p. 64.
[43] Trans. C. E. Detmold, Modern Library ed., New York, 1940, bk.
i, ch. 3, p. 117.

burnt him in effigy; to Cardinal Pole he was obviously inspired by the devil; he was put on the Index as soon as that institution was established (1557); the Protestants considered his ideas directly responsible for the massacre of St. Bartholomew. He was universally described as an atheist and an unscrupulous fiend; he was referred to no fewer than 395 times in Elizabethan drama as the embodiment of human villainy; he became, in Signor Praz's words, "a rallying point for whatever was most loathsome in statecraft, and indeed in human nature at large."[44]

When we reflect upon the matter, this violence does not, after all, seem so extraordinary. For Machiavelli's realistic view of how things actually work, his statement that the ends justify the means, the deadly practicality of his unscrupulous precepts—all these violated the idealistic order which the men of the sixteenth century had been trained to believe in from childhood. "I want to write," said Machiavelli, "something that may be useful to the understanding man; it seems better for me to go behind to the real truth of things, rather than to a fancy picture."[45] And the real truth of things, as Machiavelli saw it, had no connection with the elaborate structure of inter-related hierarchies or with the responsibility of man to the universe. For him the real truth of things concerned practical matters and particular necessities; it had no bearing on morals or ideals. If Machiavelli was right all the inherited doctrines went for nothing, and man in society could no longer reflect the order of the cosmos or the order of created beings. No wonder he was called an atheist; by abandoning the conventional belief in the law of Nature, and by thinking entirely in terms of immediate practical necessity regardless of universal truth, he denied God's government of the world: once more the destruction of one hierarchy implied the destruction of the others as well. The sixteenth-century attacks on Machiavelli were in fact a defense, sometimes in hysterical terms, of the traditional

[44] Mario Praz, 'Machiavelli and the Elizabethans," *Proceedings of the British Academy,* xiii (1928), 8. See also E. Meyer, *Machiavelli and the Elizabethan Drama,* Weimar, 1897, and Lord Acton's introduction to Burd's great edition of *Il Principe.*
[45] Quoted John Morley, *Machiavelli,* London, 1897, p. 20.

dogma, and the hysteria may be taken as an indication that, below the surface, men realized—with a fascinated conviction which they were afraid to admit—that the ideas of Machiavelli might after all be true.

5

Thus, in the immediate intellectual background of the late sixteenth century, two main attacks were being made on the idealistic picture of the nobility and dignity of man. There was the traditional attack, which described man's wretchedness since the fall, but which was still based on a firm belief in man's crucial place in the center of things; and there was the newer attack, which in a threefold way, threatened to destroy that belief itself. At the time when Shakespeare's development as a craftsman reached its climax, this conflict also reached its climax, and we shall soon attempt to discover how Shakespeare, practising the type of writing which relies on conflict, was able to use it.

But the causes which made the conflict seem so sharp at the end of the sixteenth century are more complicated than those which I have described. So far I have regarded the situation from the long-range view of intellectual history alone, and in doing so I have perhaps over-simplified it. If we come closer for a moment to the actual scene, and try to imagine ourselves breathing the emotional and intellectual atmosphere of the time, we shall have to be aware of many other considerations than those which I have outlined. For to explain why it was that the opposing views of man's nature seemed, at that time, so violently to clash, and why the gloomy view seemed more and more to be the true one, we shall have to think of local circumstances, local fashions, local impulses, which no doubt appeared more important at the moment than either the ancient conflict or the new iconoclasms which reinforced it. For one thing there was the religious situation. By discarding her allegiance to the organization of Rome, England had, as it were, broken the mould in which the old ideas had been formed, and Protestantism, as Richard Hooker realized, had to re-shape them with new purposes in mind.

211

They had been moved—to change the metaphor—from one house to another, and they had been shaken up in the process. Hence it was natural to ask that if the medium, the Roman church and its organization, through which those ideas had for centuries been expressed, could be questioned and finally discarded as a system of lies and frauds, why could not the inherited ideas themselves be questioned and discarded too?

Furthermore Protestantism, in spite of the doctrine of predestination, put a new and greater emphasis on individual choice: it was a harder and tougher kind of moral life than the Roman one; the soul was no longer guarded from God's wrath by a series of shock-absorbers or saintly intermediaries; it stood face to face with the Almighty. As we look back on the period we are tempted to ask whether Protestantism, like the earlier Platonic glorification of man's capacity to raise himself to an angelic level, did not put more responsibility on human nature than it could stand, so that, for the time being, a reaction was bound to set in. Perhaps it did: at any rate the religious changes of the age made many sensitive minds doubtful about their religious allegiance, and skepticism went hand in hand with uncertainty. As Donne writes in his *Third Satire:*

> To adore, or scorn an image, or protest,
> May all be bad; doubt wisely; . . .
> > On a huge hill,
> Cragged and steep, Truth stands, and he that will
> Reach her, about must, and about must go;
> And what the hill's suddenness resists, win so.

These are not sentiments which lead to over-confidence, and it is interesting to observe that though at the time he wrote this satire—about 1594—Donne is merely anxious about the *form* of his belief, later on, when he wrote the *Anniversaries,* in 1611 and 1612, he questions its whole philosophic content.

If the religious situation seemed uncertain and insecure, so did the political situation. By the end of the 1590's Queen Elizabeth's reign was obviously coming to a close: that particular *primum mobile* could not turn the sphere of the state for very much longer. But it was by no means

212

assured who should take her place; and without her, and the kind of courtiership which her glorious if uncertain imperiousness involved, no one knew what might happen. There were rumblings in the economic order—too many monopolies and too many enclosures of land were causing dissatisfaction among those who found their hereditary privileges or their ambition cut down or thwarted. When popular literature (outside of the drama) turned away from romance to realism, and in the early 'nineties Robert Greene found it more profitable to describe the trickeries of pick-pockets than the love affairs of princesses, a different feeling was in the air from that which had inspired Spenser, in the 'eighties, to plan a huge poem which was to form a Christian gentleman in noble and virtuous discipline. In fact (though political events lay behind it) Spenser's death in the last year of the century—as a result, it was said, of starvation—can be seen by the symbolically-minded as a microcosmic reflection of what had happened to the ideals of the early Renaissance which had originally inspired him. The 1590's had begun—in spite of their professed admiration for his genius—to turn away from Spenser. Satire, of a realistic and mordant variety, was taking the place of literary idealism, and, particularly in the writings of Donne and Marston, was turning in the opposite direction from the order implied by allegory. The cult of melancholy—which became increasingly fashionable in the period—encouraged nothing but analysis and anatomy. It was based on something more realistic—or what seemed more realistic—than the optimism of a Neo-Platonist; it had affinities with the practicality of Machiavelli and with the skepticism of Montaigne. It saw, as Marston wrote in his "Cynic Satire" (1599), that though the other orders of nature fulfill their proper functions, man alone has lost his specific virtue:

And now no human creatures, once disray'd
Of that fair gem.
Beasts sense, plants growth, like being as a stone,
But out alas, our Cognizance is gone.[46]

Yet all this emphasis on man's tendency toward evil

[46] *Scourge of Villainy,* Satire vii.

made his position only the more dramatic. It had been a commonplace of traditional humanism that what differentiated man from the other orders was that he could choose: he had free will. The angels were not called upon to choose; they were *above* choice because they directly understood universal truth through intellect. The animals were *below* choice because they failed to understand universal truth, being limited to sense. But the glory of man, who was half intellect and half sense, was that he could, through free will, decide to which level he belonged. According to Pico della Mirandola God had said to Adam —and to all other men as well—"Thou shalt have the power to degenerate into the lowest forms of life, the animal; thou shalt have the power, out of thy soul's judgment, to be reborn into the higher forms of life which are divine."[47] To Pico and the other earlier humanists, man belonged with the angels. But to Montaigne, and the satiric, melancholy, realistic writers of the 1590's, he belonged with the beasts. The reawakened emphasis on man's bestiality, on his disruption, through wrong choice, of God's order in the world, in nature and in the state, was all the more tragic because of the potentialities it at once revealed and destroyed. The earlier Renaissance had emphasized the revelation of those potentialities by comparing man with the angels; the later Renaissance emphasized their destruction by comparing man with the animals. The result, at the end of the sixteenth century, was what Robert Frost, in our own day, has described in another connection:

> As long on earth
> As our comparisons were stoutly upward
> With gods and angels, we were men at least,
> But little lower than the gods and angels.
> But once comparisons were yielded downward,
> Once we began to see our images
> Reflected in the mud and even dust,
> 'Twas disillusion upon disillusion.
> We were lost piecemeal to the animals,
> Like people thrown out to delay the wolves.[48]

[47] *Oratio de Hominis Dignitate,* trans. Elizabeth L. Forbes, *Journal of the History of Ideas,* III (1942), 348. See also G.-B. Gelli, *Circe,* bk. x.
[48] *"The White-tailed Hornet."*

In Shakespeare's time many people felt in the same fashion. For through the old orderly scheme, which the new astronomy and the ideas of Montaigne and Machiavelli were shaking to its foundations, may have given a false view of reality, at least it represented a pattern to which thought and imagination could refer. To destroy it was to shake human confidence and to emphasize man's weakness and emptiness. "Doth any man doubt," asks Bacon in his essay on Truth,

> that if there were taken out of men's minds vain opinions, flattering hopes, false valuations, imaginations as one would, and the like, but it would leave the minds of a number of men poor shrunken things, full of melancholy and indisposition, and unpleasing to themselves?

To Bacon's question only an affirmative answer was possible. The age was ripe for tragedy.

For as we reflect upon the conflict which I have described as the essential element in Shakespeare's intellectual and emotional background, it appears that nothing could have been more propitious for the writing of great tragic drama. In the periods when great tragedy has been written, two things seem to have been necessary: first, a conventional pattern of belief and behavior, and second, an acute consciousness of how that conventional pattern can be violated. The convention may be a social one, and the violation a social violation: the result is the drama of Ibsen. Or the convention may be the law of the gods, and the violation, like that of Prometheus or Orestes, may be a religious violation: the result is the drama of Aeschylus. In Shakespeare's day the convention included everything—it was the whole inherited picture of man in the system of the universe, of Nature and of the state; it was religious, moral and social; it was a vast inclusive pattern of order. The violation of this order, as I have tried to show, was being felt everywhere at the end of the sixteenth century, and it was a violation which when it occurred in any one part, was felt throughout the whole structure. It was because Shakespeare, as he developed his art, was able to see individual experience in relation to the all-inclusive conflict produced by this violation, that his great tragedies have such wide reverberations and give us so profound a picture of the nature of man.

# THE ORDER AND CONTINUANCE OF NATURE

## By Geoffrey Bush

When Sir Andrew Aguecheek and Sir Toby Belch are in admirable fooling, Sir Andrew announces proudly: "Ay, he does well enough if he be dispos'd, and so do I too. He does it with a better grace, but I do it more natural." Not all of us would say with such enthusiam that we were natural fools. But each of us belongs to nature; a part of ourselves is natural, and we are a part of the natural world.

I should like to consider what it means to Shakespeare's characters to belong to nature. Recent criticism has suggested that Shakespeare's characters, and what they do and believe, should be seen in relation to the Elizabethan idea of natural order. I would, to some small extent, take issue with this recent criticism. But others have spoken of these matters with a better grace, and I should say at once that I have no absolute conclusions to reach; there are no conclusions to be had about nature, or about Shakespeare's plays. His business is with the imagination; perhaps the most important thing we can say about his plays is that they come to no conclusions; and concerning nature John Donne wrote with some impatience: "This terme the law of Nature, is so variously and unconstantly deliver'd, as I confesse I read it a hundred times before I understand it once."

The term "nature" is variously delivered in Shakespeare's plays. But there are two ways in which nature

216

has always been understood: it means both the nature of things, and natural things in themselves. It is a name for both the law of the world, and the world itself. These are the two ways in which nature is defined in *The French Academy*: "When they speake generallie of nature, they make two principall kindes: the one spirituall, intelligible and the unchangeable beginning of motion and rest, or rather the vertue, efficient, and preserving cause of all things: the other, sensible, mutable, and subject to generation and corruption, respecting all things that have life, and shall have end."

To speak more briefly, *The French Academy* goes on, "Nature is the order and continuance of the works of god." But it is an order and continuance that has two aspects: it is an idea of natural law, and the fact of natural things. Nature means both the unchanging natural principle of the world, the preserving cause of all things, and the changing face of the world, all things that have life and shall have end. It is a name for whatever is natural, *natura naturata,* and for the reason why it is natural, *natura naturans.* In the last book of *The Faerie Queene* the Sergeant Order is a servant of the Goddess Nature; but nature is also represented as a changing pageant of the seasons and months and hours. And the Goddess Nature herself is a figure of double beauty, old and young, changing and unchanging, seen and unseen.

Nature is a fact of change and an idea beyond change; its double aspect is what places human nature in so dramatic a position, created sick, as Fulke Greville wrote, but commanded to be sound; and through this double aspect Shakespeare's characters, at their greatest moments, become involved both with things in themselves and with the meaning of things. When Hamlet waits for the fencing match, he says: "Sir, I will walk here in the hall." It is the breathing time of day with him; there is misgiving in his heart, but he says to Horatio: "If it be now, 'tis not to come; if it be not to come, it will be now; if it be not now, yet it will come: the readiness is all." We know nothing more about Hamlet that we did before; he has promised to do no more than walk in the hall; yet he seems to have come to terms with his world. It is the most mysterious moment in the play, a point of unexpected stillness and security and at the same time of strange unease, when every possibility of his natural situation is brought into our minds. There is a similar moment in *King Lear*. After the storm, when Lear wakes in the arms of Cordelia, he tells her: "You are a spirit, I know." Lear is mistaken; she is not a spirit; yet she seems so. These are points in experience when natural life seems to belong both to time and to what is beyond time; when Hamlet is acting and not acting, and Cordelia is a spirit and not a spirit; when we are made most aware of what it means to act and believe within both the aspects of natural life; and these moments are what I should like to speak of.

2

But what are we able to say of these moments? Nothing is concluded; they are events in which character is implicated in both aspects of nature at once.

It has been proposed by recent criticism that Shakespeare's vision looks toward the further aspect of nature: that it was shaped by the Elizabethan idea of natural order, the doctrine of the first chapter of *The Governor* or the first book of the *Ecclesiastical Polity,* a picture of a world of arrangement and harmony. "A doctrine of Nature," Mr. E. C. Knowlton says, "constitutes the core of the view of life held by Shakespeare," and according to this doctrine the "purposes of conduct and of art are to know Nature and to follow her." But *Hamlet* and *King Lear* are pictures of natural disorder; there is great pain attending what Hamlet and Lear come to know about nature, and there is great doubt whether they should follow nature. There is doubt, I think, whether a doctrine of natural order constitutes the core of Shakespeare's view of life. Certainly the doctrine of order is everywhere in Elizabethan writing and in Shakespeare's plays; it can be said to shape the vision of the histories and comedies, and the most famous of all its Elizabethan expressions is Ulysses' speech in *Troilus and Cressida.* Yet everywhere in Shakespeare's plays there is profound concern for the other aspect of natural life, natural things in themselves. The doctrine of order does not explain all that Shakespeare saw in *Hamlet* and *King Lear;* it is too large a philosophy, or not large enough, to explain how his vision links both aspects of the natural situation, the continuance of things and things in themselves.

There is a tendency of mind to seek out meaning: the Elizabethan doctrine of order belongs to this effort toward conclusive statement. The doctrine of order has not survived: we no longer believe in degree and hierarchy, or in the Goddess Nature; the wench is dead, and her natural law has fallen in station, through the centuries, from the decree of God in the Renaissance, to the voice of reason in the eighteenth century, to the cry of the Romantic imagination, and now to mutterings from the unconscious. The history of the great chain of being, Mr. Arthur O. Lovejoy says, "is the history of a failure; more precisely and more justly, it is the record of an experiment in thought carried on for many centuries by many great and lesser minds, which can now be seen to have had an instructive negative outcome." And while the idea of order has not survived, *Hamlet* and *King Lear* have survived: they belong to a different enterprise of the mind, concerned with matters more personal, more obscure, and more exacting of our fears and affections. They are an experiment in thought that did not end in failure; and what is striking about them is that their outcome is so incomplete and inconclusive.

Shakespeare's art is traditionally associated with nature. But the purpose of this traditional association has been to show Shakespeare's adherence to persons and events in themselves. His first editors, Heminge and Condell, said that Shakespeare was "a happie imitator of Nature." What they meant was that he wrote with a natural ease: "His mind and hand went together: And what he thought, he uttered with that easinesse, that wee have scarse received from him a blot in his papers." Perhaps there was scarcely a blot in his papers; other writers have said that their best work was written easily; and it was a remark of this sort that caused Ben Jonson to deliver his brief and notable response: "My answer hath beene, would he had blotted a thousand." Whether he did so or not, there is a quality of naturalness about Shakespeare's characters and situations, and about the art itself. A later editor, Dr. Johnson, said that Shakespeare was "above all writers, at least above all modern writers, the poet of nature." Dr. Johnson meant that Shakespeare's plays are pictures of the variety of natural fact: they are works "exhibiting the real state of sublunary nature, which partakes of good and evil, joy and sorrow, mingled with endless variety of proportion and innumerable modes of combination; and expressing the course of the world, in which the loss of one is the gain of another; in which, at the same time, the reveller is hasting to his wine, and the mourner burying his friend; in which the malignity of one is sometimes defeated by the frolick of another; and many mischiefs and many benefits are done and hindered without design." In this manner Shakespeare is a poet of nature indeed; for variety, as Sir Walter Raleigh wrote in the Preface to *The History of the World,* is a primary attribute of nature: "there being nothing wherein Nature so much triumpheth, as in dissimilitude. From whence it commeth, that there is found so great diversity of opinions; so strong a contrariety of inclinations; so many naturall and unnaturall; wise, foolish; manly, and childish affections, and passions in Mortall Men." These qualities in Shakespeare's work of naturalness and ease, and of engagement to the variety of persons and things, are what prevent conclusions, and make the vision itself, through the diversity of its opinions, seem without design.

There is another traditional judgment, besides the judgment that Shakespeare was a poet of nature; it is that he was a poet without art. When Ben Jonson wrote his memorial poem to Shakespeare, he said first, as so many others were to say later, that the Goddess Nature herself was proud of Shakespeare's designs. But in an earlier and less guarded moment Jonson said shortly that "Shakspear wanted Arte." And in our own time another severe and learned classical poet has remarked briefly that *Hamlet* is "most certainly an artistic failure." Dr. Johnson thought that Shakespeare wrote with the power of nature, but he confessed that Shakespeare seemed also to write without any moral purpose. Shakespeare does not supply us, Edward Dowden said, with a doctrine, with an interpretation, with a revelation. And most recently Mr. D. G. James thinks that Shakespeare wrote "without a philosophy," and that in *King Lear* he looked upon the world with a "bleak and merely exploratory vision." Certainly there is justice in this traditional opinion. What Dr. Johnson said of poetry in general is true especially of Shakespeare's plays—they belong to those human works of which the excellence is not absolute and definite, but gradual and comparative. There are no characters in the plays who tell us all that Shakespeare means; his imagination is both within them and without, proposing possibilities, hints and guesses, and statements that are, as it were, unfinished.

Milton wrote in *Areopagitica* that Truth came once into the world in a perfect shape, most glorious to look on, and now she is scattered in a thousand pieces. Truth displays one colored ensign, Chapman said, while the world pursues ten thousand colors. But the ten thousand colors of the world are what Shakespeare's vision makes known: his concern is with the scattered fragments of truth that reside in the actions and beliefs of particular men and women. He keeps at all times, as Coleridge said, on the high road of life, and in the main march of human affections. Mr. Alfred Harbage adds that Shakespearian tragedy is a high road leading home, telling us what we have always known. Surely this is true. But which of us knows his home? The tragic journey toward what we have always known is never completed; what is important about it is the journeying; poetry, in Mr. Archibald MacLeish's phrase, is a "continuing action," an involvement in knowing that is never ended.

The attachment to particular persons and events characterizes most of English poetry; the Western tradition in art is an endorsement of the importance of individual natural fact. Perhaps this is a result of Christianity and the other movements toward individualism in modern Western thought; whatever the reason, there is a difference between the architectural clarity of Greek tragedy and the engagement to things in themselves that is represented in the writing of even the most philosophic of Renaissance poets, Chapman or Milton. *Paradise Lost* has an epic design, but the subject is the event through which humanity forfeited a share in its own grand design; and the moment toward which Milton's vision is moving comes when Adam and Eve, hand in hand, through Eden take their solitary way. This commitment of English literature to things in themselves issues most fully in Shakespeare's plays; and through this commitment *Hamlet* and *King Lear* are a way of knowing that is itself "natural." His art, like nature, has a double aspect, an attachment to persons and events that in its final moments suggests a continuance of meaning.

## 3

We think of Shakespeare's plays as a kind of knowledge. Hamlet tells the Players that the purpose of playing is to hold the mirror up to nature; a play makes nature known to itself. And near the end of Lear's storm, after we have been an audience to the worst of Lear's suffering, Edgar says:

> When we our betters see bearing our woes,
> We scarcely think our miseries our foes.
> Who alone suffers suffers most i' th' mind,
> Leaving free things and happy shows behind;
> But then the mind much sufferance doth o'erskip
> When grief hath mates, and bearing fellowship.

There is comfort in watching the suffering of others; it is a means of knowing our own griefs, and of finding them, perhaps, in everyone. We reach a sense of community, and by the "art of known and feeling sorrows" we discover ourselves. Certainly at the end of *Hamlet* and *King Lear* there is a sense of comfort, and of knowledge; something of great importance has been discovered about natural life. But what has been concluded, and what agreement has been reached? Nothing is said in *Hamlet* and *King Lear* that has the certainty of the knowledge offered by Shakespeare's two most distinguished contemporaries in the theater. Chapman and Webster take sides, and we know where they stand; their plays are comprehensive statements about the natural condition.

In Chapman's vision things and the continuance of things are closely allied. A man is built with God's finger; the world is constructed perfect and free; and a man's chief virtue is glad obedience to the high and general cause. The world and the law of the world are a single reality; time and its continuance are joined in ourselves through right action and right reason. It is Webster's judgment, on the other hand, that the persons and events of natural life are far removed from the arrangement that gives them meaning: heaven fashioned us of nothing, and we bring ourselves to nothing; the soul in the body is a lark in a cage, looking toward a distant heaven; our natural life is a long war, a general mist of error, a slow misery that ends in the moment of fright and dazzle when we may win a kind of virtue by the manner in which we encounter death. The world and its reason are divorced, and to do and believe rightly is to flee the world and hope for grace. The positions taken by Chapman and Webster are as contrary as they could well be; they belong, more or less, to the philosophic traditions that are associated with the names of Aquinas and Augustine, and in the Renaissance with Hooker and Calvin. They are traditions that are a part of our most fundamental ways of thinking; to put the matter most simply, they are estimates of how near or how far things are from the significance of things. Things and their significance are in close conjunction in Aquinas and Hooker, and in Chapman's plays. In Augustine and Calvin things arc divided from their significance, and judgments of this sort inform the metaphysical shudder of Webster's tragedies; through the consequence of our ancient calamity in Eden there is no good in us, and what restoration is possible is the work of intervening grace.

The plays of Chapman and Webster are *drames à thèse*.

Chapman's plays are constructed to demonstrate a philosophy, and Webster's to exhibit human beings in every posture of unhappiness. "I would have these things," one of Chapman's characters says, "Brought upon stages." In the direct statements that Chapman and Webster propose, and through the open assault that their plays make upon our minds, the world and the stage become one: "I account this world," the Duchess of Malfi says, "a tedious Theatre," and another of Webster's characters kills someone in a mist —such a mistake, he says, as he has often seen in a "play." There is the same equation between life and the theater in what Hamlet tells the Players; it gives to Shakespeare's poetic and dramatic vision much of its moral weight; but it is an equation that in *Hamlet* and *King Lear* leads to a different kind of statement, and another way of knowing.

4

Two other contemporaries of Shakespeare's undertook to propose conclusive explanations of nature. Some parts of Spenser's *Faerie Queene* and Bacon's *Instauratio Magna* were written within a dozen years of each other, and within the same short period Shakespeare was carrying out his poetic and dramatic exploration of nature. This in itself, as Mr. James says of Shakespeare's work and Bacon's, is a thought to give us pause: that at the same moment in history these three great endeavors were launched, a religious explanation of nature, a scientific explanation, and a poetic and dramatic experiment that is committed wholly to neither things nor meaning.

Spenser's religious vision in *The Faerie Queene* turns toward the meaning of things. His Goddess Nature is a two-fold figure, including in herself both the world and the design of the world; the natural changes of the world are a part of her pattern. And it is toward a still greater pattern that Spenser looks in the last lines of Book VII; though the Goddess Nature can explain mutability, Spenser looks beyond her explanation to the time "when no more *Change* shall be." *The Faerie Queene* directs us beyond the natural

224

world to a religious order; the events, Spenser wrote in his letter to Sir Walter Raleigh, are "a continued Allegory, or darke conceit," standing for greater events in a further order and continuance. But it was Bacon's plan to isolate and explore natural events by themselves: to perfect (in the English of James Spedding) "a natural philosophy pure and unmixed." The *Novum Organum,* he said, was his part "towards the commencement of the great undertaking," the enterprise in which he was building in the human understanding "a true model of the world, such as it is in fact, not such as a man's own reason would have it to be." It cannot be said that Bacon's vision excludes the religious explanation of nature, or that Spenser's excludes the secular explanation; but Spenser's tendency is to join these explanations and Bacon's is to set them apart. What is in question is whether the temporal aspect of the world is an arrangement that would explain itself, if it were fully understood, or whether, because it is part of a divine arrangement, it leans on a further explanation, already partly revealed. From the history of later thought we know that Bacon prevailed. There exists now the division between religion and science that Bacon instituted when he distinguished between their two manners of understanding: "The knowledge of man is as the waters, some descending from above, and some springing from beneath; the one informed by the light of nature, the other inspired by divine revelation."

*The Faerie Queene* and the *Novum Organum* were not written in debate; Bacon was not the first natural philosopher, nor the first to distinguish between the ways of apprehending the two aspects of nature; and Spenser set down what he considered to be the common knowledge of all men. But their visions represent, at a time of philosophic change, the way that thought had taken and the way that thought was to take; they represent the explanations of nature that were made in the centuries before 1600 and that have been made since.

We are able to consider Shakespeare's plays at these crossroads of thought, when two great movements of the human spirit, endorsements of the unity or division of experience, began to go their separate ways. We can, to some degree, place Chapman and Webster on these different roads. It is clear enough that Spenser and Chapman belong together in their classical and Christian humanism; they would see things and the continuance of things as a single whole. It is less clear, but I think it can be argued, that Bacon and Webster are to be associated in their division of things and meaning. They each put their trust in a different aspect of nature—Bacon looks toward the world and Webster toward what is beyond the world—but either choice belongs to the trend of thought that has resulted in the modern view of experience as divided and fragmentary. Bacon and Webster are committed to their different conclusions, and Spenser and Chapman to another certainty; it is Shakespeare's natural and easy art that seems, in modern terms, to be "unengaged."

5

Bacon called his undertaking an "argument of hope." Both *The Faerie Queene* and the *Instauratio Magna* are arguments of hope, and efforts of the mind toward conclusions. Bacon and Spenser were aware of the incompleteness of all human knowledge, and of the cause, the far-off divine event at the beginning of the Christian history of nature; but their inquiry, as Bacon said, was "whether that commerce between the mind of man and the nature of things, which is more precious than anything on earth, or at least than anything that is of the earth, might by any means be restored to its perfect and original condition." There are loose ends in *The Faerie Queene,* and ends that will not fit, but in it Spenser included all the religious and ethical affairs of human life; Prince Arthur, Spenser wrote in his letter to Raleigh, is "the image of a brave knight, perfected in the twelve private morall vertues." Prince Arthur is a perfect image; and three years after Spenser wrote to Raleigh, Bacon wrote a letter to Sir William Cecil to explain his "vast contemplative ends" and to say that "I have taken all knowledge to be my province."

"I propose to establish," Bacon declared, "progressive stages of certainty." We know that his enterprise, though it prevailed, was not to be so successful as he dreamed. But his words are like a trumpet call; and there is a different sound to the soldiers' music that proclaims the death of Hamlet, or in Edgar's frail and hopeless flourish at the end of *King Lear*. While *The Fairie Queene* and the *Instauratio Magna* were never finished, and are only pieces of their authors' intentions, *Hamlet* and *King Lear* are in a more essential manner unfinished. When Una sees the Dwarf carrying the armor of the Red Cross Knight, she asks to hear "the wofull Tragedie." It is not a tragedy at all; the Red Cross Knight is not dead, he will conquer and marry, and his woes are comprehended in the great progression toward salvation. The story of Leyr and Cordelia is told in Book II of *The Faerie Queene,* and neither is this a tragic story; it is part of English history, and a step in the historical progress toward Elizabeth and Gloriana.

Bacon said that there are two kinds of contemplation: "the one, arduous and difficult in the beginning, leads out at last into the open country; while the other, seeming at first sight easy and free from obstruction, leads to pathless and precipitous places." *The Faerie Queene* and Bacon's natural philosophy would lead us to this open country; they would bring us, in Bacon's words, to stand upon the hill of truth, where the air is always clear and serene. Spenser's Red Cross Knight stands on the hill of Contemplation and looks toward the New Jerusalem; and Bacon was called a Moses who led his people to the verge of the Promised Land. It is "heaven upon earth," Bacon said, "to have a man's mind move in charity, rest in providence, and turn upon the poles of truth." So both Bacon and Spenser would say, looking toward heaven upon earth, or toward heaven itself.

From the hill of Truth, Bacon said, we see the errors and wanderings and mists in the vale below. Yet these are the subject of Shakespeare's plays, the errors and wanderings, and the moving accidents by flood and field; and his vision, while it seems at first sight easy and natural, and expressed in the beauty and formality of poetry, leads us at the end to pathless and precipitous places, and extremities of the human spirit. In *The Advancement of Learning,* Bacon gave his famous judgment of poetry: it is a branch of human knowledge, and one of the principal portions of learning, but "it doth raise and erect the mind, by submitting the shews of things to the desires of the mind; whereas reason doth buckle and bow the mind unto the nature of things." The kind of poetry that Bacon allowed to be nearest the truth was allegory, the poetry of *The Faerie Queene,* where things in themselves are an emblem of the nature of things. There is no such correspondence in *Hamlet* and *King Lear;* our pity and terror are for the events as they are. *Hamlet* and *King Lear* are not statements about action and belief; they are acting, and make-believe, and the vision, in Bacon's words, is "a dream of learning." In Hamlet the perfect image of the courtier, scholar, soldier is quite, quite down; his life is a story of intendments gone awry, of accidental judgments and purposes mistook. At the end he seems to have reached an agreement with his situation: but what has he done? His agreement is no more than to accept the challenge to the fencing match, and then it is neither yes nor no, but only, "Sir, I will walk here in the hall." We know only what Hamlet says about himself, and what he says is unfinished; he breaks off, he has no more time to speak, and "the rest is silence." And at the end of *King Lear* there is no image of order; the figures on the stage form a picture of distress, and we that are young shall never live so long nor see so much. It is when Lear enters with Cordelia dead in his arms that Kent asks: "Is this the promis'd end?" And Edgar asks in return: "Or image of that horror?" Shakespeare's vision does not end with a revelation or a philosophy, or with progressive stages of certainty.

6

But it was Shakespeare's first editors who said that "these Plays have had their triall alreadie, and stood out all Appeales." *Hamlet* and *King Lear,* no doubt, are Shakespeare's greatest plays; they are, at any rate, the plays in which nature is mentioned most often. They are the very seamark of an utmost sail; in *Hamlet* and *King Lear* Shakespeare explores the furthest reaches of what it means to belong both to things and to the continuance of things. And what I have to say about nature in *Hamlet* and *King Lear* is the consequence of a question asked by Mr. Arthur Sewell in his book *Character and Society in Shakespeare*. It is the question, Mr. Sewell says, around which Shakespeare fashioned his picture of the natural situation: "How shall man find the intersection between that which is in time and that which is out of time?" Or more simply: "What shall we do to be saved?"

Shakespeare's characters belong to time and the world; they have a natural constitution, natural passions, natural feeling, and natural reason. They are moved by excitements of their reason and their blood to share in the duties and pains and affections of natural life. In what they do and believe there is represented a deep involvement in persons and things; through this involvement Shakespeare's characters experience their profits and losses, and we are moved to pity and admiration by our understanding of the glories and mistakes of this involvement. Yet Shakespeare's characters are not wholly a part of the natural world. They are divided from their world; they are made to stand at one remove from their situation, and to undertake the effort of knowing and replying to the world. Their world, as it were, takes on an identity of its own; it has a shape and voice, and addresses those within it. The moral laws of nature and of nations, Hector says, "speak aloud." The Ghost speaks aloud to Hamlet, and in the storm Lear is addressed by the elements. And at their greatest moments Shakespeare's characters make their reply; at the end of the tragic progress it belongs not only to their suffering, but to their honor, that they stand apart from the world. They know the world and judge it, and they step forward to make their own address; they strike an attitude in the face of the world, and announce that they are natural fools, that "I am Bottom the weaver," or that "This is I, Hamlet the Dane."

It is at these moments that their involvement in nature becomes most complicated and precious. For to belong to nature is to be involved in an arrangement that at its most distant points touches what is beyond things in themselves. There is "terror for that which is out of time," Mr. Sewell says, "and pity for that which is in time, and they make a single experience." This single experience is the end of Shakespeare's vision; it is, as it were, the Shakespearean moment. When Lear and Cordelia in prison will be God's spies, or when Hamlet tells Horatio that there is a special providence in the fall of a sparrow, moments seem to have been reached, at some remote limit of natural life, when there is made known the possibility of a settlement between the two aspects of nature.

It is not good, Bacon said, to remain too long in the theater; and having given his judgment of poetry Bacon turned to graver matters and would not stay for an answer. But Shakespeare's vision expresses itself through the words and gestures of the theater; it reaches toward a different advancement of our learning, a way of knowing and settling with the world by which we are drawn into the continuing action of poetry and the theater. What saddens us at Hamlet's death is that he has no more time to speak, and no further words with which to record his life; but it is a great comfort, and an argument of hope, that Horatio will report Hamlet and his cause aright. He will tell Hamlet's "story" in "this harsh world." In the equation between the world and the theater, it is Shakespeare's perception that life itself is a dramatic situation of address and reply, expressed most easily and naturally in the small globe of the stage. There is a profound commerce between our lives and the gestures of the theater; it is Hamlet's most glorious accomplishment to have made his life into a "story." Shakespeare's vision reaches toward a settlement with nature that in the deepest sense is a poetic and dramatic settlement: not a moment of certainty, the point in T. S. Eliot's *Four Quartets* when through the relinquishment of things in themselves we arrive at the still center of the turning world; but a moment when natural life is addressed by every voice, by things and by the meaning of

230

things; when the possibilities of natural life go beyond even the power of words, and when it is right and proper that the rest is silence, and that Hamlet should say:

O, I could tell you—

But let it be.

## V

ELIZABETHAN INTELLECTUAL FERMENT
AND THE TRAGIC DRAMA

*The first selection, Clifford Leech's "The Tragic Picture," was originally published as part of Chapter 2 (pages 28-44) in his book* Shakespeare's Tragedies, and Other Studies in Seventeenth Century Drama. *The second selection, Irving Ribner's "Introduction," was originally the introduction to his book* Jacobean Tragedy, The Quest for Moral Order.

## THE TRAGIC PICTURE

### By Clifford Leech

A glance at W. P. Barrett's *Chart of Plays* 1584–1623[1] brings it home that nearly all the pre-Civil War tragedies of lasting value were written in the first dozen years of the seventeenth century. There belong the four major tragedies of Shakespeare, together with *Antony, Coriolanus* and *Timon,* the *Bussy, Biron* and *Chabot* plays of Chapman, Jonson's *Sejanus* and *Catiline,* Webster's *The White Devil* and *The Duchess,* Tourneur's *The Revenger's Tragedy.* Outside that period we can find Marlowe, whose strain is so different that Mr. Eliot has judged him to be a comic dramatist *in posse,*[2] and whose plays veer between an unchecked enthusiasm which the tragic writer hardly knows and a chaos of caricature which would make impossible a tragic concern with an individual's destiny; and later on we find Middleton and Massinger and Ford—Middleton very close to the great decade and almost part

[1] *Chart of Plays 1584–1623,* compiled by W. P. Barrett for the Shakespeare Association, 1934.
[2] *Selected Essays,* 1934, p. 125.

of it in his *The Changeling* and *Women Beware Women;*
Massinger a reliable but superficial dramatist, hardly
pursuing his themes with great concernment; Ford, as
individual in his way as Marlowe, the one man whose
poetic boldness made genuine tragedy possible in the reign
of Charles—though even his work has a nostalgic ring,
a forced echo which makes him an early Beddoes as well
as a late Webster. Apart from these, the later years before
the closing of the theatres have many self-styled tragedies
and many tragicomedies which alike derive from the Beaumont and Fletcher formula: with these we need not concern
ourselves, for only at rare moments, in *Thierry and Theo-
doret* for example, do we find a suggestion of the tragic
vision in the Beaumont and Fletcher plays.

If, then, nearly all the tragic work that matters comes
from a brief space within the Elizabethan and Jacobean
period, we can I think assume that there were special
reasons for this early decline of tragic drama. The primary
reason, it appears, was that during approximately the
years 1600–10 there came a phase both in the current of
Elizabethan thought and in the development of the playhouse that led men to the tragic idea and facilitated its
dramatic expression. But the remarkable brevity of the
period within which tragedy flourished was due also to
the dramatists' imperfect comprehension of their own
achievement. While writing plays that explored suffering
and evil and that found those things an ineluctable inheritance, while looking into the darkness and finding no
stay but in man's temporarily unconquerable mind, they
could still speak of "elegant and sententious excitation to
virtue" and apologise for the absence of a Chorus or
Nuntius. Their approach to tragic writing, in fact, was
instinctive, flowering almost unaided in the ground they
stood on.

Perhaps the clearest indication of this instinctive urge
towards the tragic is to be found in the prologue to
Marston's *Antonio's Revenge,* which was acted in 1599 or
thereabouts and conveniently ushers in the great decade.
In its many anticipations of the theme and the incidents
of *Hamlet,* Marston's play has some claim on a scholar's
attention, but its confusion of thought and turgidity of

manner blunt its dramatic effect. Only in the prologue does Marston speak out with a crabbed eloquence, finding first of all an appropriateness to his play's mood in the wintry season of the year, and then inviting sympathy for his characters' woes from those who have themselves known true sorrow: the pampered ones of the world, who have known only good fortune and a light heart, will be appalled by the play's darkness, will in fact recognise no link between themselves and the imagined characters. But this part of the prologue is worth quoting:

>                         Therefore, we proclaime,
> If any spirit breathes within this round,
> Uncapable of waightie passion
> (As from his birth, being hugged in the armes,
> And nuzzled twixt the breastes of happinesse)
> Who winkes, and shuts his apprehension up
> From common sense of what men were, and are,
> Who would not knowe what men must be; let such
> Hurrie amaine from our black visag'd showes:
> We shall affright their eyes. But if a breast,
> Nail'd to the earth with griefe: if any heart
> Pierc't through with anguish, pant within this ring:
> If there be any blood, whose heate is choakt
> And stifled with true sense of misery:
> If ought of these straines fill this consort up,
> Th' arrive most welcome.

The implications are several: that this kind of drama is "black visag'd," frightful; that its darkness corresponds to a darkness in actuality, not universally experienced but palpable to those who do not shut their apprehension up "From common sense of what men were, and are," who in fact "knowe what men must be"; that the effect of the play is to be achieved only if there is in the spectator a pre-existent knowledge of this darkness. There is here no suggestion of a reforming value in the drama, only the idea that the audience will understand the dramatist's picture of life if their own is not unlike it. Marston gives us no coherent theory of the tragic, no comment on the nature of the tragic hero, no suggestion of a delicate balancing between pride in human nature and terror at the image of the world presented. No more than his greater successors in tragic drama had Marston worked out his ideas, but certainly this prologue points to a state of affairs in the minds of dramatic authors which led them to write tragically about this time, led them to seek the companionship of others whose breasts were "Nail'd to the earth with griefe," whose hearts were 'Pierc't through with anguish" and whose natural warmth was "choakt And stifled with true sense of misery." The authors of *Lear* and *The Duchess of Malfi* and *Bussy d'Ambois* and even *Volpone* had become ready to slight those who had not known anguish, who from their birth had been "hugged in the armes, And nuzzled twixt the breastes of happinesse."

This preoccupation with an irredeemable darkness was the inevitable result of a weakening of faith. Dr. Tillyard has forced us to see that the Elizabethans held fast to a medieval cosmology, that their assumptions about "degree" have a religious or magical bias;[3] and the pragmatism of Machiavelli, the scepticism of Montaigne introduced only modifications of an inherited pattern. Yet it is significant that the fullest dramatic expression of the notion of "degree" comes in *Troilus and Cressida,* a play that Professor Ellis-Fermor has described as the consummate expression of an anarchic vision, a play which seems to show above all others the vanity of existence, the inherent sickness of human nature.[4] So full a formulation as Ulysses gives comes most naturally when the idea is no longer so potent in the minds of men: it is then made explicit, because it can no longer be taken for granted. Yet in the early seventeenth century "degree" was still a powerful idea, and when Shakespeare wrote *Macbeth* he was with part of his mind intent on the evils that come from usurpation, the discord that sounds with the untuning of the string. Similarly in *Lear* he thought to some extent with Sackville and Norton in *Gorboduc,* tracing the ills of the kingdom and the royal house to the king's abandonment of power and his subjecting himself to his own children.

[3] *The Elizabethan World Picture,* 1943; *Shakespeare's History Plays,* 1944.
[4] *The Frontiers of Drama,* pp. 56–76.

236

But neither *Macbeth* nor *Lear* is primarily a political tract, as *Gorboduc* is. We have already seen the oddity that Chapman could speak of "excitation to virtue, and deflection from her contrary" in relation to *The Revenge of Bussy d'Ambois*: in the same way, it is impossible for *Macbeth* to be a political tract, if the dramatist implies that the pattern of events is preordained. The insistence on the witches' most accurate foreknowledge of each step in the action puts the play into a different category from that of the histories. In Shakespeare's dramatisation of the historical events that preceded the establishment of the Tudor monarchy, he was issuing a warning against the recurrence of civil strife and usurpation: in *Lear* and *Macbeth* he shows the infringement of "degree" as fated: it is as evil in its effects as before, but is now an ill to which the world is haphazardly subject. It is not so much the diseased will of one man or of a group that leads to the disturbance of order, but rather it is Fortune who infects the individual and the whole frame of things. Sometimes, indeed, the dramatist's pessimism goes further, as when Lear cries out against the existence of Goneril and Regan, with the question: "Is there any cause in Nature that makes these hard hearts?" (III. vi), or when he sees the ranks of society and the normal processes of human justice as based on nothing more substantial than chance:

> See how yond justice rails upon yon simple thief. Hark in thine ear: change places; and, handy-dandy, which is the justice, which is the thief? (IV. vi.)

In general, however, there remains a notion of an ideal order in Shakespearian tragedy, disrupted through action discordant with "degree," but not originating simply in a human being's evil choice.

The change from the political morality of *Gorboduc* and the histories to the determinist outlook of the tragedies was doubtless in part the fruit of change in the political scene and the social structure. In Elizabeth's last years there were intrigues in plenty for the succession. The Infanta of Spain, the Earl of Derby, Essex were among those who in the minds of many had claims as impressive as those that

237

James VI could produce, and the fire which the Essex rebellion lit in the hearts of some must have scorched the paper on which the canons of "degree" had been laboriously set out. And when James VI had inherited, it was no longer so easy to see magic in sovereignty: Elizabeth could be hated, but she had a magnetism and an isolation that James signally lacked, qualities that primacy seems naturally to demand. Moreover, society's change from the land-basis to the money-basis was becoming increasingly apparent. In Peele's *The Old Wives' Tales,* acted about 1592, the magician Sacrapant has conjured up a Friar, "the veriest knave in all Spain," to entertain his fair captive Delia: when she asks the Friar: "Which is the most greediest Englishman?" the answer comes pat and without comment: "The miserable and most covetous usurer." In Greene's *James IV,* of about the same time, there is a scene (V. iv) which appears to have got into the play by accident, being merely a conversation between a Divine, a Lawyer and a Merchant on the bad condition of the time: as each of the three professions represented is blamed in turn, the debate is inconclusive, but its occurrence in the play suggests an increasing awareness that something was unhealthy in the social structure. There is an equally noticeable irrelevancy in *Romeo and Juliet,* acted about three years later, when Romeo buys poison from the Apothecary and tells him that the gold he is parting with is more noxious than the mortal drug he is receiving (V. i). A year or two later, there is at least a kind of seriousness in *The Merchant of Venice* when we are shown that the golden casket does not contain the prize and that the usurer's trade can put a man's life in jeopardy. But after the turn of the century the attacks on gold become more virulent in the drama of the time. Lear and Timon see it as the universal corrupter, the trafficker in justice and honour; Volpone and Face lead men to their undoing by holding up the gilded bait. But among the metals gold had the primacy, as the lion among beasts, the eagle among birds, the king among men. If gold was corrupting and deceitful, men might come to see rottenness in other sovereign things, might come at last to question whether the hierarchies had been rightly conceived.

Such inchoate scepticism might well be directed towards the political order, especially now that James was on the throne, and in *Bussy d'Ambois* Chapman goes out of his way to praise the court of Elizabeth as a model to Europe and a contrast to the French court. King Henry says:

> Assure you, cousin Guise, so great a courtier,
> So full of majesty and royal parts,
> No queen in Christendom may vaunt herself.
> Her Court approves it, that's a Court indeed,
> Not mixt with clowneries used in common houses,
> But, as Courts should be, th' abstracts of their kingdoms,
> In all the beauty, state, and worth they hold,
> So is hers, amply, and by her inform'd.
> The world is not contracted in a man
> With more proportion and expression,
> Than in her Court, her kingdom. Our French Court
> Is a mere mirror of confusion to it:
> The king and subject, lord and every slave,
> Dance a continual hay; our rooms of state
> Kept like our stables; no place more observed
> Than a rude market-place.     (I. ii.)

He goes on to add that the English will soon realise the difference if they change their court-form to one like the French, and Monsieur, his brother, adds the sharp comment:

> No question we shall see them imitate
> (Though afar off) the fashions of our Courts,
> As they have ever aped us in attire.

This goes to the roots of things in a way that Spenser's satirical comments on court life do not, for Chapman's criticism by implication does not spare the ruler himself. Such criticism was not reserved for the temporal hierarchy: as tragedy was so often set in southern lands, the dramatists might consider themselves 'icensed to make free with Italianate cardinals, but often their thrusts have an anti-ecclesiastical direction. In *The Duchess of Malfi* the dramatist seems fully in sympathy with his Duchess when she asserts that her solemn exchange of vows with Antonio makes the formal blessing of the church supererogatory. "What can the church force more?" she asks, and later: "How can the church build faster? We now are man and wife, and 'tis the church That must but echo this." (I. i.) Towards the ends of the play, the Cardinal says of Antonio: "Although he do account religion But a school-name" (V. ii), and our feeling is strengthened that Webster's world-picture is to a considerable extent antinomian. Not entirely so, for *The Duchess of Malfi,* like *Macbeth,* shows the dreadfulness that follows on a breaking with 'degree': Antonio and the Duchess have neglected the specialty of rule. But Webster's sympathy with them is far greater than his reprobation, and the dominant impression left by the play is that the hierarchies among men are unsound.

The goodness of the natural and the supernatural order was not the only article of faith available for an Elizabethan. There was too the typically Renaissance belief in the splendour of human life, that belief which dominates Italian painting and sculpture at its finest, which provides the motive-force for the early plays of Marlowe. Burckhardt, in his *The Civilisation of the Renaissance in Italy,* makes us understand how in the fifteenth century men became imbued with a new consciousness of power, a keener delight in its employment. His account of Leon Battista Alberti should be one of the starting-points for a consideration of Jacobean tragedy, for the great peal that rings in Alberti's life is both dimly echoed and denied by Shakespeare and Chapman and Webster:

> In all by which praise is won, Leon Battista was from his childhood the first. Of his various gymnastic feats and exercises we read with astonishment how, with his feet together, he could spring over a man's head; how, in the cathedral, he threw a coin in the air till it was heard to ring against the distant roof; how the wildest horses trembled under him. In three things he desired to appear faultless to others, in walking, in riding, and in speaking. He learned music without a master, and yet his compositions were admired by professional judges. Under the pressure of poverty, he studied both civil and canonical law for many years, till exhaustion brought on a severe illness. In his twenty-fourth year, finding his

240

memory for words weakened, but his sense of facts unimpaired, he set to work at physics and mathematics. And all the while he acquired every sort of accomplishment and dexterity, cross-examining artists, scholars and artisans of all descriptions, down to the cobblers, about the secrets and peculiarities of their craft. Painting and modelling he practised by the way, and especially excelled in admirable likenesses from memory. Great admiration was excited by his mysterious "camera obscura," in which he showed at one time the stars and the moon rising over rocky hills, and at another wide landscapes with mountains and gulfs receding into dim perspective, and with fleets advancing on the waters in shade or sunshine. And that which others created he welcomed joyfully, and held every human achievement which followed the laws of beauty for something almost divine. To all this must be added his literary works, first of all those on art, which are landmarks and authorities of the first order for the Renaissance of Form, especially in architecture; then his Latin prose writings—novels and other works—of which some have been taken for productions of antiquity; his elegies, eclogues, and humorous dinner-speeches. He also wrote an Italian treatise on domestic life in four books; and even a funeral oration on his dog. His serious and witty sayings were thought worth collecting, and specimens of them, many columns long, are quoted in his biography. And all that he had and knew he imparted, as rich natures always do, without the least reserve, giving away his chief discoveries for nothing. But the deepest spring of his nature has yet to be spoken of—the sympathetic intensity with which he entered into the whole life around him. At the sight of noble trees and waving cornfields he shed tears; handsome and dignified old men he honoured as "a delight of nature," and could never look at them enough. Perfectly formed animals won his goodwill as being specially favoured by nature; and more than once, when he was ill, the sight of a beautiful landscape cured him. No wonder that those who saw him in this close and mysterious communion with the world ascribed to him the gift of prophecy. He was said to have foretold a bloody catastrophe in the family of Este, the fate of Florence, and the death of the Popes years before they happened, and to be able to read into the countenances and the hearts of men. It need not be added that an iron will pervaded and sustained his whole personality; like all the great men of the Renaissance, he said: "Men can do all things if they will."

And Leonardo da Vinci was to Alberti as the finisher to the beginner, as the master to the *dilettante*. Would only that Vasari's work were here supplemented by a description like that of Alberti! The colossal outlines of Leonardo's nature can never be more than dimly and distantly conceived.[5]

That this underlies *Tamburlaine* is at once obvious: the delight and the ambitions of Alberti come to be Tamburlaine's appetite for greatness, for splendour of setting and the homage of men, for the divine Zenocrate, for riding in triumph through Persepolis, for the sweet fruition of an earthly crown, for recognition as the scourge of God. And if we find some coarseness of temper in Tamburlaine's dreams, that is not surprising. The Elizabethan playhouse, the Reformation, the formulation of practical politics that we associate with Machiavelli—these all united in taking away from the Renaissance temper something of fineness. And perhaps because the dream of human greatness was less golden, was snatched from under the eyes of the reformers, was with difficulty harnessed with a delight in political intrigue, was expressed in the still primitive theatrical terms of the 1580's, it was less enduring than Italy had known it. Even in *Tamburlaine* itself, the defection of Calyphas in Part II, his wanton truancy from his father's battles, raises awkward questions. His preference for a game of cards over witnessing yet another of his father's victories is so obviously sensible when the spectators themselves have been sated with Tamburlaine's long line of triumphs; his brutal execution at his father's hands therefore seems to hint that Marlowe was growing weary of his own dream, would be ill-content with a repetition. If *Faustus* is Marlowe's next play, it is significant that there the aspirations of the individual are given to us in a morality-framework, that there is an uneasy balance between ortho-

[5] Jacob Burckhardt, *The Civilisation of the Renaissance*, 1944, pp. 86–7.

doxy of religious belief and antinomianism. Later Marlowe was to turn to the more orthodox view of things, and in *Edward II, The Jew of Malta* and *The Massacre at Paris* there are many assertions of the sacredness of "degree": the thirst for power is shown in the Jew and Mortimer and the Guise only to be reprobated. It is as if Marlowe had at least partially abandoned the worship of man for the worship of divine decree.

But if the splendour of earthly aspiration grew tarnished in Marlowe's hands, it was indeed a crumbling idol for the Jacobeans. Chapman's Bussy tells us that advancement comes because it must and not because we will it, that great place brings greater vulnerability and closer contact with the antics of the court; Jonson parodies the Renaissance man in Sir Epicure Mammon; men are the stars' tennis-balls, flies at the mercy of the wanton gods, asses to be led by the nose, players strutting at the playwright's beck, bodies that rot into dust and souls driven in a black storm. Yet, just as the notion of "degree" underlies the Jacobean cosmology, so the Renaissance dream of greatness is the necessary foundation for the tragic heroes of the time. The dramatists inherited a cult of stoicism from Seneca, but it is not for their imperturbability that we admire Lear and Othello and Hamlet: in the end, it is true, they learn to stand up to Fortune's blows and to go out with dignity and a conventional gesture of resignation; but we must remember that Macbeth dies in despair, Othello in terrible remorse, and Lear with his nerves stretched beyond breaking-point by his hope that Cordelia may yet live. It is not so much their capacity for endurance as their sharp sense of their own being that marks them out as exceptional. Hamlet, Lear and Macbeth come to greater self-knowledge, and Hamlet throughout the play has the many-sidedness of the typical Renaissance figure: he is the scholar, the expert with his rapier, the connoisseur of the stage, the poet too, and likely, had he been put on, to have proved most royally. If Othello has not the self-knowledge of the others, he has at least a superabundance of vitality; he exults in his power, his eloquence, his animal vigour, his regality of gesture to the very end. Even for Jonson the Renaissance dream was not entirely dead: he was fasci-

243

nated by the aspiring Sejanus and Catiline, though he hated them too, and he could show the fascination of power and sensuality in Volpone while at the same time giving him the comic shiftiness of the fox and bringing him at last into fetters.

As we pass beyond the first decade of the seventeenth century, we find that the Jacobean scepticism becomes ultimately destructive of tragedy. Major works of literature seem to depend on a tension between two ways of perception. We have seen that, according to Professor Ellis-Fermor, there is in tragedy an equilibrium set up by the opposition of a divine and an anthropocentric interpretation of the universe: the tragic writer is as it were wrestling with his salvation before ultimately surrendering to it.[6] This would seem to be a simplification, for *Macbeth* and *Othello* hardly suggest the notion of a benevolent overseer. But there appears to be in Jacobean tragedy a state of balance between a conception of the universe as order and a conception of the universe as chaos, between the notion of man's dignity and the notion of his insignificance. When the equilibrium is destroyed, the movement may be towards a despair of order and dignity, as in *Timon of Athens,* or towards a reassertion of traditional beliefs, as in Shirley's *St. Patrick for Ireland.* In the drama that followed the short period of great tragedy, we have the drama of indifference, as in Beaumont and Fletcher and their followers, the conventionally built but fundamentally unthoughtful drama of Massinger, and the approach to complete antinomianism in Ford. Life has become a languid pageant of woe in *The Broken Heart,* and it requires the fierce rebelliousness of Giovanni to bring back the tension once again: in one Caroline play, *'Tis Pity She's a Whore,* we thus recapture the Jacobean equilibrium, but tragedy recovers like a spent taper, for a flash, and instantly goes out. The nullity of Caroline tragedy as a whole is forcibly illustrated in Shirley's *The Cardinal,* the last tragedy to be acted before the Civil War: it is a competent piece of work in its kind, but the mechanical approach of the dramatist is shown in his frequent echoes of Jacobean writing, and in his picture of

[6] Cf. above, p. 7.

244

the villainous Cardinal. There would be a piquancy in the drawing of such an ecclesiastical villain by James Shirley, a convert to the Church of Rome, were it not that we feel how derivative the portrait is. In seventeenth-century drama cardinals had become traditionally fair game, and the play did not mean enough to Shirley for him to make it consonant with his new allegiance. The Cardinal dies echoing Vittoria Corombona:

> now it would be rare,—
> If you but waft me with a little prayer;
> My wings that flag may catch the wind; but 'tis
> In vain, the mist is risen, and there's none
> To steer my wandering bark.   (V. iii.)

and the difference of the wording makes us realise again that Shirley is following a dramatic pattern rather than communicating a personal vision. Orthodoxy, indifference, and something very close to unbelief itself, can all be found in the later Jacobean and Caroline plays, but except momentarily in Ford there was not the balancing of belief and scepticism, of order and chaos, of human splendour and corruption.

But in another way we find an equilibrium of forces in Jacobean tragedy. On the other hand, there is a strong sense of determinism, as we have seen; on the other, the characters have that degree of lifelikeness that makes it seem always possible for them to exercise free will. Here, indeed, we touch on one of the problems of tragic writing: the dramatist is presenting a picture of the world in which man is subject to the operations of cosmic forces, blind or purposive, and cannot carve out his own future. But if he is merely one of the stars' tennis-balls, it is difficult to see how we can preserve an idea of his dignity: if he is a manipulated doll, the world becomes something between a Bartholomew Fair and a *Walpurgisnacht*. In sixteenth-century drama the foreordaining of event is heavily under-lined. Material from historical sources lent itself to this kind of handling, for the development of the action was necessarily determined by the actual sequence of events, and in plays with entirely fictional plots the dramatist

245

would go out of his way to make us realise that the end was settled simultaneously with the beginning: in *The Spanish Tragedy* the presence of Andrea's Ghost and Revenge throughout the play serves as a permanent assurance that revenge will be accomplished; in *Romeo and Juliet* the initial chorus foretells the love and its doom; in *James IV* and *The Old Wives' Tale* the use of the induction makes it clear that what is being presented belongs already to the past and is therefore settled in its every detail. The use of the induction is, indeed, highly significant in the development of dramatic technique at this time, and we must later examine it from that angle: for the moment we shall notice it as underlining the powerlessness of the dramatic characters to change the course of events. But in none of these plays is the tragic spirit fully apparent: there is sensational incident, and an occasional touch of that darkness of experience which Marston speaks of in his prologue to *Antonio's Revenge*; but we get neither the notion of human greatness in adversity nor the long persistence of terror. In *Tamburlaine,* indeed, there are latent the forces that in tragedy balance one another, but that play is so brimmed with eloquence, so pageant-like a series of triumphs, until the end, that the tragic problem is there unobtrusive. In Jacobean drama, on the other hand, we have a kind of dual vision of the action: simultaneously it appears foreordained and dependent on the characters' choice. Only in *Macbeth* among the great tragedies does Shakespeare labour the idea of predestination, and even there Macbeth and his wife are drawn so convincingly as human beings that, as in actuality, it appears always that freedom of choice exists even though we may have decided that the overall pattern is not of our making. In Greek tragedy the events are decreed, the reactions of the characters are free. In Shakespeare and the best of his contemporaries, action is not separated from thought and feeling: each is foreordained, yet each seems always a new birth. We feel simultaneously that Desdemona is doomed and that she may escape, that Macbeth's sin is decreed and that the temptation could be resisted, that Lear must die and that Edmund's repentance may come in time.

One cannot say that the tragedies that followed the great

246

ones are characterised by a one-sided stress on free will. The later writers modelled themselves too closely on their predecessors to forgo the generally fatalistic air. But at least the tragicomedies in the Beaumont and Fletcher style illustrate well enough the breakdown of this equilibrium too. *A King and No King* is only the most notorious example of a haphazard putting of things to rights; the action seems destined for disaster until the last act, when an unexpected revelation offers a fortunate conclusion. When Edmund Waller in the late seventeenth century altered *The Maid's Tragedy* and gave that too a happy ending,[7] he was only making the play consistent with others of its kind: if Arbaces can escape his doom, there seems no reason for Amintor to suffer. The situation is rather different in Shakespeare's romances, when we have the suggestion that a providence safeguards the main characters from ultimate harm: this, however, is a return to the earlier stressing of predestination. Only in the major tragedies, those of the great decade, is the balance preserved.

I have tried to suggest certain features of the picture of the world seen by the early seventeenth-century tragic writers. Standing between a belief in natural order and a growing perception of chaos, between the Renaissance enthusiasm for living and an ever-darkening disillusion, between the twin poles of Fate and Chance, of predestination and free will, they went through mental experiences of a peculiar intensity, knew the darkness and the terror all the more keenly for the light that still remained in a diminishing fragment of the heavens. And because their feelings were so deeply stirred by the contradictions in their experience, they were led to the writing of tragic literature. It was almost coincidental that this should be the time when the development of playhouse technique had made tragic drama possible. Until around 1595 the dramatic medium was insufficiently subtle, and after 1615 or thereabouts it had acquired characteristics which made great tragedy far more difficult to achieve. That second major reason for the brevity of the tragic period I wish to examine next. Even without the change in technique, however, the tragic world-

[7] Cf. below, p. 108.

view would not have lasted long. A delicate equilibrium is soon gone when the winds of heaven blow, and because the tragic dramatists of James's time were barely conscious of their own aims, the equilibrium was precarious indeed.

# JACOBEAN TRAGEDY: AN INTRODUCTION

## By Irving Ribner

The most important writer of tragedy in the Jacobean era, of course, is William Shakespeare. Not only do such plays as *Othello, Lear, Macbeth* represent the highest reaches tragedy has attained in any age by the perfection with which they mirror a vision of man's relation to his universe, but the plays of Shakespeare served also as models for his Jacobean contemporaries to emulate. Beaumont and Fletcher, Heywood, Webster and Ford all reveal the influence of their master. But Shakespeare, while he taught his contemporary dramatists much of their craft, is still not one of them. While they imitate his language and ape his situations, the writers of tragedy in the early years of the seventeenth century generally find it difficult to accept without question the view of man's position in the universe which gives to Shakespeare's greatest tragedies their most significant form.

Thomas Heywood is one exception. Conservative like Shakespeare, he continued to espouse throughout his career a view of the universe as the harmonious creation of an ever-loving God, the parts of creation observing order and degree, with every element enjoying its proper function as part of the divine plan. Man was at the centre of the universe, the noblest work of God, his life guided and controlled by the power of divine providence. In such a view of the world evil was real and active, and Heywood like Shakespeare is not afraid to portray its operation, but the means of overcoming evil are always available to man, and although sinners like Macbeth might suffer damnation, the movement of the cosmos was towards a constant rebirth of good out of evil. The end of tragedy written in terms of such a cosmic view was always reconciliation, with the forces of evil at least temporarily vanquished in spite of the horror they have wrought. In *Patterns in Shakespearian Tragedy* I have tried to suggest that Shakespeare's tragedies represent successive attempts to embody in drama steadily more comprehensive visions of the eternal conflict of man against the forces of evil in the world, so as to lead to an affirmation of order and design in the universe, and that they do this in terms of the optimistic Christian humanism of the early Renaissance which stressed always the dignity of man and the providence of God.[1]

But Shakespeare wrote his profoundest plays in an age when their philosophical assumptions already were beginning to appear anachronistic, when Christian humanism was losing its dominance in the more thoughtful minds, and newer, more pessimistic notions of man's position in the universe were gaining supremacy. The seventeenth century is one in which man, as F. P. Wilson has written,

> revised his conception of the external universe and of his relation to it, revised also his conception of himself and of the powers of his mind. . . . Where the emphasis had been upon order and degree, hierarchy and discipline, man's duty to God and the Prince, some now placed it on rights—the rights of the individual conscience, of criticism, of reason.[2]

It is an age out of which finally was to emerge in triumph at the end of the century the new belief in progress and

[1] See Herschel Baker, *The Dignity of Man* (Cambridge, Mass., 1947); Douglas Bush, *The Renaissance and English Humanism* (Toronto, 1939); Hardin Craig, *The Enchanted Glass* (New York, 1936); E. M. W. Tillyard, *The Elizabethan World Picture* (London, 1943).
[2] *Seventeenth Century Prose* (Berkeley, Calif., 1960), p. 1. See also Wilson's brilliant analysis of the cleavage between the Elizabethan and Jacobean eras in *Elizabethan and Jacobean* (Oxford, 1945). Perhaps the most comprehensive study of the decline of Christian humanism in the seventeenth century is Herschel Baker, *The Wars of Truth* (Cambridge, Mass., 1952).

human perfectibility which Francis Bacon had heralded, and it was to be the true beginning of our modern era, but the seventeenth century had to go first through a period of doubt, confusion, and profound pessimism. The Jacobean dramatists do not reflect the new scientific optimism of Bacon, although in Webster's emphasis upon the dignity of human life in spite of the world's corruption there may be some suggestion of what finally is to come. Jacobean tragedy more generally reflects the uncertainty of an age no longer able to believe in the old ideals, searching almost frantically for new ones to replace them, but incapable yet of finding them.

The early seventeenth century is the age of paradox. This is a dominant literary exercise of the time, developed in the best of Jacobean prose, and a cardinal element in its metaphysical poetry. I have already indicated that Shakespeare, in his final tragedies, *Antony and Cleopatra* and *Coriolanus,* when he had thoroughly explored the implications of his own Christian humanism, came at last to a paradox which he could not resolve.[3] These final plays reveal a world in which man may be destroyed by evils which are the inevitable concomitants of those very virtues which make him great, and in which the lust of Antony or the pride of Coriolanus—examples of vice in traditional terms—may have an heroic quality to which we cannot help but give our emotional acquiescence while we recognize the corruption of divine order from which it springs and its utter sinfulness in terms of traditional morality. Shakespeare brought his hero at the end of *Coriolanus* to a point where he could not renounce sin without also renouncing virtue. In these final plays of paradox, and not in the great positive affirmations of *Othello, Lear,* and *Macbeth,* Shakespeare reveals his affinity to the Jacobean dramatists who were his fellows and successors.

We are not to assume that the tragedy of the Elizabethan period was universally orthodox in its moral position. There has been intellectual division and dissent in every era in human history, and among the Elizabethan dramatists there was an important tradition of scepticism

[3] *See Patterns in Shakespearian Tragedy* (London, 1960), pp. 168–201.

whose leading exponent was Christopher Marlowe. He had questioned the order and perfection of the universe and the workings of divine providence in all his plays; even in *Dr Faustus,* with its outward framework of religious belief and its morality play technique, Marlowe had protested against a system of values which decreed damnation as the price of knowledge and the power inherent in it. Professor Una M. Ellis-Fermor has indicated the spirit of Marlovian tragedy, with its steadily increasing sense of human limitations and its tone of human defeat, as that which comes to dominate the Jacobean era, and she has seen this "mood of spiritual despair" as the product of Marlowe's continuing exploration of the political system of Niccolò Machiavelli.[4]

Although Machiavelli had tried to divorce politics from ethics as two separate areas of human concern, he did not entirely succeed in doing so. The inevitable ethical implications of his political creed tended to emphasize a new materialistic view of the universe in direct opposition to the divinely oriented Christian humanism of Richard Hooker and William Shakespeare, and this new materialism, Miss Ellis-Fermor holds, fostered the spiritual uncertainty of Jacobean tragedy. But the emergence of Machiavelli in Italy in the early years of the sixteenth century is merely one evidence of the spirit of scepticism which is as much a part of the Renaissance as its Christian humanism. Bruno and Montaigne exerted a wide influence as well, and the new astronomy in the early seventeenth century was a direct challenge to all which men traditionally had believed about the permanence and immutability of the heavens.

The brief career of Christopher Marlowe may serve as a kind of index to the shifting currents of Renaissance thought. He came up to Cambridge as a Parker Foundation scholar, destined for the Anglican ministry and presumably committed to its doctrinal position which he must have absorbed at the King's School in Canterbury. After his wide reading of theology in the library at Corpus Christi College, he seems to have turned to the new Renaissance scepticism, and in his *Tamburlaine* we find an enthusiastic

---

[4] *The Jacobean Drama* (London, 1936), pp. 1–5. See also Wilson, *Elizabethan and Jacobean,* pp. 100–1; Robert Ornstein, *The Moral Vision of Jacobean Tragedy* (Madison, Wis., 1960), pp. 24–31.

espousal of the premises of Machiavelli, coupled with an exuberance and faith in the potentialities of mankind. He breathes the spirit of Renaissance vitality and optimism. But in the second part of *Tamburlaine* we find already a painful awareness of the limitations placed upon mankind by the very fact of mortality. As he grows older his disillusion steadily increases until in *Edward II* we find him rejecting his earlier faith in the fall of Mortimer,[5] and if *Dr Faustus* is his final play, as is now generally supposed, it may be also his most pessimistic statement of human limitation and frustration. Marlowe began, in short, embracing the new challenge to the old orthodox, and he ended disillusioned with the new but still incapable of accepting the old. He arrived at the spirit of negation and disillusion which is the mark of Jacobean tragedy.

Seventeenth-century literature reflects this lack of spiritual certainty in its concern with death, time, and mutability, and in the pervasive spirit of melancholy already fully drawn in Shakespeare's *Hamlet,* the subject for pseudo-scientific analysis in Burton's *Anatomy,* and surviving in the quiet sadness of Ford's *Broken Heart.* There is a renewed interest in a notion which has its roots in the waning of the Middle Ages, but which in the seventeenth century becomes an important source of controversy and a leading motif in literature: the idea that the world is in its antiquity, nearing the end of a long period of progressive decay which had begun with the fall of man, and rapidly approaching total dissolution. It has been argued that the revival of this belief owed much to the new astronomy.[6] The discovery in 1572 of a new celestial body among the fixed stars led men to question the very notion that there were fixed stars. The heavens no longer appeared to be the immutable evidence of an unchanging, perfectly unified

[5] I have dealt with these matters in 'Marlowe and Machiavelli,' *Comp. Lit.,* VI (1954), 349–56, and *The English History Play in The Age of Shakespeare* (Princeton, 1957), pp. 127–36.
[6] George Williamson, 'Mutability, Decay and Seventeenth Century Melancholy,' *ELH,* II (1935), 121–50. See also D. C. Allen, "The Degeneration of Man and Renaissance Pessimism,' *SP,* XXXV (1938), 202–27; R. F. Jones, *Ancients and Moderns* (St. Louis, Mo., 1936), a condensed version of which appears in *The Seventeenth Century* (Palo Alto, Calif., 1951), pp. 10–40.

creation, in which the destiny of mankind, past and future, could be read. The continuing discoveries of the astronomers culminated in Galileo's discovery in 1612 of spots in the sun, which seemed to indicate that the heavens themselves were subject to decay. Dr Godfrey Goodman in 1616 proclaimed his thesis of a decaying world in his widely influential *The Fall of Man,* in which he related this decay to the fall of Adam and Eve from Paradise, as Sir Walter Ralegh had related it some two years before in his *History of the World.* Goodman was answered in 1627 by Dr George Hakewill in his finally more important work, *An Apology of the Power and Providence of God in the Government of the World,* which espoused instead the idea of human progress.

Hakewill's position finally was to triumph, but it is not a position which is reflected in the tragedies of the period, for these reflect a search for moral order in a world which seems in its senility, giving constant evidence of death, decay, and eternal change. In this fact Jacobean tragedy is not associated with that movement in seventeenth-century thought which is best represented by Hakewill and Bacon. It is associated rather with the despair for humanity which runs through Ralegh's *History of the World,* the concern with death and decay and the corrosion of time which are constant motifs in the poetry of John Donne, and the melancholy tone of Sir Thomas Browne's *Urn-Burial,* which has aptly been called the age's great funeral sermon for a world in dissolution.

As part of this melancholy vision of human destiny, we find a renewed interest in the ancient notion of the four ages of man, of which every schoolboy read in Ovid's *Metamorphoses.* The present is seen as the "iron age," and the "golden age" comes to be identified with the period before the fall of Adam and Eve from Paradise, when the forces making for decay and degeneration had not yet been set in motion. There is a tendency also to look back with nostalgia upon classical antiquity—long accorded a special place by the Renaissance humanists—as a time when the world was inhabited by a nobler race of men, less defiled and vitiated by the process of deterioration. The dominant philosophy of the Jacobean era comes to be one which had

253

emerged in different forms in the most pessimistic times of the ancient world, in the Hellenistic period of Greece and in the Rome of the later emperors. This is the philosophy of stoicism, which was perhaps most influentially proclaimed in the Renaissance by Justus Lipsius in his *De Constantia* of 1583, a work which embraced the theory of the world's deterioration and offered as the only means of survival in such a world a stoic control of human emotions and a consequent imperviousness to pain, with an awareness that the destruction of the world was part of the inevitable scheme of things. This work was translated into English by John Stradling. It went through several editions and was widely influential in disseminating the ideas both of the degeneration of the world and of how man might live in spite of it.

These notions are reflected with a particular clarity in the tragedies of George Chapman. His *Bussy D'Ambois,* as I shall try to show in the following chapter,* is based upon the assumption of a degenerate decaying world in which virtue is incapable of survival. To make his point Chapman uses the concept of the "golden age" of prelapsarian perfection, for Bussy reflects the qualities of man in such an age, and his tragedy is the tragedy of all of us who must live in a world where such virtues can no longer exist. These motifs are repeated in the *Byron* plays, with further emphasis upon the corroding force of the world's evil, and with a slowly developing stoic insistence on the need for authority to regulate a degenerate humanity. In *The Revenge of Bussy D'Ambois* and *Caesar and Pompey* Chapman sacrifices everything else in the plays to his need to proclaim, almost frantically, the virtues of the stoic ideal. There is little stoicism in his final play, *The Tragedy of Chabot,* but his theme is the inability of justice to survive in a vitiated world, and the mood is that of the early *Bussy D'Ambois.*

Chapman's career as a writer of tragedy may illustrate that drive which produced also the greatest plays of the other dramatists with whom the following chapters will be concerned. It is a drive to find a basis for morality in a world in which the traditional bases no longer seem to have

* *Jacobean Tragedy, The Quest for Moral Order,* Irving Ribner.

validity. The greatest tragedians of the Jacobean era seek in their various ways to discover some meaning in human suffering, some kind of affirmation which can make life possible in a world which seems to give reason only for despair. This quest, I believe, has been the traditional mission of tragedy as an art form, and it is the goal which Shakespeare in his way most triumphantly achieved. The dramatists we are here considering all seek ways of their own, and although none is so successful as Shakespeare, in the moral earnestness of their striving, and in the poetic imagination with which they reflect the tensions of their world, we have what gives to their works their distinctive character.

D. C. Allen has written that whereas human suffering in the Middle Ages could be accepted as the road to heaven, the Jacobean era could look upon it with no such certainty, and he has attributed the pessimism of the age to the failure of Renaissance philosophers to create out of conflicting modes of thought a synthesis as satisfying as that which Aquinas had shaped for their medieval forebears.[7] This failure of synthesis is what ties the Jacobean era to our own and gives to its literature so much immediacy. It is a failure, we must not forget, which has not been without its compensations, for it has made possible the idea of progress and enlarged the possibility of scientific advance and a perhaps someday to be hoped for amelioration of the human condition.

Far as the seventeenth century may be from the Middle Ages in this respect, the writers of the Jacobean period tend to fall back upon motifs particularly characteristic of the medieval mentality. Of this fact the two plays attributed to Cyril Tourneur may offer most striking evidence. Here we have all the symbols traditionally associated with medieval asceticism; the human skull, the charnel house, the seven deadly sins paraded across the stage, the bitter excoriations of lust and gluttony, and a world whose evils are drawn with such brutal exaggeration that they would be merely ludicrous could we not see them in terms of medieval *contemptus mundi* as the author's

[7] *SP*, XXXV (1938), 202–27.

way of arguing that man must place his hopes in the world to come.

Tourneur is unique in his age for the moral fervour with which he uses the drama to espouse a primitive Christianity more closely related to that of the medieval world than to that of the seventeenth century. It is not, however, a philosophy entirely of escape from the evils of the world, for implicit in it, as I shall try to show, is the means of overcoming these evils. Tourneur employs the weapons developed by medieval and Renaissance satirists, but his final goal is something more than a plea for social improvement; it is a larger vision of man's relation to the cosmos. His Christianity is of another sort than that of Thomas Heywood, with his faith in the essential goodness of man and in the power of love and divine providence to overcome the evils of the present world. Tourneur's Christianity is based upon the assumption of a decaying universe and a corrupt and degenerate humanity. His primary concern is the salvation of the soul, as that part of man which can survive and transcend the chaos of the world. Heywood also, as *A Woman Killed with Kindness* may superbly illustrate, is committed to the Christian thesis that the soul's fate must be man's most significant concern.

Generally, the Jacobean dramatists are firmly Christian in their orientation, although their Christianity may take different forms, as we may see by a comparison of Heywood with Tourneur. In some dramatists such as Chapman, Christian belief receives so little emphasis that the possibility of human salvation is virtually excluded from the moral framework of their plays. This is true also of John Webster who, while he refers constantly to heaven and hell in conventional terms and fills his plays with commonplaces of Christian sentiment, nevertheless creates a world which is incompatible with any system of religious belief. Webster is nevertheless among the dramatists who succeed most notably in their search for moral order. He bases this order not upon divine influence in human affairs, but in a celebration of the dignity of human life which renders man superior to his world, and he finds his basis for morality in the need to preserve this dignity which separates man from beast at any cost, for it is man's only weapon against the

256

chaos of the world. In this attitude Webster is related to the current of his age which points out of Jacobean uncertainty and despair towards the future, for it was in terms of man's human strength and initiative that men like Francis Bacon sought to resolve their age's dilemma.

Thomas Middleton, on the other hand, is as fully Christian in his orientation as Heywood or Tourneur. His moral categories are clear and precise. There is never any question of the reality of evil or of its absolute distinction from good. Nor is there any doubt of the punishment the sinner must suffer inevitably in a world governed by an inexorable force of divine retribution. But Middleton's is neither the optimistic religion of Heywood nor the heaven-oriented Christianity of Tourneur. His vision is one of hell and damnation. His world is gloomier far than that of Webster, for he offers little hope for human triumph. There is, as I shall suggest, a Calvinistic strain in Middleton which grows more and more marked as we move from *The Changeling* to *Women Beware Women*. In both plays he is concerned with the revelation of an evil which man is incapable of escaping. His constant theme is man's slow awareness of his own damnation, which he is able to portray with a psychological realism unique in his age. In *Women Beware Women* we seem to have a symbolic vision of the damnation of all mankind.

The final dramatist with whom we will be concerned is John Ford. His literary career begins near the end of the Jacobean period, and his great tragedies all belong to the age of King Charles. But Ford looks back as surely as any of his contemporaries to the great Elizabethans for his inspiration, and among his plays the echoes of Shakespeare's language are perhaps most frequent. In Ford we find a melancholy nostalgia for the Elizabethan age which he imitates but of which he never can be a part. His tragedies reveal an acute awareness that the world of Shakespeare is no more, and this awareness lends the characteristic note of sadness to his plays. Ford reflects both the scepticism of his own age and a longing for the kind of ordered moral universe which this scepticism rejects. His tragic heroes stand literally between two worlds, the one dead and the other incapable of being born, and his tragic vision is a view of mankind incapable of achieving the kind of moral order without which survival is impossible. Ford's moral earnestness has not been sufficiently recognized by his critics, although they have usually pointed to the negation which is the only resolution of which he is capable.

The dramatists we are considering express their visions of man's relation to his universe in different ways. Of primary importance in all of them is the shaping of a particular story so that its parts, in the usual manner of myth, will combine to give expression to a moral statement, and so that particular characters may stand for particular moral positions, and in their conflict with one another opposing moral commitments be resolved. Some rely upon specific moral preachment. Tourneur's *Atheist's Tragedy* carries this method to an extreme, and this is one reason why this play is so much inferior to *The Revenger's Tragedy,* where the moral substance of the play is more perfectly conveyed in the total dramatic structure. Tourneur relies heavily upon his poetic imagery to emphasize his themes and to establish the tone of his plays, as does Webster in both of his Italian tragedies and Middleton in *Women Beware Women,* although *The Changeling,* a far greater play in most respects, is comparatively weak in this. Heywood and Ford are barren in poetic imagery when compared to Webster or Tourneur. Chapman shapes his total play as a reflection of a specific philosophical point of view. To this end, even in his most successful plays, he sacrifices consistency of character and plot, and he does not hesitate to insert long speeches of didactic commentary to further his philosophical argument at the price of his dramatic structure. His diction is complex and involved, and he packs his poetry with constantly recurring symbols, those of the tree and the ship at sea being two of his favourites. These occur in different contexts in almost every one of his plays. I propose in the following chapters to examine the moral vision of six dramatists by means of a close analysis of selected plays, and each play will be approached according to the particular technique upon which the individual dramatists most heavily depend.

In spite of their diversity of technique, what all of these writers of tragedy have in common is that their moral purposes are controlling factors in their plays, shaping character, plot and poetry so as to give expression to the presiding moral statement. This is generally true of Elizabethan and Jacobean tragedy. Only in Shakespeare, and occasionally in a dramatist like Middleton or Webster, is a moral vision expressed in terms of characters who have much resemblance to men and women we might have known or in situations which are likely to have occurred.[8]

I shall stress in the following chapters, as I stressed in *Patterns in Shakespearian Tragedy,* the conventional, symbolic dimension of the Jacobean stage, with its roots in the medieval drama, and its constant use, in the medieval manner, of the specific symbol to express the universal truth. I will suggest that these dramatists, like Shakespeare, are always more interested in mankind than in individual men, and that they rarely hesitate to sacrifice the consistency of character portraiture to the needs of the larger symbolic statement which is the play as a whole. We cannot hope to understand the horrors of Tourneur or Webster while we try to see their plays as realistic accounts of events which might have occurred, and forget that the painted skull at the lecher's lips was a traditional symbol with connotations deeply rooted in medieval iconography.

I have been able to analyse in the following chapters only a handful of the tragedies of the Jacobean era. There are some powerful and important products of multiple authorship, such for instance as *The Witch of Edmonton,* to which I have paid no regard, largely because such works tend to reflect a vision which is unlike that of any of the individual contributing authors, and it is upon the total attitudes and developments of individual dramatists that I wish to place my emphasis. There are also some dramatists of towering importance in their time whose works I have not chosen to dwell upon. It is impossible to

[8] Wilson, *Elizabethan and Jacobean,* pp. 100–8, has stressed this point, as has M. C. Bradbrook, *Themes and Conventions of Elizabethan Tragedy* (Cambridge, 1935).

overestimate the influence of men like Marston, Jonson, Beaumont and Fletcher. I do not believe, however, that any of the dramatists I am excluding from full consideration ever succeeded in conveying a total vision of the relation of mankind to the forces of evil in the universe; the impulse behind their tragedies was smaller and generally directed towards immediate social rather than larger cosmic issues. Those dramatists upon whom I am concentrating my attention all reflect a total—and therefore a truly moral—vision of the destiny of mankind, and this vision they are capable of conveying with the truth inherent in the greatest of poetry. Thomas Heywood admittedly never reaches the heights attained by the others, but I have included him as the dramatist who most perfectly illustrates the survival of a conservative tradition against which the greater plays of his contemporaries may be measured. If *The Rape of Lucrece* is a bad play, it is nevertheless a sincere attempt to express a view of mankind which we cannot ignore if we are to have any true understanding of the Jacobean age.

John Marston is in many ways a greater dramatist than Heywood, and he certainly left a heritage which his contemporaries more assiduously imitated. It could be argued, in fact, that next to Shakespeare Marston is the most influential dramatist of his age. In his plays we find the devices which are to be used with greater artistry by Webster, Tourneur, Middleton and Ford. The hero of the atrocious *Antonio's Revenge* shows his influence in Tourneur's Vindice, and we probably could not have had Webster's Bosola and Flamineo without the example of Marston's Malevole. Marston created the pattern for the malcontent; he developed the Machiavellian villain, and he is Kyd's great successor in revenge tragedy. He showed his followers how to end a play in the bloody holocaust of a final masque scene. He is a master of dramatic irony, and the technique of *The Malcontent,* with its central omnipotent character manipulating the action, is reflected in later days of such diversity as *The Revenger's Tragedy, Measure for Measure,* and *The Tempest.*

Yet Marston, in spite of his influence on others, wrote no play himself which is truly significant among the tragedies of his age. This is true in spite of the indignant, crusading spirit which marks everything he wrote. Marston succeeds only in being moralistic, never in attaining the truly moral vision. This is so because his impulse is essentially satiric rather than tragic. He is concerned with attacking vice, painting it in its most horrible and revolting forms. He is not concerned with the relation of good and evil to one another within the cosmos, or with the relation of human suffering to human joy. He is incapable of that kind of acceptance of the fact of evil which is implicit in any total cosmic vision. Behind his plays is always the impulse to destroy evil by revealing how horrible or ludicrous it truly is, and thus his end is not the understanding of the human condition, but rather the improvement of social life by the eradication of vice. In this distinction is much of the difference between tragedy and satire.

*Antonio's Revenge* and *The Insatiate Countess,* while they deal with suffering and death, and in spite of the greatness of much of their poetry, arc rendered absurd by Marston's satiric impulse. The only one of his plays which really can be called a tragedy is that neglected play he wrote at the end of his literary career, before he abandoned the stage and disappeared into the obscurity of the church. This play is *Sophonisba, or The Wonder of Women,* which T. S. Eliot in a rather surprising reversal of the usual judgment, has called the greatest of Marston's works.[9] But the very qualities which lead Eliot to praise this play are, I believe, what render it also so unlike the plays with which we are here concerned. *Sophonisba* does not seem to spring from any attempt to reconcile the confusion and uncertainties of the Jacobean age; it springs rather from Marston's admiration for the ancients, for it is above all else an exercise in Senecan imitation. Eliot is perceptive in pointing to the greatness of much of its poetry, but the play's moral statement is little more than the typical Senecan acknowledgment of the supremacy of fate and the need for man to face his destiny with stoical courage and acceptance. It reflects the moral dilemma of Marston's age only to the extent that it illustrates that tendency to look to the classical world for models of an excellence which men in the de-

[9] *Selected Essays* (London, 1951), pp. 230–3.

generate present may strive to emulate, and it is similar to Chapman's *Caesar and Pompey*. It does not reflect that agonized struggle with the realities of the dramatist's own age which marks Chapman's greater and more successful plays. Eliot writes that one must come to this play fresh from Corneille and Racine, that it belongs with the French and English classicists rather than with the Shakespearians. This fact sets it apart from that current in Jacobean tragedy with which we are concerned.

What is true of *Sophonisba* is in large measure true also of Ben Jonson's two Roman tragedies, for they also are the products of classical imitation, the only essays in tragedy of a dramatist whose greatness lay in other areas. Not the tragic but the satiric spirit is the key to Jonson's greatness, and it is why he achieved his stature as one of the greatest writers of English comedy. He knew how to attack the evils of mankind, and he did so effectively in comedy, his goal being always the satirist's object of social improvement. His conception of the goals of tragedy is clearly outlined in the address to the readers which he prefaced to the 1605 edition of *Sejanus,* where he listed among its essential qualities, "truth of argument, dignity of persons, gravity and height of elocution, fullness and frequency of sentence." In these principles Jonson is following not his own native dramatic tradition, but the neo-classical critics of France and Italy, Scaliger and Castelvetro. All of the qualities he lists are evident in his *Sejanus* and *Catiline,* but these remain among the last read of all his plays. They do not reveal the kind of struggle for a vision of man's role in the universe which is an essential feature of the greatest tragedies. Jonson's Roman plays belong, perhaps, more closely in the tradition of Roman satire than they do in that of English tragedy.

*Sejanus* and *Catiline* remain the scholar's attempts to achieve a classical ideal in tragedy, and like Marston's plays they are moralistic rather than moral, for they do not use the events of Rome to reflect, as Shakespeare always does in his Roman tragedies, upon the larger questions of mankind in general. Roman history is used for the parallels it may afford to the specific political vices of Jonson's own day. His supposed tragedies reveal the same impulse towards social correction which more properly governs Jonson's comedies. He is concerned not with mankind but with the corruption in the court of King James. His "fullness and frequency of sentence" becomes not a statement of general moral truth, but simply the repetition of commonplace moral injunctions gleaned from the ancients, and primarily from Seneca. His "truth of argument" gives to his plays perhaps a greater validity as history than as tragedy, while his "dignity of persons" and "gravity and height of elocution" firmly link his plays to the Senecan ideal he is imitating, with its heavy reliance upon essentially sterile devices of rhetoric. *Sejanus* and *Catiline* in many respects are interesting plays, and they deserve perhaps a greater place than usually has been accorded to them in critical estimates of Jonson's achievement, but they do not belong in the company with which we here are concerned.

The final years of the Jacobean era are dominated by the influence of Beaumont and Fletcher, through the plays they wrote individually and together, and through those which they produced in collaboration with Massinger, Field and Shirley. Their influence is strong upon John Ford, and I shall suggest that only as he learned to overcome this influence did Ford write the kind of truly moral tragedy which links him rather with Shakespeare and Webster. Although the tragedies of Beaumont and Fletcher are concerned with ethical and political problems, and although their work is an intimate reflection of the age which produced it, the kind of tragedy they wrote—of which *The Maid's Tragedy* is the finest example—is incapable of expressing the kind of moral vision with which we are concerned.

J. F. Danby has pointed to Beaumont and Fletcher as the dramatists who best express a nostalgia for Elizabethan values—the elegant aristocratic life of the great house—which can no longer survive in the seventeenth century, and he has called *The Maid's Tragedy* a perfect reflection of the tensions of the Jacobean world.[10] There is much truth in this, and it is possible to see Aspatia, as Danby sees her, as a symbol of the rejected Elizabethan values, and Amintor as the symbol of an honour which consists

[10] *Poets on Fortune's Hill* (London, 1952), pp. 152–206.

only in outward appearance, and thus is only a debased shadow of the true code of honour represented by Melantius. Beaumont and Fletcher might have written truly moral tragedy. I would suggest that they failed to do so because of their very attachment to a past social ideal which may never have fully existed except in men's minds, and because the ethical paradoxes they examine are related only to artificial—and ultimately unimportant—patterns of social conduct, and never to the larger problem of the relation of good to evil in the world. There is, moreover, no real working through of these paradoxes in their plays, no evidence of real intellectual and emotional involvement, what Eliot has called a struggle for harmony in the soul of the poet. The paradoxes which form the central conflicts of their plays are resolved by dramaturgy, the clever manipulation of situation, with a masterly control of shock and suspense. There is no real quest for moral certainty in their plays, only the facile reduction of artificially contrived paradoxes, with no attempt to resolve moral issues.

*The Maid's Tragedy* rings its many changes on the themes of honour, love and friendship, values dear to the Elizabethan world of Wilson and Penshurst, but in this play reduced to a specious shallowness. Amintor is torn at first between his love for Aspatia and his loyalty to the king, two conflicting absolute values, and we must remember that Beaumont and Fletcher are as conservative as Heywood in their doctrine that the king, no matter how evil he may be, must be unconditionally obeyed. Amintor must sacrifice the honour of his betrothed for his loyalty to the king. When he learns that Evadne is the king's whore, he is again torn between duty and honor, for he cannot oppose the king who has made him a cuckold. The shallowness of the ideal of honour to which these characters so thoroughly are committed is revealed by Evadne: she has married Amintor to preserve an honour which in truth already has been forfeited, and to do so she must destroy the honour of her husband by making him a cuckold. In the same way Amintor must be a knowing bawd to his wife in order to preserve his own honour because to reveal his cuckoldry is to destroy his reputation and thus his honour. Honour here is a meaningless pretence.

Similarly, Melantius, when Amintor calls Evadne a whore, must kill his friend to preserve the non-existent honour of his sister. When Melantius, moved by friendship, finally offers to kill the king to preserve the honour of Amintor, his friend draws his sword against him, for an exposure of the king will destroy Amintor's reputation. Melantius is faced with the paradox that to preserve the already forfeited honour of his family he must destroy the already forfeited honour of his friend.

Such paradoxes have no validity in moral terms because they are merely explorations of the nuances of a code of behaviour which has no relation to reality, and it is a code from which no character is capable of the slightest departure. Their absolute stances represent no real moral positions, merely varieties of pretence. The paradoxes must be resolved if the audience is to be satisfied, and for this purpose Beaumont and Fletcher use the simple device of having Evadne undergo a sudden reformation and then murder the king. The conflict of absolutes upon which the play is constructed is in no way resolved. No moral statement emerges, although in the death of Aspatia there may be, as Danby holds, a lament for the beauties of a world which can be no more.

The great popularity of such drama may signal the decline of tragedy of real moral intensity. In the plays of Beaumont and Fletcher we see the triumph of theatricality over philosophical substance. This may be related to the growing dominance of the particular coterie theatre for which these dramatists wrote, the influence of the court with its particular tastes and attitudes, and the gradual relegation of the great popular theatre for which Shakespeare wrote to the confines of the lower middle class audiences at the Red Bull.

It is also true that in the age of Shirley and Massinger many of the intellectual conflicts of the Jacobean era were ceasing to have the intensity they had had when Chapman, Tourneur and Webster were writing their plays. The great issues of the seventeenth century were approaching some resolution. The idea of human progress had begun to triumph; the new scientific age was coming into its maturity, and England was becoming more deeply involved in the political and social problems which in 1642 were to bring

265

the theatres to a close. The plays of Massinger and Shirley are no longer vehicles for profound self discovery and philosophical statement. They are exploitations for the sake of an amusement-loving court of the theatricality learned from Beaumont and Fletcher. A play like Shirley's *The Cardinal,* although brilliantly constructed and no doubt extremely effective upon the stage, is merely the shallow imitation of only some external features of Webster's Italian tragedies. These men succeed most notably in facile court comedy. The great age of English tragedy had come to a close with John Ford, some ten years before the closing of the theatres.

# VI

## THE ELIZABETHAN AGE: A SYNTHESIS

*Patrick Cruttwell's "The Society of the Shakespearean Moment" is taken from this book,* The Shakespearean Moment. *It is the fourth chapter of this book.*

## THE SOCIETY OF
## THE SHAKESPEARE MOMENT

### By Patrick Cruttwell

If the essential features of this poetry [of the Elizabethan Age] be the abilities to include everything and to concentrate many orders of experience on to a single point, then it is clear that such poetry will be possible only in a society which both provides plenty to include and provides it in such a way that it *can* be brought together. The first requirement will be a view of life which does not specialize and does not exclude.

"Does not specialize" means, for our purpose, that sets of emotions and ideas which for us are non-transferable from one context to another, were in that age, for the kind of mentality that Donne and Shakespeare represent, fully transferable. It was always possible—and they were always attempting it—to build bridges from subject to subject, emotion to emotion; these bridges, increasingly fragile in the domains of pure ideas and practical politics, still held in that of poetry—and just because of their fragility in other domains, they were all the more tempting and precious. Between the spiritual and the political, for instance. A passage not yet looked at* in the *Second Anniversarie*

* The reference is to Chapter 3, "The Poetry of the Shakespearean Moment," in Cruttwell's book, *The Shakespearean Moment*.

gives a perfect example. In the section "Of our company in this life and in the next," Donne evolves a series of elaborate conceits to establish a parallel between "her" and a sovereign State, all of whose functions she (in metaphor) performed: she made war and peace, she "did high justice," she gave pardons, she coined, she gave protections; and hence

> As these prerogatives being met in one,
> Made her a soveraigne State; religion
> Made her a Church; and these two made her all.

These lines touch one of the nerve-centres of the seventeenth century, and in particular of the kind of poetry we are analysing now. Without this intense feeling for a nexus, an absolute identity, between the spiritual, the political, and the personal—it could be, as here, the feminine, quasi-amorous personal—the poetry of the Shakespearean moment would not be what it is. These three things—spiritual, political, personal—are united, in a way essentially the same, in Ulysses' words to Achilles in *Troilus and Cressida:*

> The providence that's in a watchfull State,
> Knowes almost every graine of Plutoes gold;
> Findes bottome in th' uncomprehensive deepes;
> Keepes pace with thought; and almost like the gods,
> Does thoughts unvaile in their dumbe cradles:
> There is a mysterie (with whom relation
> Durst never meddle) in the soule of State;
> Which hath an operation more divine,
> Than breath or pen can give expressure to.
>
> (III,3)

What Ulysses is talking about may seem to a modern mind somewhat inappropriate as basis for a passage of such mysterious, almost mystical, solemnity; he is assuring Achilles that the Greeks' Military Intelligence is well aware of his goings-on with the Trojan Polyxena. Spying, in fact; but this in no way debars Shakespeare from feeling and expressing the same union of spiritual and political that Donne felt: "providence," "like the gods," "mysterie," "divine"—the recurring key-words keep hammering at the

268

spiritual note. Through poetry such as this—and through it alone—we can go some way towards restoring the flesh and blood of emotional reality to the dry bones of the clichés in the history textbooks. "Church and State," "divine right," "no King, no Bishop"—the twentieth century is apt to read them as if they were mere political slogans, on the level of "Votes for women" or "No taxation without representation": and so reading, fatally misunderstands them.

Divine right, it is true, was a Tudor, not a medieval invention; but it can be said that it was an invention in the medieval mode. It belongs to the same kind of thinking, represents the same sort of ambition, as that which made Dante see the fall of Troy as an event which led to Aeneas' founding of Rome, which led to the Roman Empire, which existed so that in due time—in God's name—a framework of political order might be ready for the reception of the spiritual order of Christianity: which double order should still (if things went right) be the pattern for Emperor and Pope to follow. The society of Donne and Shakespeare, still medieval at least in this part of its mind, still pursued the medieval dream of synthesizing all things to a single system, with the spiritual at its head; it tried to realize, for the smaller field of England, and the Church of England, what had been a dream for Europe. It is by remembering the existence of this dream that we can understand what may seem to be—sometimes are—absurd excesses of sycophancy bordering on the blasphemous: such things as Donne's confident anticipating, for the benefit of his sovereign, the verdict of the Almighty (he is speaking of Queen Elizabeth and King James):

> Though then these two great princes (of whom the one con-regnat Christo, reigns now with Christ, the other reigns over us vice Christi, for Christ) were near in blood, yet thus were they nearest of kin, quod uterque optimus, that they were both better then any other, and equal to each other.
>
> (Sermon preached on 24 March, 1617)

Poets who thought and felt in this way would always be inclined, in their poetry, to unite rather than divide, amalgamate rather than distinguish; hence the conceit—most characteristic poetic weapon of the Shakespearean moment —is above all a device for uniting disparate things. And especially for uniting the concrete and the abstract, the sensuous and the spiritual; we have seen how this poetry is sensuous through and through, how it roots the transcendental in the earthy and renders in physical terms its mental and spiritual states. Of such a mentality the ecclesiastical concomitants are obvious: colour and music and ritual in the Anglo-catholic service. What goes with it in politics is equally clear: a reluctance to secularize, an instinct for seeing political processes as more than matters of merely rational "policy." Of all three the real meaning is the same: a preservation—precarious, soon to be lost, but alive for all that—of the medieval heritage. It is quite clear that to Donne, for example, it was the traditional theology of the Middle Ages, and not the new science, which "came home to his business and bosom"; it was the former, and not the latter, which was linked with his bodily and emotional life; the latter, not the former, which for him was the dry abstraction. "Medieval heritage" is a meaningless cliché in itself: what, in our context of a poetry which is permeated by the sensuous, did it actually mean? It meant, above all, a way of thinking about the human creature which united body and soul. This way of thinking was not in the least vague; it was thoroughly systematic and "scientific," however badly wrong. It could be, and was, systematized (the Middle Ages systematized everything), and a glance at it in the realm of physiology, at its view of the human body, will illuminate more than that realm alone.

Medieval physiology was also psychology. Its bases, of course (derived from Galen), were the four elements and the four humours. They in themselves need no elucidation. But for our purposes the point is that the humours were thought of as strictly and literally physiological realities. Their use as "metaphors" for human behavior was secondary and very closely linked to the physiology which lay behind them. They were produced by the liver; they were liquids, spread through the body in the blood. The psychological conditions which resulted from an excess of one

270

or the other were thought of as physical diseases, which drugs or dieting could deal with. Choler, for instance. When Hamlet tells Guildenstern (who has reported that the King "is in his retirement marvellous distempered . . . with choler") that he, Guildenstern, would do better "to signify this to his doctor," and when Petruchio remarks that he cannot eat mutton—"for it engenders choler, planteth anger"—neither is being fanciful: both are reproducing the medical commonplaces of their age. (Rhubarb was for choler a favourite prescription, as Webster's Ferdinand knew.) So with melancholy: this was seen as a "drosse and thicking" in the blood[1]—a physical condition, as Shakespeare sees it in *King John:*

> Or if that surly spirit melancholy
> Had bak'd thy bloud, and made it heavy, thicke,
> Which else runnes tickling up and downe the veines . . .
>
> (III, 3)

This kind of physical-psychical parallelism runs all through the thought of the age, and is constantly appearing in its imaginative writing. A hot and moist humour led to (and was a symptom of) lechery: Othello brooding over Desdemona's hand ("give me your hand; this hand is moist, my Lady . . ."), and Cleopatra's maids joking with the soothsayer, are all referring to this:

> —There's a Palme presages Chastity, if nothing els.
> —E'ne as the o're-flowing Nilus presageth Famine . . .
> Nay, if an oyly Palme bee not a fruitful Prognostication . . .
>
> (I, 2)

[1] The phrase comes from Sir Thomas Vicary's *Profitable Treatise of the Anatomie of Mans Body*, published in 1548:the first text-book of anatomy and physiology printed in English. Vicary was a royal surgeon to four Tudor monarchs (from Henry VIII to Elizabeth); he was Master of the Barber Surgeon's Company and a governor of Bart's. His treatise (which I have drawn on extensively in this and following pages) is thoroughly representative of the orthodox medical ideas of the age. It goes back to a four-teenth-century MS. which in turn goes back still earlier. But the fact that the sixteenth century regarded it as authoritative is shown by its republication in 1577 (after Vicary's death) by the surgeons of Bart's; it seems to have been used as a textbook for at least a century more.

271

The colour of the cheeks was symptomatic of the humour prevailing. If the cheeks are "full, ruddy, and meddled with temperate whiteness," the nature is "sanguin and temperat"; if they are "white coloured, without medling of rednes," it is "flematike"; if "browne in colour," choleric; if "as it were blowen in colour" (a livid yellowish pallor, presumably) then melancholy is the temperament.[2] So, when Agamemnon in *Troilus and Cressida* asks the assembled Greeks "Princes: what greefe hath set the Jaundice on your cheekes?" and when Viola talks of the "green and yellow" melancholy of her imaginary and lovesick sister, neither expression is merely figurative, as a modern reader is inclined to take them; both are literal, physiological as well as psychological. The "spirits," natural, animal, and vital, which in all this medical theory come second in importance only to the humours, are, like the humours, physical substances, conveyed in the blood. Liver, heart, and brain, regarded as the master-organs of the body,[3] produce the spirits: the animal spirit, produced by the brain, is that which makes Antony feel he is still young enough to fight:

What Gyrle, though gray
Do somthing mingle with our younger brown, yet ha' we
A Braine that nourishes our Nerves, and can
Get gole for gole of youth.

(IV, 8)

If the humours of the brain be not properly balanced, then comes trouble:

Wherefore (sayth Aristotle) when it happeneth that the Brayne is eyther too drye or too moyst, then can it not worke his kinde; for then is the body made colde; then are the spirites of lyfe melted and resolued away; and then foloweth feebleness of the wittes, and of al other members of the body, and at the last death.
(Vicary, op. cit.)

[2] All from Vicary, op. cit.
[3] Cf. *The liver, heart, and braine of* Brittaine, *By whom I grant she lives*. (*Cymbeline*, V, 5.)

272

On which physiology Falstaff bases his defence of sherris sack:

> It ascends me into the Braine, dryes me there all the foolish, and dull, and cruddie Vapours, which environ it . . .

(2 *Henry IV*, IV, 3)

What all this amounts to is a link between body and character so close that it might almost be called behaviourist—would be behaviourist, indeed, but for belief in the soul. There seems a contradiction here: perhaps there is. On the one hand, this body-soul integration, based (as they thought) on real fact, exact science; on the other hand, the theology which (as seen in the *Second Anniversarie*) drew a very clear line between body and soul and in fact represented them as hostile. It was certainly a much-debated question of the age, just where the soul could be fitted into this framework so precisely marked out; Sir John Davies gives us some of the rival theories in the introduction to his poem *Of the Immortality of the Soul*:

> In judgment of her substance thus they vary,
>   And thus they vary in judgment of her seat;
> For some her chair up to the brain do carry,
>   Some thrust it down into the stomach's heat;
> Some place it in the root of life, the heart;
>   Some in the river-fountain of the veins;
> Some say, she's all in all, and all in every part,
>   Some say, she's not contained, but all contains.

The soul, then, was thought of both as something which fought against the body and aspired to escape from it, and as a part of the body; and it was this kind of thinking—there seems no doubt that Donne and Shakespeare and the rest thoroughly shared in it, took it for granted, indeed, as we take for granted (without, most of us, really comprehending) the existence of vitamins and their effects on our bodies—it was this that made it not only possible and easy, but inevitable, for the poets of the Shakespearean moment to fuse the physical with the spiritual. They still held the medieval integration. Their ideas on man's body, on his

273

character and soul, on his religious and his political activities, still formed a whole—and formed it not merely in the sphere of metaphor but in that of science. In such a mental climate, it was not fancifulness to draw parallels between the order of the planets and that of human society (as it ought to be) and between the disorders of a troubled State and the diseases of a man's body. The poets who drew such parallels believed that all this was *true*. The forces which were to prove that in the sphere of science almost all of it was nonsense, and in the spheres of politics and religion all of it could be torn apart and defeated, were gathering and strengthening; the tension was steadily tightening, but the break was not yet.

Parallels between politics and literature should always be made with caution and received with scepticism; but perhaps it is not accidental that the age of the Shakespearean moment was one of comparative settlement between two great upheavals: the Reformation and its consequences before it, the Civil War after it. The settlement was highly precarious, what with Roman Catholic fanatics in the basement of the Houses of Parliament and Puritan or Arminian fanatics in half the pulpits of the land; the tension was held but only just held. And this is exactly the quality of the age's poetry. A poem like the *Second Anniversarie,* or a play like *King Lear,* maintains, but only just maintains, control over the clashing elements which compose it. Chaos is very near; its nearness, but its avoidance, gives the poetry its force. And the poetry delights in it; it takes the pure pleasure of the dramatist-as-artist in giving the maximum power and persuasiveness, the greatest possible chance of victory, to those forces which the dramatist-as-individual regarded as "enemies." Such art—the art of true tragedy—is possible only to those whose view of life is tragic but not pessimistic; they must have no delusions, no wishful-thinking, about the actual behaviour, capacities, and fates of men on the human level, but must believe that there exists another level on which those fates are redeemed. If they have the delusions, they sentimentalize; if they do not have the faith, the tragedy turns to mere sadism—or masochism. For Christians, the terms by which the tragic sense can be kept are original

274

sin (for the lack of delusions on the human level) and redemption (for the faith on another). By the former, one was disembarrassed from any hope that mankind, in this existence, would ever "progress"; by the latter, one felt no need for such a hope, since another, and better, was believed to be available. The dramatist could give the devil a good long rope—and thoroughly enjoy his capers at the end of it—because he knew that at last, the devil would hang.

Hence the poetry of the Shakespearean moment—which is shot through with the tragic sense—sprang from, and depended on, a view of politics essentially conservative, and a view of religion essentially orthodox: these two making up a view of humanity tragic but not hopeless. By such a view it was possible to give full value to all sides of human nature: which the progressive and optimistic mentality—represented, as the following chapters will argue, by the Puritan and the rationalist—could never do; for that mentality must always be tempted to minimize, or shut its eyes to, or try to suppress, some parts of the human variety.

Variety is one of the essentials of the poetry we are studying, and only a society which was various in itself could feed such poetry. But the variety must have some meaning: not chaotic, but ordered. And such was the variety of seventeenth century society: aristocratic but not snobbish; hierarchical without being petrified. The age of the first two Stuarts saw the English aristocracy reach a kind of distinction—not so easy to define but quite unmistakable—which, like the age's poetry, has a quality of its own. It seems—again, like the poetry—to get the best of all worlds, to be poised with a delicate force between extremes. The flamboyance, brutality, and whimsicality which so often give to the Elizabethan aristocracy an air of adolescence, are now toned down to a real refinement, but a refinement still far from the over-elaborate artificiality to which the aristocracy of the eighteenth century tended to bring it.

These aristocrats, the men of the early Stuarts, compared with their forebears or their descendants, seem much more often and more successfully in tune with the best of the spiritual and artistic worlds of their age. And hence the patron-writer relationship, notoriously one of the trickiest of all human associations, "comes off" then surprisingly well. Clarendon, for instance, testifies to Falkland's success with that most difficult member of the irritable genus, Ben Jonson:

> He seemed to have his estate in trust for all worthy persons who stood in want of supplies and encouragement, as Ben Jonson, and many others of that time, whose fortunes required, and whose spirits made them superior to, ordinary obligations; which yet they were contented to receive from him . . .

But the harmony went deeper than a tactful bestowal and a dignified acceptance of patronage; the relationship was often such that the very words "patron" and "patronage" seem hopelessly inappropriate. Imagine for a moment how utterly impossible it would be that a poet of the eighteenth century—or in fact after the Restoration—should feel for his patron anything like the depth and quality of emotion that Shakespeare felt for his Mr. W. H. Into such relationships—that of Shakespeare and Mr. W. H. was not the only one—there entered a warmth and sometimes a passion which did not destroy feelings of reverence and inequality —on the contrary, those feelings were intensified—but gave to the relationships a genuine value in themselves, not merely in the benefits they conferred. They could be, as they were for Shakespeare, not only the means by which the poet could live, but a valuable material for his poetic creation. So with Donne—though *his* patrons were apt to be women. For Magdalen Herbert (George Herbert's remarkable mother) Donne felt a complex of emotions which, allowing for the differences caused by the difference in sex and ages and by a strong devotional tone, are by no means incomparable with Shakespeare's feelings for Mr. W. H. The latter were a subtle and changing blend of love and tenderness for a beautiful and gifted young man, reverence and gratitude for a noble patron; Donne's feelings for Mrs. Herbert were a strange amalgam (strange to us, not to them) of a devotion almost religious, a respectfulness almost courtly, and a love which may or may not have had some tinge of the sexual. The sermon he

276

preached at her funeral service gives the first of these aspects:

> For, as the rule of all her civil actions, was religion, so, the rule of her religion, was the Scripture; and, her rule, for her particular understanding of the Scripture, was the church.

The lines in his verse-letter to her, which say to the paper on which the letter is written

> But when thou com'st to that perplexing eye
> Which equally claimes *love* and *reverence*

(the emphasis is Donne's), give the courtliness and the love. And why "perplexing"?—because, presumably, Donne himself is not sure whether "love" or "reverence" is the right emotion. Jealousy too (as Shakespeare's Sonnets abundantly prove) could enter into such relations; the crowding of writers round a favourite patron could be thought of as if it were the attracting of lovers to a famous beauty. Donne again—still addressing his paper—sees it in Mrs. Herbert's cabinet, among its rivals, as if in a bundle of *billets doux*:

> Who knowes thy destiny? when thou hast done,
> Perchance her Cabinet may harbour thee,
> Whither all noble ambitious wits doe runne,
> A nest almost as full of Good as shee.

Even the cantankerous and commonsensical Jonson is not above such feelings; his epistle to the Countess of Rutland includes a few lines on Lucy, Countess of Bedford (also Donne's patroness):

> . . . Lucy the bright,
> Than whom a nobler Heaven itselfe knowes not.
> Who, though she have a better verser got,
> (Or poet, in the court account) than I,
> And who doth me (though I not him) envy . . .

Who the rival may be is not clear—it might be Donne, except that one can hardly imagine Donne "envying" Jonson—but the feelings there, of a rivalry felt as something more personal than a mere competition for hard cash,

277

are akin to Donne's for Mrs. Herbert, and akin to Shakespeare's for Mr. W. H. There is a vital difference between the literary-social world of the seventeenth century and that which we of the twentieth know and are conditioned to—a difference very obvious but rarely given its full value in criticism: the fact that in the seventeenth century a writer's public, those whom he wrote for and whose tastes counted in what he wrote, were actual individuals personally known to himself.[4] To this almost the only exceptions were the audiences for the popular drama and the public for pamphlets and broadsheets: once a writer left these worlds—as Shakespeare left the former in the Sonnets—he was committed to a kind of life in which personal relationships and personal emotions were inextricably involved with his literary career.

Such emotions, when blended with literary ambitions and a writer's career, the modern mind finds hard to comprehend: it asks with some bewilderment if Shakespeare was "in love" with Mr. W. H. and if Donne was "in love" with Mrs. Herbert? if she was his mistress? and if so, in what sense? Sir Herbert Grierson thought she was—in some sense or other; Professor Garrod, with indignation, declared she was not—in any sense at all.[5] Donne and Mrs. Herbert, one imagines, would have been much surprised, and somewhat amused, at such debatings. Of course (Donne himself would have answered) he loved Mrs. Herbert; but the word "love" had other and wider meanings than it has to-day, and its very narrowing indicates an impoverishment in a wider sphere than that of language alone.

[4] Poetry in the 1950's seems to be reverting to this condition. But since it is doing so not willingly but *faute de mieux* (*faute de* anyone willing to buy the stuff), the actual results may not be so happy.

[5] Walton's remark (in the *Life* of George Herbert) seems to show, by its protesting tone, that some contemporaries were a trifle dubious:

> This amity, begun at this time and place, was not an amity that polluted their souls; but an amity made up of a chain of suitable inclinations and virtues; an amity like that of St. Chrysostom's to his dear and virtuous Olympias; whom, in his letters, he calls his Saint . . .

The point is, for our purposes, that the word could be employed, without scruple and without insincerity, in a patron-poet relationship. When a poet of the early seventeenth century said that he loved his patron, male or female, more often than not he meant no less than he said.

And the patrons—the best of them—deserved it. Two of them we may take as specimens: Lucius Cary, Viscount Falkland, who was perhaps the best of all, and William Herbert, Earl of Pembroke—who may have had the most famous of "lovers."

For both of them the best source is Clarendon [1609-1674]: best for our purpose, of imaginative reconstruction, as much as for factual information. For Clarendon himself came of this strain of Jacobean and Caroline gentry; his judgments and his emotions drew from the same sources as fed those men who read and rewarded Shakespeare and Jonson and Donne. His praises of Falkland, whom he loved more than he did any other man, make some of the greatest passages of English prose; that in the *History of the Rebellion* begins with two noble sentences which at once set the tone of the whole:

> But I must here take leave a little longer to discontinue this narration; and if the celebrating the memory of eminent and extraordinary persons, and transmitting their great virtues, for the imitation of posterity, be one of the principal ends and duties of history, it will not be thought impertinent, in this place, to remember a loss which no time will suffer to be forgotten, and no success or good fortune could repair. In this unhappy battle was slain the lord viscount Falkland; a person of such prodigious parts of learning and knowledge, of that inimitable sweetness and delight in conversation, of so flowing and obliging a humanity and goodness to mankind, and of that primitive simplicity and integrity of life, that if there were no other brand upon this odious and accursed civil war, than that single loss, it must be most infamous, and execrable to all posterity.

> Turpe mori, post te, solo non posse dolore.

This is the monumental style, the weighty Ciceronian

eloquence, the kind of prose which one feels should be carved on a tomb—and that, in words, is just what Clarendon has set himself to make. The spirit it expresses was a vital ingredient in the emotion which the age felt (or wished to feel) for those who stood at the apex of its social order: the classical conception of greatness, the classical and Renaissance conviction that poet and historian must celebrate such greatness "for the imitation of posterity." It takes us back to that sonnet of Petrarch which tells how Alexander, coming to the tomb of Achilles, wept at the thought that he, Alexander, had no trumpet as great as Homer to keep his fame alive; and that in turn goes back to the lines of Horace:

> Vixere fortes ante Agamemnona
> multi; sed omnes illacrimabiles
>     urgentur ignotique longa
>     nocte, carent quia vate sacro.

The spirit in which the Renaissance read and thought of its ancient history Clarendon can transfer—not unselfconsciously but not unnaturally—to the consideration of his own times and the praise of his own most deeply-loved friend. It is not incomparable with what we have seen Shakespeare doing in the Sonnets: transferring to the young man, and seeing in him embodied, all the glamour of medieval chivalry.

But this alone—the monumental reverence—would not be enough; more is needed, to account for the love that Falkland evoked. What he possessed was the power of uniting worlds which in our age seem irretrievably disparate, and of doing so not because he thought it his duty (though no doubt he *did* think so), but because he wanted to, because his deepest interests embraced those worlds. Though he himself (it would have to be "though" nowadays) was an aristocrat, a man of great wealth, and a politician (Member of Parliament, and Secretary of State), "his familiarity and friendship," says Clarendon, "for the most part, was with men of the most eminent and sublime parts, and of untouched reputation in point of integrity; and such men had a title to his bosom." He was a patron and friend to wits and poets—"he was a great cherisher of wit, and fancy, and good parts in any man"— and also to scholars (these worlds also were not then separate): "his house being within ten miles of Oxford, he contracted familiarity and friendship with the most polite and accurate men of that university."

His own intellectual life followed a pattern not unlike Donne's. It began in the tradition of the Renaissance courtier who was also an amateur writer—as Anthony Wood puts it:

> His first years of reason were spent in poetry and polite learning, into the first of which he made divers plausible sallies which caused him therefore to be admired by the poets of that time.

But—typical of his kind—theology was his deepest concern. The son of a Roman Catholic mother who made enormous efforts to convert her children (and succeeded with almost all save the best of them, Falkland himself), he regarded, as Donne did, the decision on the question— which church is the true Church?—as the most vital of all decisions. Medieval scholasticism was still alive for his mind: "he had read" (Clarendon again) "all the Greek and Latin fathers; all the most allowed and authentic ecclesiastical writers." But however deeply involved in theological controversy, in that age when such controversy was even more than normally un-Christian in spirit, he kept his tolerance and charity, his dislike of violence and rancour. In his own words: "Truth in likelyhood is where her author God was, in the *still voice,* and not the *loud wind.*"[6] And although his opinions settled down as those of a moderate Anglican, he was very far from uncritical admiration of the Laudian party then dominant in the Church; Clarendon is rather worried by his dislike of Laud, and his speech in the Commons debate on the Root and Branch and the Ministers' Petitions contains as fierce an

[6] From Falkland's one work of theology, *Of the Infallibility of the Church of Rome.*

attack on the bishops' excesses and deficiencies as even a Milton could hope for—though Milton would not have approved its conclusion, that the men should be reformed, not the institution abolished. His friends among the clergy, the members of the *convivium philosophicum* which met at his house near Oxford, seem all to have had this moderation and decency: such men as John Hales [1584-1656], whose opinions Clarendon describes:

> Nothing troubled him more than the brawls which were grown from religion; and he therefore exceedingly detested the tyranny of the Church of Rome; more for their imposing uncharitably upon the consciences of other men than for the errors in their own opinions: and would often say that he would renounce the religion of the Church of England to-morrow if it obliged him to believe that any other Christians should be damned.

—and Chillingworth, whose own words show the same spirit:

> Take away this persecuting, burning, cursing, damning of men for not subscribing to the words of men as the words of God; require of Christians only to believe Christ, and to call no man master but him only; let those leave claiming infallibility that have no title to it, and let them that in their word disclaim it, disclaim it likewise in their actions. In a word, take away tyranny, which is the devil's instrument to support errors and superstitions and impieties in the several parts of the world, which could not otherwise long withstand the power of truth.
>
> (*Religion of Protestants a safe way of Salvation*)

That spirit was characteristic, if not of the age as a whole, at least of that part of it which not only seems, but in fact was, linked with metaphysical and Shakespearean verse. Such tolerant commonsense was also Donne's:

> You know I never fettered nor imprisoned the word Religion; not . . . immuring it in a Rome, or a Wittemberg, or a Geneva; they are all virtuall beams of one sun.

282

This is the equivalent, in theological thought, of the dramatists' art of seeing and valuing all sides.

And Falkland's politics were as decent and moderate as his theology; when the war began, he took—as his birth and background made certain he must take—the royalist side; but his intellectual sympathies were at least as much with the Parliament, and he told the King of his errors and deficiencies with a freedom which the latter did not always enjoy. His one desire was for peace. The war changed, as Clarendon most movingly describes, his very demeanour and appearance:

> From the entrance into this unnatural war, his natural cheerfulness and vivacity grew clouded and a kind of sadness and dejection of spirit stole upon him, which he had never been used to . . . and he, who had been so exactly unreserved and affable to all men, that his face and countenance was always present, and vacant to his company, and held any cloudiness, and less pleasantness of the visage, a kind of rudeness or incivility, became on a sudden less communicable; and thence very sad, pale and exceedingly affected with the spleen. In his clothes and habit, which he had intended before always with more neatness, and industry, and expense, than is usual to so great a mind, he was not now only incurious, but too negligent. . . . When there was any overture or hope of peace, he would be more erect and vigorous, and exceedingly solicitous to press any thing which he thought might promote it; and sitting among his friends, often, after a deep silence and frequent sighs, would, with a shrill and sad accent, ingeminate the word *Peace, Peace;* and would passionately profess, "that the very agony of the war and the view of the calamities and desolation the kingdom did and must endure, took his sleep from him, and would shortly break his heart."

Trevelyan remarks that Falkland, with his negligence of clothing, unaccountable behaviour, and "spleen," behaved in this crisis with something of the manner of Hamlet in *his* crisis; he might have added that just as Hamlet was, before the fatal duel, so Falkland was plainly "fey" on the morning of his last day. He was killed at Newbury in September 1643; "in the morning of the fight he called for a clean shirt, and being asked the reason of it, answered, that if he were slain in the battle they should not find his body in foul linen."[7] His death, if not quite suicide (as many contemporaries thought it was), was certainly the action of someone who was less than normally anxious to live: he rode his horse at a gap in a hedge which was lined—as he knew—by musketeers. "He died," says Clarendon, "as much of the time as of the bullet; for, from the beginning of the war he contracted so deep a sadness and melancholy that his life was not pleasant to him; and sure he was too weary of it." Carlyle and Macaulay (as one might expect) both hold him in great contempt; no prophet certain of his own rightness, and no politician certain of his party's, could fail to do so.

The tragic sense: that is clear in all the men of Falkland's kind. That his behavior should resemble Hamlet's is not entirely fortuitous and insignificant; it signals his affinity to the way of feeling which lay behind Elizabethan and Jacobean tragedy; it proves him, a Caroline, to be still a true child of the Shakespearean moment. Men of his kind, confronted with the brutal reality of civil war, responded as the tragic poets had responded to the imaginary form of it they evoked in their plays. The imagination of the Elizabethans had been haunted by a presentiment of what reality brought to their children; their plays of civil wars, medieval or Roman, were felt and presented as ominously, potentially topical. So the tragic sense, which is in Falkland, is also in Clarendon who loved and praised him, and in Andrew Marvell, on the other side in politics, but united to them by this common quality which makes him also a poet of the Shakespearean moment. What Clarendon thought of his country in civil war (he is writing of its happiness before the war broke out):

> . . . whilst the kingdoms we now lament were alone looked upon as the garden of the world

[7] Bulstrode Whitelocke: *Memorials.*

echoes exactly the lines of Marvell in *Appleton House*:

> Oh Thou, that dear and happy Isle
> The Garden of the World ere while . . .

The tragic sense is seen again—and here the dramatic vision is explicit—in the letter which Sir William Waller, the Parliamentary general, sent to his royalist friend Sir Ralph Hopton, whose defeat and wounding he was fated to bring about at the battle of Landsdown:

> The great God who is the searcher of my heart knows with what reluctance I go upon this service and with what perfect hatred I look upon a war without an enemy. The God of Peace in his good time send us peace, and in the meantime fit us to receive it. We are both on the stage, and we must act the parts that are assigned to us in this tragedy.

And the spirit of all of them had found its voice in Shakespeare's histories, in which the tragedy of civil war in itself is a theme felt far more deeply than attachment to one cause or the other; the image of the violated garden, the wrecking of innocence and fruitfulness, is in Shakespeare too, in the talk of the gardeners in *Richard II*.

Falkland's was a character of exceptional beauty; as an individual, he would never, in any age, be typical. But the elements to which he gave a special beauty of his own can be found in others, whose characters were made out of earthier stuff—such as William Herbert, whom Clarendon thus describes:

> William earl of Pembroke was next, a man of another mould and making, and of another frame and reputation with all men,[8] being the most universally loved and esteemed of any man of that age; and, having a great office in the court, he made the court itself better esteemed, and more reverenced in the country. And as he had a great number of friends of the best men, so no man had ever the wickedness to avow himself to be

[8] The contrast is with the Earl of Arundel.

his enemy. He was a man very well bred, and of excellent parts, and a graceful speaker upon any subject, having a good proportion of learning, and a ready wit to apply it, and enlarge upon it; of a pleasant and facetious humour, and a disposition affable, generous and magnificent. . . . He lived many years about the court, before in it; and never by it; being rather regarded and esteemed by king James, then loved and favoured. . . . As he spent and lived upon his own fortune, so he stood upon his own feet, without any other support than of his proper virtue and merit. . . . He was exceedingly beloved in the court, because he never desired to get that for himself, which others laboured for, but was still ready to promote the pretences of worthy men. . . . He was a great lover of his country, and of the religion and justice, which he believed could only support it; and his friendships were only with men of those principles. And as his conversation was most with men of the most pregnant parts and understanding, so towards any, who needed support or encouragement, though unknown, if fairly recommended to him, he was very liberal. And sure never man was planted in a court, that was fitter for that soil, or brought better qualities with him to purify that air.

Yet his memory must not be so flattered, that his virtues and good inclinations may be believed without some allay of vice, and without being clouded with great infirmities, which he had in too exorbitant a proportion. He indulged to himself the pleasures of all kinds, almost in all excesses. To women, whether out of his natural constitution, or for want of his domestic content, and delight (in which he was most unhappy, for he paid much too dear for his wife's fortune, by taking her person into the bargain) he was immoderately given up. But therein he likewise retained such a power and jurisdiction over his very appetite, that he was not so much transported with beauty and outward allurements, as with those advantages of the mind, as manifested an extraordinary wit, and spirit, and knowledge, and administered great pleasure in the conversation. To these he sacrificed himself, his precious time, and much of his fortune. And some, who were nearest his trust and friendship, were not without apprehension, that his natural vivacity and vigor of mind began to lessen and decline by those excessive indulgences.

Whether or not this *was* Mr. W. H., there is no doubt at all that it *could* be. Clarendon's portrait fits to perfection the character one deduces from the Sonnets: the charm, elegance, splendour, and wit, the independence and wilfulness, the generosity to men "of parts and understanding," the susceptibility to women and notorious proneness to amorous excesses,[9] and even the preference for women whose attractiveness (like that of the dark lady) came more from "character" and wits than from beauty of the chocolate-box order. This is clearly a man far removed from the almost-saintliness of Falkland; but the two have more in common than we could expect, or than most times could show, in characters on such different levels. The power of evoking not merely "esteem" but love; the unforced preference for the company of men of intellect; the insistence on a moral and political soundness (as he saw it), as well as intellectual distinction, in the men to be chosen for friends and beneficiaries:[10] these he had in common with Falkland. Herbert was born, one might say, with a patron's purse in his mouth. Son of that Countess of Pembroke for whom Sidney (her brother) wrote the *Arcadia* and whom Aubrey calls "the greatest patronesse of witt and learning of any lady in her time," tutored in his youth by Samuel Daniel, he was patron or friend or both to Donne and Chapman and Jonson (to whom he sent an annual £20 for the purchase of books)—as well as to Shakespeare: he was co-dedicatee with his younger

---

[9] Cf. the lines in the 95th Sonnet:

> That tongue that tells the story of the daies,
> (Making lascivious comments on thy sport) . . .

[10] *If* Herbert was the young man of the Sonnets (we do know, of course, that he was Shakespeare's patron), and *if* Clarendon is correct in saying that he confined his favours to men whose opinions on Church and State coincided with his (that is, Anglican and royalist), one may have here a clue to Shakespeare's opinions. But two if's don't make one certainty.

brother of the First Folio, whose editors describe the two Herberts as having "prosequted both of them [*sc.* Shakespeare's plays] and their Author living, with so much favour . . . for, so much were your Lordships' likings of the severall parts, when they were acted, as before they were published, the Volume ask'd to be yours." And there is no reason to doubt the evidence of Heminge and Condell: or to doubt the verdict of Aubrey upon the elder Herbert—"the greatest Maecenas to learned men of any peer of his time or since."

A quality of this aristocracy which counted for much in its value for the poets was that which the age called "magnificence": splendour and display, "conspicuous consumption" in the phrase of Veblen. To this the poets took up a doublefaced attitude, a characteristic blending of old and new, Christian-ascetic and Renaissance-aesthetic. They accepted—it is one of the commonplaces of their political thinking—the classical theory that "luxury" was the great destroyer of States; they accepted also the medieval Christian denunciation of it as a wrong to the poor and a distraction from thoughts of the life to come: but neither prevented them from not merely enjoying it but also giving it a value that can be called spiritual. Both Falkland and George Herbert—characters near to saintliness—show it, as Clarendon tells us of the former:

> In his clothes and habit, which he had intended before always with more neatness, and industry, and expense, than is usual to so great a mind . . .

and Walton of the latter:

> His clothes seemed to prove, that he put too great a value on his parts and parentage.

If one puts these with Sir Richard Baker's description of the youthful Donne—"not dissolute, but very neat"[11]—and with Ophelia's description of Hamlet before his troubles— "the glass of fashion and the mould of form" one sees

---

[11] "Neat" had a wider and stronger meaning than it has to-day; its modern equivalent would be something like "finely dressed."

that magnificence, a taste for finery, was not alien, on the contrary it was natural, to minds of unusual refinement and power. It had even, it seems, an association with emotional intensity. Falkland's calling for a clean shirt on the morning of Newbury has a curiously close parallel in King Charles' conduct on the morning of his execution. "Herbert," he said to his attendant, "this is my second marriage-day. I would be as trim to-day as may be; for before night I hope to be espoused to my blessed Jesus." *The Spartans on the sea-wet rock sat down and combed their hair*: an anthropologist would no doubt see all these actions as deriving from the ceremonial washing and dressing of the sacrificial victim. Magnificence was allied to "nobleness," was its outward expression, as Clarendon sees it in William Herbert:

> ... but all [*sc.* his great wealth], served not his expense, which was only limited by his great mind, and occasions to use it nobly.

And "to use it nobly" did not mean to use it with senseless extravagance. Vulgar ostentation, avaricious "new men," and shameless profiteers, abounded then as much as at any time, and received their proper treatment at the writers' hands (Ben Jonson's plays are full of them, and Shakespeare's *Timon* is an essay on indiscriminating expenditure); but just as Falkland could denounce the misdeeds of the bishops without demanding the end of episcopacy, so in this matter of magnificence the writers of the age contrived to keep their moral judgments without losing their sensuous appreciation of the colour and variety which magnificence brought into life. They made it, as they strove to make all things, into a kind of symbol: magnificence was the symbol of the "great mind" and the "noble occasions." It gave them—or their imaginations so transformed it that it could give them—yet another field in which to make concrete and actual their spiritual perceptions—in this case, their perception that there must be a hierarchy in all things; and of the hierarchy in human society, magnificence was the outward show. Just so its equivalent in the Anglo-catholic service was the outward show of the spiritual hierarchy. The "philosophy" which linked the two may be seen in this passage from Donne's *Devotions upon Emergent Occasions:*

> In Heaven there are Orders of Angels, and Armies of Martyrs, and in that house, many Mansions; in Earth, Families, Cities, Churches, Colleges, all plurall things.

That was the theory; the practice is shown in the following account of the Laudian regime in the Church where the "conspicuous consumption" for the spiritual end is perfectly clear, and the natural symphony between a monarchy, a magnificent aristocracy, an Anglo-catholic church, and a sensuous poetry, appears in a concrete example:

> The churches or chapells of all the colleges are much beautifyed, extraordinary cost bestowed on them; most of them newe glazed, richer glasse for figures and painting I have not seen, which they had most from beyond the Seas . . . excellent pictures, large and great church worke of the best hands they could gett . . .[12]

"The Barge she sat in, like a burnisht Throne burnt on the water: the Poope was beaten Gold . . ."—the collocation is not inappropriate.

When such men as Falkland and William Herbert—and such women as Magdalen Herbert—were the flesh and blood embodiments of "nobleness," whom the poets of the age knew and wrote for and loved, then it becomes comprehensible that the word and the concept of "nobleness" should have gained, as it did, such richness and power in their writings. For Shakespeare in particular the epithet of "noble" is, above all others, that which renders both social and moral distinction—*the* word for the kind of conduct expected from those who are above the common herd, by station and no less (so, as least, it should be) by soul. Through *Anthony and Cleopatra* the word rings like a refrain. It is Cleopatra's word for her own suicide,

[12] From a letter by George Garrard, describing a royal visit to Oxford in 1636: cited by Mathew, *Social Structure in Caroline England*, p. 82.

the act which is to prove her worthy of her queenliness
and of Anthony's love:

> What poore an Instrument
> May do a Noble deede . . .
> He words me Gyrles, he words me, that I should not
> Be Noble to my selfe.

It is her praise for Antony:

> Noblest of men, woo't dye?

Antony's for her:

> My Queene and *Eros*
> Have by their brave instruction got upon me
> A Noblenesse in Record.

And Antony's for himself:

> Bruised peeces go,
> You have bin Nobly borne.

Two things were combined in this concept of nobleness:
high birth on the one hand, and on the other an inherent
superiority which was (or ought to be) the consequence
of high birth, and which, in those individuals worthy of
their rank, became a quality both physical and spiritual.
We have seen that it was this inherent "nobleness" which
broke the boy Mamillius' heart when he heard of his
mother's disgrace; it shows also in his sister, even when
she is thought to be a shepherd's daughter. "Nothing she
do's, or seemes," say Polixenes, "but smackes of something greater than her selfe, too Noble for this place"; and
when the old shepherd reveals that she is a foundling, this
same quality is cited as one of the proofs of her royal
blood—". . . the Affection of Noblenesse, which Nature
shewes above her Breeding."

Modern readers may be apt to find this not only incredible, but a trifle sycophantic. And so, of course, in real
life, it very often was; when the rewards for pleasing a

nobleman might be as great as they frequently were, sycophantic adulation would not be lacking. But at its best—and we are entitled to think of it at its best, since we are concerned with it as refined into art—it was not mere worldly wisdom or snobbery, because it was never disjoined from moral judgment. Just as Willian Herbert, in Clarendon's words, "lived many years about the court, before in it; and never by it," and held himself aloof from the King's favourites, so both Donne and Shakespeare—and indeed all the poets of their age and kind—could combine a deep reverence for the Court, thought of as ideal centre of the country's soul, with a bitterly accurate perception that the real Court, more often than not, was a centre of vice and intrigue; and Shakespeare's reverence for the true thing, the real "nobleness," did not exclude a thoroughly critical attitude towards its abuses. The King's speech in *All's Well* gives the Renaissance theory, which one finds also in Castiglione: that noble birth, if unaccompanied by noble conduct, loses its title to reverence:

> That is honour's scorne,
> Which challenges it selfe as honours borne,
> And is not like the sire: Honours thrive,
> When rather from our acts we them derive
> Than our fore-goers: the meere word's a slave
> Debosh'd on everie tombe, on everie grave:
> A lying Trophee, and as oft is dumbe,
> Where dust, and damn'd oblivion is the Tombe
> Of honour'd bones indeed.
>
> (II, 3)

The point is made, in another key, by the brilliantly farcical dialogue of *The Winter's Tale*, ending the scene in which Perdita's true identity has been discovered and her inherent nobleness accounted for. Enter then the Shepherd and Clown, who proceeded to explain that they are now "gentlemen born. . . and have been so any time these four hours"; and the Clown announces that since he is a gentleman, he is perfectly entitled to tell lies and swear to them:

—You may say it, but not sweare it.

292

—Not sweare it, now I am a Gentleman? Let Boores and Franklins say it, Ile sweare it.

—How if it be false (Sonne)?

—If it be ne'r so false, a true Gentleman may sweare it, in the behalf of his Friend.

(V, 2)

The low, as so often in Shakespeare, criticize by parody and by comic misunderstanding—which is yet, in another sense, only too accurate understanding—the pretensions of the high.

When one looks at the men whom the great patrons favoured, one sees what seems to us a strange jumble of types: poets and wits, men of learning, scholars, divines. "Wit" and "learning"—by which the age meant, roughly, what we would mean by "imaginative writing" and "scholarship"—are equally the objects of patronage or friendship; the Sucklings and Carews—raffish and witty amateurs—jostle with the Shakespeares and Jonsons—professional and popular playwrights—with the Donnes and Earles—writers who lived and wrote in both secular and clerical worlds—and with the Chillingworths and Hales—scholars and theologians. Wherever one turns in this age, one comes across these blending groups. Donne is linked with Lord Herbert of Cherbury, poet and proto-Deist philosopher, and with his younger brother George, poet and divine; Jonson with Donne; Donne is a lifelong friend of Sir Henry Wotton, diplomat and Provost of Eton; Jonson is a protégé of William Herbert, who is also a patron of Shakespeare and of Chapman; Chapman is a member of Sir Walter Raleigh's circle in which, earlier, was Marlowe; Jonson again is a protégé of Falkland, who is the friend of Earle, author of *Microcosmographie* and future bishop, and of Chillingworth, most notable of Caroline Anglican theologians. The materials of the pattern are always the same, though the variants are manifold: Church, aristocracy and gentry, the scholarship of the universities, poetry and drama.

An extraordinary cultural and spiritual unity: that is the irresistible impression, and the impression is true. This society, the dominant though not all-embracing society of

293

the early seventeenth century, shows a short-lived and wonderful converging of elements which had been separate and were to be separate again. It shows, for example, the perfecting of a process the beginnings of which we saw in the 1590's. The popular drama of the London theatres finally grew out of the dis-esteem in which it had been held by the courtly and the scholarly; the Shakespeares and Jonsons were not despised by the heirs of the Sidneys (for the gentry) and the Halls (for the Church): they were admired, courted, and favoured. For Jonson, the evidence is overwhelming: he, more than any other man, perhaps, bridged this particular gap, for he alone of the dramatists had a weight of learning and a classical integrity that nobody could affect to despise. (And hence it is his name that is always recurring, more often than others, in the kind of groups described above.) But the bridging is equally clear for Shakespeare, in spite of his lack of "learning": for which we have the unimpeachable evidence of Dryden—later, of course, but not too late to have had it first-hand:

> . . . The consideration of this made Mr. Hales of Eaton say that there was no subject of which any poet ever wrote but he would produce it much better done in Shakespeare . . . and in the last King's court, when Ben's reputation was at its highest, Sir John Suckling, and him the greater part of the courtier's, set our Shakespeare far above him.
>
> (*Essay of Dramatic Poesy*)

"Mr. Hales of Eaton" is that Rev. John Hales, [1584-1656] friend of both Falkland and Clarendon, whose theological tolerance has been already cited; the "last King" is of course Charles I (Dryden is writing in the 1660's). Milton too, somewhat condescendingly, contributes his evidence to the same effect, in *Eikonoklastes:*

> I shall not instance an abstruse Author, wherein the King might be less conversant, but one whom we well know was the closet companion of these his Solitudes, *William Shakespeare* . . .

Church, courtliness, and popular drama have come to-gether; scholarship also has joined them, for Hales was (in Clarendon's phrase) "the greatest scholar in Europe."

What this converging meant, in modern terms, was a bridging of the gulf between highbrow and lowbrow, Third Programme and Light. In the Elizabethan years, there had been such a gulf: one can see it in many things—in the utterances of Sidney and Hall on the drama, in the con-scientiously "Senecan" closet-dramas of Fulke Greville and others,[13] and in the three "Parnassus" plays, which seem to set up, for a University audience, the correct and learned Jonson against the ignorant, amorous-mellifluous, popular Shakespeare. Why the gulf was bridged requires no elaborate explanation; it was bridged simply because the popular theatres began to turn out plays which deserved the admiration of the "judicious"—and the latter had suffi-cient sense and freedom from highbrow prejudice to admire as they should. The result of it is the extraordinary range of levels—it *is* extraordinary, when one thinks of it—which mature Shakespearean drama exhibits. It is incredible—to us—that poetry of the utmost difficulty and complexity, poetry such as this—

> Affection? thy Intention stabs the Center.
> Thou do'st make possible things not so held,
> Communicat'st with Dreames (how can this be?)
> With what's unreall thou co-active art,
> And fellow'st nothing. Then 'tis very credent,
> Thou may'st co-joyne with something, and thou do'st,
> (And that beyond Commission) and I find it,
> (And that to the infection of my Braines,
> And hardning of my Browes).
>
> (*Winter's Tale,* I, 2)

[13] Greville on his own plays is firm that they were not "intended for the stage": with a glance back at his adored Sir Philip, he writes:

> And if in thus ordaining and ordering matter, and forme together for the use of life, I have made these Tragedies, no Plaies for the Stage, be it known, it was no part of my purpose to write for them, against whom so many good, and great spirits have already written.
>
> (*Life of Sidney*)

—should be not only in, but the very stuff of, dramas full of action and melodrama, full of horseplay, slapstick, and bawdy, dramas which—to reach the climax of incredibility—were produced with the greatest financial success in a London theatre. Because Shakespeare in his maturity wrote for, and was appreciated by, an audience—that is, a society—which ranged from the most vulgar to the most refined, his drama could be, and had to be, of corresponding range. It would be profitless to inquire which came first in this process—whether he deliberately deepened the tone and thickened the complexity of his verse in order to win the appreciation of the more educated tastes (the Sonnets seem to indicate a feeling that he *ought* to attempt this), or whether he won over his educated admirers because his work developed as it did. That we shall never know: presumably there was a constant and fluctuating interaction. It seems to have been round the turn of the century that highbrow and scholarly opinion began to show him favour. Gabriel Harvey's remark—

The younger sort take much delight in Shakespeare's *Venus and Adonis*; but his *Lucrece,* and his tragedy of *Hamlet, Prince of Denmark,* have it in them to please the wiser sort.

may be interpreted as a sign of this beginning, though one cannot much admire the critical judgment which links *Lucrece* with *Hamlet*; and in *Hamlet* itself—the Prince's talks with the players about the gagging of the clowns, the ranting of certain actors, and that "excellent play" which was "caviare to the general"—one sees a self-consciousness, an anxiety about the verdict of the "judicious," "those whose judgments in such matters cried in the top of (his)": put this together with the acute dissatisfaction voiced in *Henry V* (written about 1599, a year or two earlier than *Hamlet*) concerning the limitations and absurdities of the stage he had to work for; put both with the general uneasiness about his work that the Sonnets reveal, and the total picture is clear and coherent—of a writer who strove for, and obtained, the approval of those whom he regarded as both socially and intellectually the most gratifying of

296

admirers. And it might be conjectured that his success in gaining this approval, the fulfilling of the ambition revealed in those of the Sonnets which deal with the subtler, more up-to-date rivals, was one of the causes which led to that re-establishing of settled values perceptible in the mature tragedies, when contrasted with the "problem-plays." The Sonnets show a Shakespeare uneasy about his status in society, as well as about many other things; for his later life we have no such "personal" document, but plays like *Macbeth* and *Antony and Cleopatra* show an easy certainty in portraying their courtly milieux as well as a firm foundation of moral values. Shakespeare shared in what he had greatly helped to bring about: the rise of the drama in all spheres, spiritual and intellectual as well as social. It is one of the surest signs of the fineness of Jacobean and Caroline society, that a rise in the first two spheres should have meant a rise in the third.

How it happened may be matter for doubt; what is clear is that it did happen; and this combination—of a thorough-going intellectualism prepared to go to any lengths of obscurity and subtlety, and a firm base of the popular and colloquial—is a vital component of all the poetry of the Shakespearean moment. The popular is of course more blatant in Shakespeare than it is in non-dramatic verse, since he had a directer incentive (the approval of his pit) to keep it prominent; but it is really no less in the sermons of Donne, with their purple passages of emotional rhetoric, and their jokes and puns, and in the poems of George Herbert, with their domestic imagery and colloquial language. When such blendings are no longer possible, the Shakespearean moment has come to an end. And they were possible only on the basis of a society with such spiritual unity as has been described.

Of this society and the attitudes to life which lay underneath it, what are the essential features from our point of view—the features which explain, as far as such things can explain it, the poetry which the society produced? First, it was a society which brought together, more successfully than most do, things which always tend to fly apart or to quarrel: spiritual and political, spiritual and physical, reverence and criticism, magnificence and simplicity; the hierarchical and the individualist, the popular and the esoteric. It was a society full of tension, ominousness, doubt of itself and its future; full, in consequence, of the tragic sense. But the traditional bases were still firm in men's minds; it had the medieval unity of thought without the medieval rigidity and fixed limitations. The feverishness and *naïveté* of the early Elizabethans were quietened and deepened; out of the turmoil of the 1590's— an incomparably fertile growing-time rather than one of full maturity—emerged this short-lived but perfect balance. It is not that the age was in any sense a Golden Age—in any case, the kind of society and mentality which this chapter describes was only part of the age's whole, as the following chapters will argue—it was just as imperfect as any other age, as full as any other of corruptions and brutalities. But this kind of society *was* dominant in the age, and it *was* peculiarly well-fitted—it is in this that its "perfection" lies—for the production of great poetry.

For poetry at its best is the least specialized of the arts; it employs a medium which everyone uses, its "technique" is of a sort which everyone has had a smattering of, inasmuch as everyone has learned his language. This fact, which should make it the least specialized of the arts, makes it also that most sensitive, since it uses a medium always liable to be corrupted by those wider corruptions in society which damage the society's language. Poetry is therefore peculiarly dependent on having a wide field of unspoiled stimuli available, on being in the midst of a society which excites the poet, excites him beneficially, and is excited by the poetry which both esteems the art and can be esteemed by the artist. An age which largely rejects the poet and is largely rejected by him may produce a few good poems; it will never be a great age of poetry.

It seems also to be highly beneficial to poetry that it should be taken seriously but not solemnly, regarded as an art of the highest dignity, worthy of the full-time devotion of the finest spirits, but also as an occasional recreation for ordinary educated men. Hence one of the most reliable criteria for the state of poetry at any given time is the quality of its minor and "amateur" versifying, since that is an index of how near those who ought to be the best readers are, in spirit and comprehension, to the real and "full-time" poets. By that criterion, the early seventeenth century has no rival. Its Herricks, Sucklings, Wottons, and Lovelaces score the occasional bullseyes which are all that the part-time poet can hope to score, with a frequency and a satisfying confidence that her equivalents in other times can never achieve.

> You meaner beauties of the night
> That poorly satisfy our eyes
> More by your number than your light:
> You common people of the skies . . .

These lines, the work of a professional diplomat (written, it seems, while he was preparing in great haste and flurry to go on a highly important mission), written by a man for whom the writing of verse was a very occasional amusement, have an expertness of phrasing and rhythm which seems truly "professional." The English language, like so much else in the age, was not yet specialized.

Nor, in particular, was the language of poetry. For one thing, verse was still a natural and public medium: the medium for topical balladry and knockabout bawdy as much as for tragedy and devotional meditation. One of the reasons, no doubt, for the odd fact previously mentioned, that Shakespeare's intensely complex verse could be the medium for very popular theatrical successes, was simply that Jacobean audiences were far, far more sophisticated, in the matter of hearing verse, than the audiences of the twentieth century. The latter are completely at sea; either they listen with a strained awareness that this is something "special," or else—usually with the assistance of the actors' methods of delivery and often with that of the poet's rhythms—they do their best to forget that what they are hearing is verse at all. The Jacobean audiences must have been hearing verse all the time; the ballads and songs which they heard outside the theatre were part of their training for what they heard inside it. Inside the theatre, they expected verse; a play in prose would be for them the disconcerting exception. Looked at from the viewpoint of the audience, the whole extent of Elizabethan and Jacobean drama, from the jog-trot stuff of, say *Ralph Roister Doister* through the rhythms of Kyd and Marlowe to those of mature Shakespeare, can be looked on as a long course of ever-increasing difficulty in the art of hearing verse. By the time of the Shakespearean moment their sophistication was complete.

The state of the language reflects it. In the early seventeenth century the language was poised between two extremes. It had outgrown the adolescence of early Elizabethan English, reflected in such whimsicalities as Euphuism, in shapeless outpourings like Nashe's prose, and in naïve pedantries like the experiments in classical metrics; it had not grown into the impoverishing "refinement" which overtook it after the Restoration. It stood between two "poetic dictions." Coleridge's brilliant remark about the metaphysical poets—they express "the most fantastic out-of-the-way thoughts, but in the most pure and genuine mother English"—(though one may doubt if the "thoughts" are really so "out-of-the-way") shows a true perception of the quality of their language.

# APPENDIX

## THE ELIZABETHAN VOICES

*Francis Bacon's "The Character of Queen Elizabeth," as reprinted here, is the last item in a miscellaneous collection of his works, published under the title The Essays, . . . of Sir Francis Bacon, Lord Verulam, Viscount St. Albans (London, 1696).*

*The selection from William Camden is from* The History of . . . Elizabeth, Late Queen of England, *third edition (London, 1675), pp. 658-661.*

# THE CHARACTER OF QUEEN ELIZABETH

## WRITTEN BY WAY OF ESSAY.

### By the Lord *Verulam.*

*Queen Elizabeth* was one, whom *Nature* and *Fortune* had made the Wonder of her *Sex,* and an Ornament to *Crowned Heads.* For the truth of this we need not appeal to the Testimony of any *Monk,* or of any such like *Solitary Recluse:* For tho these men write acutely, and have extraordinary judgments; yet being wedded to, and byased [i.e. biased] by their own faction, they can never be faithful in transmitting a thing of this nature to posterity. But this is a Province that more properly belongs to men of the *first Rank,* to such as have had the management of the *Government* in their own hands, and have been acquainted with the Secret Springs and motions of Civil Affairs. Every Age has look'd upon a *Female Government* as a Rarity; if *prosperous* as a Wonder; but if *prosperous* and *long,* almost as a Miracle. Whereas tho she reign'd full four and forty years, yet she outliv'd not her *happiness.* Of the *happiness* of her Reign I design to say something, without running

301

out into high Encomiums. For Praise indeed is the Tribute of *Men,* but Happiness the Gift of *God.*

I take this to be the first step to her *happiness,* that from a Private condition she was rais'd to the Administration of the *Regal Power.* Forasmuch as 'tis a standing Rule in the Morality and common Sense of Mankind, that those things are to be look'd upon as our greatest happiness, which come beyond our hope and expectation. But this is not what I mean. That which I aim at is this, that *Princes,* who are bred up in *Courts* as the undoubted Heirs of a Crown, are so far debauch'd by a soft, indulgent and effeminate Education, that they frequently become less capable of managing the State: Whereas those have proved the best and most excellent Princes, who have been under the Discipline of both Fortunes. We need not go far for instances, *Henry* the *Seventh* in *England,* and *Lewis* the *Twelfth* in *France,* within our own memory, and almost at the same time, mounted the Throne, not only from a Private, but also from an Adverse and harass'd Fortune; and the one prov'd famous for his *Prudence,* the other for his *Justice.* This was the Case of *Q. Elizabeth;* whose Fortune was as inconstant as the first, as at last, when she came to the Crown, it prov'd Constant and Even. For at her *Birth* she was declar'd Heiress to the Throne, afterwards, disinherited, and at last despis'd: during her *Brother's Reign* she enjoy'd a more serene and favourable Fortune, but whilst her *Sister* swayed the Scepter the Clouds and Storms return'd upon her again. Nor was she advanc'd on a sudden from a Prison to a Throne, thereby to render her haughty after the Provocation of her Sufferings: But being restor'd to her Liberty, and rais'd in her hopes, she at last quietly and happily mounted the Throne, without any Opposition or Competitor.

These things I have mention'd, to shew how careful *Divine Providence* was of this best of *Princes,* by preparing her for a Crown by such methods of Discipline. Nor ought the misfortune of her *Mother* [i.e. Ann(e) Boleyn, 1507–1536] to Eclipse the glory of her *Birth:* especially since 'tis abundantly evident, that *Henry* the *Eighth* was engag'd in a new love before he gave way to his Anger against Q. *Ann:* nor is posterity a stranger to the nature of that

*King,* which was so very prone to Love and Jealousie, and prosecuted both even with the effusion of Blood. To this we may add, that she was cut off by an Accusation grounded on slight Conjectures, and on the improbable Testimony of a wicked Accuser: all which was mutter'd privately at that very time; and Q. *Ann* herself with an undaunted mind, and noble presence, protested her Innocence at the time of her Death. For having (as she thought) got a faithful and generous Messenger, she just before her execution dispatcht him away with this Message to the King; *That the King had very well observ'd, and would still keep his promise good to her, that was now going to be invested with new honors: since from a Private Person he rais'd her at first to the dignity of a Marchioness, and then advanc'd her to be the Partner of his Bed and Throne; and now, when he could raise her no higher on Earth, design'd to promote her an Innocent to the Crown of Martyrdom.* But the Messenger durst not tell this to the *King,* who was devoted to another Love, tho *Fame,* the Asserter of Truth, has transmitted it to *Posterity.*

Another part of the Happiness of Q *Elizabeth* seems to consist in the Period and Course of time wherein she reign'd: Not only that it was *Long,* but because it was such a Part of her Life, as was most fit for managing the Affairs of State, and governing a Kingdom. For she was five and twenty years old when she began her Reign (at which Age she was out of her Guardians Jurisdiction) and she continu'd to Reign to the 70th year of her Age. So that she neither experienc'd what it was to be a *Minor,* and under a Governors power; nor did she labour under the Inconveniences of an extreme and miserable *Old Age.* An Age, which even to Private men brings too many troubles along with it; but to Kings, beside the ordinary Miseries of human Life, it comes attended with the Decay of their States, and is back'd with an *inglorious Exit.* For there has scarce been a King, that has liv'd to an extreme and infirm old Age, but what lost much of that Power and Esteem, which he formerly had. Of this we have a notable Instance in *Philip* the *Second,* King of *Spain,* a Prince very potent, and one very well skill'd in the Art of Governing: who in his latter days, labouring under the Impotency of old Age, deeply

303

experienc'd the truth of what we asserted. He quitted all his Conquests in *France,* made a Peace with that Nation, and endeavour'd to do the same with others, that so he might leave all things in quiet and compos'd to his Successors. On the other hand, Q. *Elizabeth's* Fortune was so Constant and Vigorous, that no declension of Affairs follow'd her lively, tho declining Age. Nay more, for a standing and most certain monument of her happiness, she died not before a Victory in *Ireland* had put an end to the Rebellion there, so shining and so uniform was her Glory in all its Parts! Besides, I think it very material to reflect, over what sort of People she bore the sway, for had her Government been over the *Palmyrenians,* or any other soft and unmanly Nation of Asia, it had been a less wonder, since a Female in the Throne would be suitable enough to an *Effeminate* People, but to have all things move and be directed by a Woman's Nod in *England,* a Nation so fierce and warlike; this, I say, justly raises our highest admiration.

But tho the *Genius* of her Subjects was so desirous of War, and so impatient of Peace, yet this did not hinder her from maintaining it strictly all her Reign. And this natural inclination of hers, join'd with success, is what I reckon redounds to her highest Commendation. For this conduc'd much to the Happiness of her own Life, to the Honor of her Sex, and to the Peace and Quiet of her Conscience. About the tenth year of her Reign, an Insurrection was indeed attempted in the *North,* but it was soon hush'd and suppress'd. All the rest of her time *England* enjoy'd a secure and profound Peace. And I account it a most glorious Peace, upon these two accounts; which tho they make nothing to the *Merit,* yet contribute very much to the *Glory* of a Peace. The first is, that it appear'd the more Conspicuous and Shining by the Calamities of its Neighbours, which were all in flames round about it. Another is, that even in the Blessings of Peace there still remain'd so much martial Glory, as by its famous Actions not only retain'd, but likewise increas'd the honor of the *English* Nation. For the supplies sent into the *Netherlands, France,* and *Scotland*; the Voyages that were made to the *Indies,* and round the whole World; the Fleets that were sent to infest *Portugal* and the Coasts of *Spain,* and the *Irish* Rebels so often conquer'd and cut off, were all sufficient Testimonies, that *England* had remitted and lost nothing of its Ancient Glory in the Field of War.

It was likewise an addition to her *Glory* and *Deserts,* that by her timely supplies, the Neighbouring Princes were maintain'd in their Thrones; and the Suppliant States, who by a conduct unbecoming Princes, were expos'd to the Cruelty of their Ministers, to the fury of the Rabble, and to all manner of Ravage and Slaughter, were at last reliev'd by her, and plac'd in that posture of Affairs, wherein they now are. Nor were her *Counsels* less beneficial than her *Supplies*: witness her frequent admonitions to his *Catholick Majesty,* to moderate the displeasure he had conceiv'd against his Subjects in the *Netherlands,* and to restore them to that mildness of Government which they formerly enjoy'd: and witness her earnest importunities with the Kings of *France,* putting them often in mind of the *Edicts* wherein they had promis'd to preserve the Peace. It must indeed be acknowledg'd that her advices prov'd ineffectual. For the common interest of *Europe* oppos'd the first, lest the Ambition of *Spain,* freed as it were from its confinement, should enlarge it self (as affairs then stood) to the great prejudice of the Kingdoms and States of the Christian World. And the *Latter* was prevented by the Massacre of so many Innocent Persons, who with their Wives and Children were butcher'd in their own Habitations by the barbarous Rabble, who like so many Beasts of prey seem'd to be Animated, Armed, and sent out by Publick Authority: So that the Blood which was shed cry'd aloud for *Revenge,* that the Kingdom, stain'd by so notorious a Villany, might be purg'd by mutual Slaughters and Bloodshed. However she perform'd the Office of a *Faithful, Prudent,* and *Generous Ally.*

There is still another Reason, why we should admire the peaceful Reign of Queen *Elizabeth,* namely, because the Peace which she enjoy'd, was not owing to the inclination which the age she liv'd in had to it, but wholly to her own Prudence and wise Conduct. She struggled with an *Inbred Faction* at home, upon the account of Religion; and the strength of the Kingdom, like the common Bulwark of all *Europe,* seem'd to oppose the growing Greatness of the *Spaniard,* and his Ambition so formidable at that time; so that upon these accounts, there was a sufficient Cause of War: but by her Forces and Policy she surmounted these difficulties. This was demonstrated by one of the most memorable Events, that ever happened in the whole course of Affiairs of our age. For when the *Spanish Armada* rode upon our Seas, to the terror of all *Europe,* with so much noise, and so much assurance of success; it took not the least Fisher-boat, nor burnt the least Cottage, nor so much as touched upon our Coast: but being routed in an Engagement, was dispers'd by a miserable flight, and with frequent storms; and so left *England* and her Sea Coast in an unmov'd and undisturbed Peace. Nor was she less fortunate in disappointing the secret Plots of her private Foes, than in Conquering and Routing the Forces of an open Enemy: For tho there were many Conspiracies laid against her Life, yet were they most happily discovered and defeated. Nor was she upon that account more fearful or anxious of the safety of her Person; her Guards were not increas'd, nor did she confine her self in her Palace, without appearing abroad: But secure of her self, and trusting to her Subjects, she remembered her *Deliverance,* but forgot the *Danger,* and alter'd nothing of her usual Management and Behavior.

It is likewise worthy our Observation, to consider in what sort of times she flourish'd. For some Ages are so Barbarous and Ignorant, that Men have been Govern'd with as much ease, as a Shepherd drives and manages his Sheep: But this Princess liv'd in a most Learned and Polite Age; wherein it requir'd great parts and a high degree of Vertue [i.e. strength] to be excellent. A *Female Government* is likewise very often eclips'd by *Marriage,* and all the Praises and Conduct is bestow'd upon the *Husband:* whilst those who live unmarry'd, have no sharers or partners in their Glory. And in this was our Queen the more to be commended in that her Throne stood upon no other *Basis,* than what she her self had erected. She had no *Brother,* no *Uncle,* nor any other of the *Royal Family,* to partake of her Cares, or share in her Government. But even those whom she did advance to any places of Trust, were so manag'd and kept in such awe, that each of them was solicitous how to please her; so that she was always *Mistress of her self.* She was indeed *Childless,* and left no issue of her own Body to succeed her: But this has been the case of the most fortunate Princes, of *Alexander the Great,* of *Julius Cæsar,* of *Trajan,* and several others: which has been variously censur'd and has always been a matter of Dispute. For some have look'd upon it as a Diminution of *human Happiness,* as if men could not be compleatly happy, unless they were so both in their own persons, and in the propagation of their Species: but others have esteem'd it as the greater Happiness, because then it seems to be compleat, when it is not any longer subjected to the various turns of Fortune: which 'tis impossible to secure, when a Posterity is left behind.

To all this we may add her *Outward Embellishments;* she was tall of *stature,* well shap'd in her Body, and had in her Face the mixture of *Sweetness* and *Majesty;* and always enjoy'd a very *Sound Health.* Beside all this, she was strong and vigorous to the very last, never experienc'd the Changes of Fortune, nor the miseries of old Age, and at last by an easy and gentle death she obtain'd that *Euthanasia,* which *Augustus Cæsar* was us'd so passionately to desire. This also is Recorded of *Antoninus Pius,* one of the best of Emperors, whose death seemed to be nothing else but a quiet and sweet slumber. Just so in Q. *Elizabeth's* Distemper, there was nothing that was deadly, or ominous, or unsuitable to humane nature. She was not desirous of Life, or impatient under Sickness, nor disturb'd with the tortures of any Pain: No direful, no pestilential Symptom appear'd, but every thing seem'd rather to prognosticate the decay of Nature, than either the corruption or disparagement of it. For some few days before her Death, being weakened by the driness of her Constitution, and the cares of the Government, having not so much as drank any Wine, or taken any moist diet, she was seiz'd with a *Dead Palsy,* but yet (which is not usual in that Distemper) she retained her Speech, her Sense, and her Motion, tho not so brisk and lively as before. Nor was she long in this condition, so that it did not seem to be the *last Act* of her Life, but rather the *first step* to her Death. For tho 'tis esteemed a misery to live a long time in the loss of the use of our faculties; yet to be prepar'd for Death, by a gradual decay of our senses, is certainly a very sweet and pleasant *Dissolution*.

Another remarkable addition to her *Happiness,* is this, that she was not only very happy in her own *Person,* but likewise in the Worthiness of her *Ministers of State.* For she made choice of such men, as this *Island* perhaps was never so happy in before. But *God* that favours Kings, raises them up *Ministers* and adorns their Minds.

There remain two *Posthumous Felicities,* which seem to attend the more Noble and August Passages of her Life: The *One* is that of her *Successor,* the *Other,* that of her *Memory.* For she has got such a Successor, who, tho by his *Masculine Virtue,* and *Off-spring* and *late Accession to the Throne,* he may excel and eclipse her Glory; yet is so far a favourer of her *Name* and *Esteem,* and is so willing to transmit her actions to posterity, that he has made little alterations, either in the *choice* of *Ministers,* or in the *method of Governing.* So that hardly any *Father* has been succeeded by his *Son,* with less noise, disturbance or alteration. As for her *Memory,* 'tis so much in the mouths, and so fresh in the minds of all men, that *Death* seems to have extinguished Envy, and put her Fame in a clearer light, and now the *Happiness* of her *Memory* does as it were strive to outvie that of her *Life.* For tho through mens love to any Party, or upon the account of the difference of Religion, any factious report may be spread abroad, yet 'tis such as seems to be fearful of it self, is not sincere, and can never last long. And 'tis upon this account especially that I have made this collection of things, that relate to her happiness, and are marks of the Divine favour: that so no foul-mouthed Libeller might dare to stain so great blessings of God, by the venom of his scandalous Tongue. If any one should now say, as one did to *Cæsar, quæ miremur, habemus; sed quæ laudemus, expectamus; we do indeed see cause to Admire, but none to Praise:* to this I answer, that I look upon *Admiration* as the superlative degree of *Praise.* Nor could that *Happiness* we have been describing, be attained by any, but such as are supported and highly indulged by the Divine favour; and such as in some measure by their *Morals* and *Vertue* are the Establishers of their own *Fortune*. However I thought fit to subjoin some few hints with respect to those *Morals* of the Queen, which seem to have been most exposed to the lash of malevolent Tongues.

In *Religion,* Q. *Elizabeth* was *Pious* and *Moderate, Constant* and *Steady,* and a profest Enemy to *Novelty.* As for her *Piety,* tho the chief strokes of it appeared in the Actions and Affairs of State; yet some signs of it were to be seen in the course of her Life, and her ordinary Conversation. She was seldom absent from *Divine Service,* either in her *publick or private Chappel.* She employed much of her time in reading the *Scriptures* and the *Writings* of the *Fathers,* especially of S. *Augustin.* She compos'd some Prayers her self, upon some occasions, and for some extraordinary purpose. Whenever she mentioned the name of *God,* even in ordinary discourse, she generally added the title of *Creator;* and shewed some sort of humility and reverence in her looks and countenance, which I my self have often observed. As for that which some have reported, that she was so far from thinking of her *Mortality,* that she could not endure to be told of *Old Age* or *Death,* it is absolutely false: since she her self, several years before her Death, would frequently with much facetiousness call her self *the Old Woman:* and would often discourse about the *Inscription,* she had a mind should be upon her *Tomb*: She gave out, that she was no lover of Glory and pompous Titles, but only desired her Memory might be recorded in a line or two, which should very briefly express her *Name,* her *Virginity,* the *time of her Reign, the Reformation of Religion, and her Preservation of the Peace.* 'Tis true, in the flower of her Age before she was past Child-bearing, when she was importun'd by some to declare her *Successor,* she did make answer, *that she could by no means endure to have a Shroud held before her Eyes while she was living.* However, some few years before her Death, when she was more thoughtful, and meditated (as 'tis probable) on her *Mortality,* as one of her bosom friends told her, that many and great Places and Offices of Trust in the Commonwealth, would be too long vacant; she rose up, and with more than ordinary concern said, *that she was sure her place would not long be Vacant.*

As for her *Moderation* in *Religion,* perhaps in this her *Character* will deem deficient, because of the *severity of those Laws,* which were made against her Subjects of the *Romish Religion;* but we will produce such things, as are well known to us, and carefully taken notice of by us. This is certain, that she was always averse from laying any constraint on mens Consciences: but yet she could not allow that the Government should be endanger'd under the pretence of *Conscience* and *Religion.* Hence it was that she thought nothing but a certain destruction would ensue, if she should at the first grant a liberty and toleration of two Religions by publick Authority to a fierce and headstrong people, who would soon upon their private Animosities fall together by the ears. Even in the beginning of her Reign, when all things looked with a suspicious face, she kept some of the *Prelates,* which were of a more turbulent and factious spirit, Prisoners at large, tho she had the Law on her side: and to the rest of both Orders, she used not any sharp inquisition, but by a generous Connivance kept them under her Protection. This was the posture of affairs at first. Nor did she swerve much from this her *Clemency,* tho provoked by the Bull of *Excommunication,* thundered against her by *Pius the Fifth.* This indeed might have raised her indignation, and have been the occasion of new modelling the State, but still she re-retained her own generous Temper. For this Prudent and Courageous Woman was not much moved at the noise of such Threatnings, being secure of the Fidelity and Affection of her Subjects, and not fearing any harm from the *Romish Faction,* which was too weak to attempt any thing unless seconded by a foreign Enemy.

But about the three and twentieth year of her Reign, the face of Affairs was quite chang'd. Nor is this Period of time, feigned to serve a turn only, but mentioned in the *Publick Records,* and engraven as it were in *leaves of Brass.* Nor were her Subjects of the *Romish Religion* punished with any severity before that year, tho several Laws had formerly been enacted against them. But at this time it was by degrees discovered what vast and am-

310

bitious designs were laid by *Spain,* to conquer this Kingdom. A great part of this design was to raise a faction in the very heart of the Nation, which being no friends to the Government, and desirous of alteration, should join with the Enemy upon his Invasion. This was hoped would be effected upon the difference there was in Religion; whereupon they resolved to improve that breach, and Priests were sent over from the young *Seminaries,* to raise and increase Mens Love for the *Romish Religion,* to teach and inforce the Validity of the *Popes Bull,* which absolved the Queens Subjects from their Allegiance, and to excite and prepare the Minds of men for an Alteration in the Government.

Much about that time, *Ireland* was openly invaded, and the *Name* and *Government* of Queen *Elizabeth* vilified by various and Scandalous Libels; and affairs were in such a strange ferment, that they prognosticated a greater Commotion. Nor indeed will I say, that every *Priest* knew of the design, or were conscious of what was to be done, but certainly they were the wicked Instigators and Promoters of the Villainy others were to commit. And this is certainly true, (as appears by several Confessions) that almost all the Priests, who were sent into *England* from the year abovemention'd, to the thirtieth year of Queen *Elizabeth's Reign* (wherein the Design of *Spain* and the *Romanists* was to be put in Execution, by that memorable preparation of a Fleet and Land-forces) I say 'tis certain, that all, who were sent over within that time, among other things had this likewise in their Orders, That they should insinuate, *That Affairs could not last long in the same posture; that they would put on a new Face within some short time; and that the* Pope *and the Catholick Princes would take care of the* English *State, provided the* English *were not their own hinderance.* Nay, some of the Priests were manifestly engag'd in the Plots and Contrivances which were laid for the Subversion and Ruin of the *Government*: and which is still more, the whole Train of this Design was discover'd by Letters which were intercepted from all parts: wherein it was written, *That the Vigilancy of the Queen and her Council over the Catholicks would be baffled: For she only seem'd concern'd, that the Faction should not be headed by any Nobleman or Person of Quality; whereas the Design they laid was such, as was carried on by Private Men of no Note; who never met and conspir'd together in numbers, but order'd and dispos'd all things in the private way of Confession.* These were the *Artifices* which were then us'd, and were so customary and familiar to those Men, as might be seen in a fresh and parallel case.

In a time of so much danger, Queen *Elizabeth* was obliged by a kind of fatal necessity to enact severe Laws, thereby to restrain those of her Subjects, who being averse to her Government, and grown past the hopes of being cur'd, began to grow rich by the private Life they led, being exempted from the charge and burden of publick Offices. The Original of this spreading Evil was charg'd upon the *Seminary Priests*; who were bred up in foreign parts, and maintain'd by the Charity and Benevolence of *Foreign Princes* the profest Enemies of the Realm: who had liv'd in places, where the best Titles they could bestow on Queen *Elizabeth* were those of, *Heretick, Excommunicated, and Damnable Fury*; who, tho they themselves were not engag'd in treasonable practices, yet were known to be the intimate Friends of such as were guilty of those Villanies, and who, by their Artifices and poysonous Methods had depraved the very Sacrifice of the *Mass,* which before was a sweet and harmless thing; and had as it were infected it with a new kind of Ferment and pernicious Malignity. Whereupon the only Expedient to put a stop to this growing Evil was thought to be the prohibiting these Men from coming into the Land upon pain of Death; which was accordingly enacted in the seven and twentieth Year of her Reign. Nor did the Event itself, when so great a Storm broke out upon, and threatned the Nation, in the least take off from the Envy and Hatred of these Men, but rather increas'd it; so far had they divested themselves of the Love they ow'd their Country. Afterwards when our fears of *Spain* (the true occasion of this severity) were over and vanisht; yet the Memory of the former times was so deeply fixt in the Minds and Senses of most Men, and to have abrogated the Laws that were once made would have argued so much *Inconstancy,* or to

312

have slighted them would have been a sign of so much *Indifferency*; that Queen *Elizabeth* as cases then stood, did not think it safe for herself, that things should return to the same posture they were in before the three and twentieth year of her Reign. To this may be added the *Industry* of some to increase the Revenues of the *Exchequer,* and the *Care* of those *Ministers of Justice,* who are us'd to mind no other Safety of their Country than what is contain'd in the Laws: both which requir'd and call'd loudly for the Laws to be put in Execution. However, she (to the Glory of her good Nature be it spoken) did so far blunt the edge of the Laws, that but very few Priests suffer'd Death upon that account. Nor do we speak this by way of defence, for these matters stand in need of none: since the whole Safety of the Nation depended upon this Conduct, and the Method and Measure of all this Severity was far from being bloody, and is a thing that no Christian need to be asham'd of; for it proceeded more from the Arrogance and Wicked Practices of others, than from any necessity the Nation lay under, and it stands for a Monument of Disgrace to the *Romanists*. But not to forget what we first asserted, we think we have abundantly demonstrated, that she was *moderate* in points of *Religion,* and that the Alteration which did happen, was not owing to her Nature, but to the Iniquity of the times.

Of her *Constancy* in *Religion* and the *Worship* thereof, the greatest proof is, That with an undaunted Mind and little Assistance she extirpated and abrogated the *Romish Religion,* as being disagreeable to the *Word of God,* the *Primitive Purity,* and her own *Conscience*: notwithstanding in her *Sister's Reign* it was established by Publick Authority and a great deal of Care, and had taken deep root, and was strengthned with the Consent and Approbation of all that were in Authority and Places of Trust. Nor did she do this hastily or in a heat, but cautiously and by degrees. The truth of which appears, not only in her whole Conduct of Affairs, but also in that Answer which she once made to a *Courtier* upon the like occasion. For in the beginning of her Reign, when according to the Custom the *Prisoners* were to be releas'd, to grace and honor her first Accession to the Throne; as she was going to Chappel she was accosted by a certain *Courtier,* who took more than ordinary freedom, being of a pleasant and facetious Nature. He, either prompted to it by his own private Inclination, or set on by a Wiser Head, deliver'd a *Petition* into her hand, and in a full Concourse of People with a loud Voice expressed himself thus, *That there were still four or five kept Prisoners, and that for no reason at all: That he came to petition for their Freedom, as well as for the rest: That they were the Four Evangelists, and the Apostle S. Paul, who had been long confin'd in an unknown tongue, as it were in a Prison, and were not suffer'd to appear abroad in the World.* The Queen gave him this very cautious Reply, *That it was best to consult them first, whether they were willing to have their Freedom yet, or no.* And thus she kept every thing within her own Power, by giving such a doubtful Answer to so surprizing a Demand. Nor did she carry on things fearfully, and by fits and starts, but gravely, orderly, and maturely: A Conference first had between the Parties, and a *Parliament* first call'd; and at last, within the compass of a year, she so far order'd and establishe'd all things which concern'd *Religion,* that she did not suffer the least Tittle of them to be alter'd, during all her Reign. And it was always her Publick Admonition in almost every Session of *Parliament,* that no Innovation should be made in the *Discipline* and *Ceremonies* of the *Church.* Thus far of her Religion.

Now if any of the *graver Sort* should object these *Levities*: "That she was contented and desirous to be Admir'd, to be Courted, and upon the Account of Love to be Prais'd and Extoll'd; and that she continu'd these Levities even to an Age wherein they were unbecoming her." Yet if you take even these in a milder sense, they are not without their due *Admiration,* since they are such things, as often are to be found in the *fabulous Narrations* of Poets and others. Thus 'tis recorded of a certain Queen in the *Fortunate Islands,* who in her Court and Government entertain'd that soft thing call'd *Love,* and yet forbad *Lust* to enter there. But if a harsher construction should be put upon them, yet they are to be admir'd, and that very highly too, since these *Softnesses* cast but little blemish on her *Fame,* and none at all upon her *Grandeur*; did no

Injury to her Government, and hinder'd not the Publick Administration of Affairs. For these sort of things are usually joyn'd to the most Noted Fortune. But, to conclude this Essay; she was certainly a *good, moral Princess,* and as such she desir'd to appear: She was a hater of *Vice,* and study'd to grow famous by *honorable Methods.* And truly at the naming of her *Manners,* something comes into my mind, which I will here declare. When she had order'd an Express to be written to her Embassador, concerning certain Instructions, which he was privately to impart to the Queen Mother of *France* at *Valois,* and her Secretary had incerted a certain Clause, that the Embassador to ingratiate himself the better should say, *That they were two Female Princes, of whom, in the Management of Affairs, and in the Art and Skill of Governing, as great things were expected as from the best of Men*; she could not endure the Comparison, but order'd it to be struck out, and said, that *she us'd quite different Arts and Methods in the Administration of the Government.* And she was extreamly pleas'd, when any one by chance dropt out such an Expression as this, *That she would have liv'd and excell'd in the Eye of the World, tho she had spent her days in a private and mean Station:* So desirous was she that nothing of her *Virtue* and *Praise* should be owing to the *Grandeur* of her *Fortune.* But if I should enter upon her Praises, either *Moral* or *Political,* or should touch only upon her *Virtues,* which would be a Disparagement to so great a Princess: or should I endeavour to set them in their clear and proper light, I must run out into the *History* of her Life, which requires more leisure, and a larger Genius, than I can pretend to. For I have here given you her character in short. But it must after all be said, That only *Time* will bestow a true Encomium on this Excellent Woman: since no Age since the Creation, could ever shew her *Equal* in her own *Sex,* that was so fit to manage the Affairs of a State.

# THE DEATH OF QUEEN ELIZABETH

## By William Camden

The Queen, who had hitherto enjoyed her Health without Impairment, by reason of her Abstinence from Wine and observing a temperate Diet, (which she usually said was the noblest part of Physick,) being now in her Climactericall Year, to wit, the Seventieth Year of her Age, began to be sensible of some Weakness and Indisposition both of Health and Old age, which the Badness of the Weather increased, whilst upon the last of *January,* which was a very windy and rainy day, she removed from *Westminster* to *Richmond,* there to enjoy and refresh herself in her Old age, and more freely to attend the Serving of God. Upon which day (whether thinking on her Death, or presaging what would ensue,) she happened to say to the Lord Admirall, whom she always dearly affected, *My Throne hath been the Throne of Kings, neither ought any other than he that is my next Heir to succeed me.* And the Courtiers observed, that she never before more frequented Prayers and the Service of God then now. Who also report, that she then commanded that Ring wherewith she had been as it were joyned in Marriage to her Kingdome at her Inauguration, and had never since taken off, to be filed off from her Finger, because it was so grown into the Flesh, that it could not be drawn off. Which was taken as a sad Omen, as if it portended that her Marriage with the Kingdome, contracted by that Ring, would now be dissolved. In the beginning of her Sickness the Almonds in her Throat swelled, and soon abated again; then her Appetite failed her by degrees; and withall she gave herself over wholly to Melancholy, and seemed to be much troubled with a peculiar Grief for some Reason or other: whether it were through the Violence of her Disease; or for

the Want of *Essex,* (as *Essex* his Friends persuaded themselves;) or that, after so great Expenses in the Irish War,
she was prevailed with to pardon the Rebell *Tir-Oen;*
or that she had heard some Whisperings, and had also
been advertised by the French King, that many of the
Nobility did by underhand Letters and Messengers seek
to curry Favour with the King of *Scots,* that they adored
him as the rising Sun, and neglected her as being now
ready to set. Which (as the female Sex and Old age are
apt to be suspicious) she easily believed, and that not
without good Cause: for some of the Lords of the Court,
(to say nothing of the Ladies,) who had least Reason of
all to have done it, ungratefully in a manner forsook her,
whilst she altered not from herself, but they from their
Opinion of her, and Respect to her; either because they
saw her now very aged; or were weary of her long Government, (for things of long Continuance, though never
so good, are tedious;) or out of a credulous Desire of
Novelty and Change, hoping for better Times, despising
the present, and forgetting Favours past, (the Remembrance whereof is a Burthen to Unthankfull persons;) finding Fault with the state of things, haply out of a Mystery
and Art of Court, to win Favour with her Successor, falsly
believing that the Dispraise of the Predecessour is a grate-
full and delightful Hearing to the Successour. And this
they did so openly, that they quarrelled one with another
about it: and others propounded to have the Successour
sent for, whilst her Recovery was yet doubtful; so as they
seemed to have fled over to him in their Hearts, though
their Bodies stayed at Home in *England.* Hereupon she
looked upon herself as a miserable forlorn Woman, and
her Grief and Indignation extorted from her such Speeches
as these: *They have yoaked my Neck; I have none whom
I can trust; My Condition is strangely turned upside down.*
And, to increase this her Grief and Dissatisfaction, they
made her believe that her Authority among the People
sensibly decayed: whereas the People (in whom there is
always a murmuring and querulous Dislike of such as are
in Authority) complained of nothing so much as that
the Power of some near the Queen, if not above her, was
grown too great; and that others were too hasty in catching

317

and snatching for themselves (as is usuall in such cases) now they saw her grown old.

When the Report now grew daily stronger and stronger that her Sickness increased upon her, and that, as she had done always before in the prime of her Age, so now much more she refused all Help of Physick, incredible it is with what great Speed the Puritans, Papists, Ambitious persons and Flatterers of all kinds, and other sorts of men, all of them prompted by their particular Hopes, poasted night and day by Sea and Land into *Scotland,* to adore the rising King, and get into his Favour. Whose Title to the Succession the Queen (though out of Prudence she declared it not openly, yet) always really and from her Heart favoured, as Justice and Equity required: the like did all men of all Degrees and Qualities, who with great Satisfaction and Content had fixed their Eyes and Hearts upon him as her undoubted Heir; though false Rumours were spread abroad of a Marriage of the Lady *Arabella* his Uncle's Daughter; and the French Embassadour did what he could to raise Disturbances, lest the two yet divided Kingdoms of *Britain, England* and *Scotland,* should be united into one. In the beginning of *March,* an heavy Dulness, with a Frowardness familiar to Old age, began to seize upon her, insomuch as she would sit silent, refrain from Meat, fixing her Mind wholly upon her Meditations, and would not endure any Talk unless it were with the Archbishop of *Canterbury,* with whom she often prayed with great Fervency and Devotion, untill by little and little her Speech failed her; and after she willingly heard him praying by her. About this time the Lord Admirall telling the rest of the Privy Council what the Qu. at her departing from *Westminster* had said to him by the Bye concerning her Successour, they all thought that good that he with the Lord Keeper and the Secretary should wait upon her, and put her in Mind thereof, and acquaint her that they were come in the name of the rest of the Councill to understand her Pleasure touching her Successor. The Qu. made Answer with a gasping Breath, *I said that my Throne was a Throne of Kings, that I would not have any mean Person succeed me.* The Secretary asking her what she meant by those words; *I will* (said she) *that a King succeed me: and who should that be but my nearest Kinsman, the King of Scots?* Then being put in mind by the Archbishop to think upon God; *That I do,* (said she) *neither doth my Mind at all wander from him.* And when she could no longer pray with her Tongue, with Hands and Eyes lift up she directed the Thoughts of her pious Heart to God; and in this very thing she prayed, by sorrowing inwardly that she could not pray, as was plainly to be gathered by some Signs observed by the Standers by.

On the 24. of *March,* being the Eve of the Annunciation of the Blessed Virgin, she (who was born on the Eve of the Nativity of the same Blessed Virgin) was called out of the Prison of her earthly Body to enjoy an everlasting Country in Heaven, peaceably and quietly leaving this Life after the happy manner of Departure which *Augustus* wished for, having reigned 44 Years, 4 Months, and in the 70. Year of her Age; to which no King of *England* ever attained before.

The sad Miss which she left of herself to the *English* was much lessened by the great Hope conceived by the Vertues of King *James* her Successour, who a few Hours after was proclaimed King with the joyfull Shouts and Acclamations of all the People. No Oblivion shall ever bury the Glory of her Name: for her happy and renowned Memory still liveth, and shall for ever live in the Minds of men to all Posterity, *as of one who* (to use no other then her Successour's Expression) *in Wisedome and Felicity of Government surpassed* (without Envy be it spoken) *all the Princes since the days of* Augustus.